JAWBREAKER

Dear Mel Harris

I hope you enjoy
my book. He who dares
wins! I look forward
to meeting you.

Best Regards

Gary Bernsen

Dec 21, 2006

JAWBREAKER

THE ATTACK ON BIN LADEN AND AL-QAEDA:
A PERSONAL ACCOUNT BY THE CIA'S KEY FIELD COMMANDER

GARY BERNTSEN
AND RALPH PEZZULLO

CROWN PUBLISHERS / NEW YORK

Maps courtesy of Mapping Specialists

Copyright © 2005 by Gary Berntsen and Ralph Pezzullo

Library of Congress Cataloging-in-Publication Data is available upon request.

ISBN-13: 978-0-307-23740-8
ISBN-10: 0-307-23740-0

Printed in the United States of America

Design by Leonard Henderson

10 9 8 7 6 5

First Edition

Dedicated to the brave men and women of our clandestine service, their families (including my own), and the people of Afghanistan

CONTENTS

Author's Note and Acknowledgments   ix
Glossary   xi
Key Characters   xiii
Maps   xix

1   THE ATTACK—7 AUGUST 1998   1
2   THE DECLARATION   28
3   DEPLOYMENTS   42
4   CTC/▪▪▪▪▪▪▪▪   65
5   NEGOTIATIONS   88
6   PANSHIR VALLEY   102
7   SHOMALI PLAINS   123
8   MAZAR-E SHARIF   133
9   AMIR   154
10   THE FALL OF KABUL   164
11   KABUL   183
12   TEAM JULIET   202
13   BILAL   222
14   GENERAL TOMMY FRANKS   233
15   QALA-I JANGI FORTRESS   245
16   TORA BORA   255
17   THE BATTLE OF MILAWA   265
18   ADAM KHAN   278
19   HAMID KARZAI   289
20   ESCAPE   305
21   CONCLUSIONS   311

Index   316

AUTHOR'S NOTE AND ACKNOWLEDGMENTS

This is a book that the CIA didn't want you to read. In May 2005, I submitted the manuscript to the CIA's Publication Review Board for review. I was told it would take approximately thirty days for them to redact those passages that they felt compromised active Agency sources and methods. In working with my co-author, I had been careful not to reveal sensitive material beyond what the CIA had already approved in other books.

As an experienced CIA Chief of Station and one loyal to the Agency's mission, I have absolutely no interest in undermining our nation's intelligence effort. But I also believe that freedom of speech is fundamental to all of our liberties, and that a timely and fair review of manuscripts by the Agency's Publications Review Board and Clandestine Service is essential if current and ex-Agency employees are to have a relevant voice in our national debate.

That same month, May 2005, I decided to retire from CIA's Clandestine Service after twenty-three years of service and an additional four years in the U.S. military. It had been a privilege to serve in the Directorate of Operations alongside brave men and women who helped me combat al-Qaeda and other terrorist groups.

Despite the fact that the CIA had recently approved another book by a retired Agency officer about the war in Afghanistan and had briefed authors Steve Coll (*Ghost Wars*) and Bob Woodward (*Bush at War*), they held up my manuscript for months. Finally in mid-July 2005, in what turned out to be the most surreal and frustrating experiences in my life, I was forced to file a lawsuit against my former em-

ployer. When a Federal judge ordered the Agency to release the manuscript in late August, they told me I had to redact over forty pages of
material, including the mileage between cities in Afghanistan and the
name of CIA officer William Buckley, which has appeared in hundreds of publications since his death in 1987.

When I asked the Agency to restore some of the material that had
already appeared in other publications that had been cleared by
them, I had to file another injunction in Federal Court before they
would respond. A Federal judge will ultimately rule if segments of the
book that have been blacked out by CIA censors will be added to future editions. For the sake of readability, my co-author and I have
tried to give the reader a sense of the subject matter of excised material. Blacked out lines of text that run more than two lines often indicate redacted segments which run for several pages.

I am privileged to have served alongside very brave men from the
CIA and the U.S. Military's Special Operations community while in
Afghanistan. As in many past conflicts, many of them were American
immigrants—especially, Muslim Americans from South Asia and the
Middle East—who stepped up and were the most critical component
of our intelligence collection effort. Those Muslim Americans reminded me about how special our country is and the liberties we
sometimes take for granted.

May God bless America and, especially, those who fight and sacri-
fice to defend it. I would also like to thank my wife and children for
their love and support over so many years, and extend thanks to Jim
Tyler of DOD and retired Lt. Colonel Mark Brightman for historical
and military context.

Gary Berntsen

Ralph Pezzullo would like to thank Gary, our agents, Wendy Silbert
and Harvey Klinger, our editor, Rick Horgan, and Julian Pavia, Tina
Constable, Brian Belfiglio, and the other very capable people at Crown,
and his wife, two sons, and two daughters for their love and support.

GLOSSARY

ADDO . . . . Associate Deputy Director of CIA Operations

AWACS . . . . Airborne Warning and Control System

CAS . . . . Close Air Support

CENTCOM . . . . U.S. Armed Forces Central Command based in Tampa, Florida

COS . . . . Chief of CIA Station

CTC . . . . CIA's Counterterrorism Center

CTC/▮▮▮ . . . . Counterterrorism Center/▮▮▮▮▮▮▮▮▮▮▮
▮▮▮▮▮▮▮▮▮▮▮

DCI . . . . Director of the CIA

DDO . . . . CIA's Director of Operations

DDST . . . . CIA's Deputy Directorate of Science and Technology

EDT . . . . Emergency Deployment Team

GPS . . . . Global Positioning System

GPC . . . . CIA's Global Response Center

IJO . . . . Islamic Jihad Organization

ISID . . . . Pakistan's Inter Service Intelligence Directorate

JSOC . . . . Joint Special Operations Command

▮▮▮▮▮▮▮▮▮▮▮▮▮▮▮▮▮▮▮▮▮▮

MOIS . . . . Iran's Ministry of Intelligence and Security

NA . . . . Afghanistan's Northern Alliance

NGO . . . . Non-governmental organization

NID . . . . National Intelligence Daily

SAD . . . . Special Activities Division—the paramilitary division of CIA Operations

SAS . . . . British Special Air Service

SF . . . . Special Forces, the Army's unconventional forces; not to be confused with JSOC Special Operations Forces

SIGNIT . . . . Signals intelligence, or intelligence derived from intercepting radio, telephone, computer or other electronic communications

SNI . . . . Shelter Now International

SOCOM . . . . Special Operations Command

SOFLAM . . . . Special Operations Forces Laser Acquisition Marker

KEY CHARACTERS

(■ The following names have been changed to guard their identity.)
(❑ The following names have been changed at the direction of CIA censors.)

CIA

■ A.C. . . . . Black-bearded tech wizard from Science and Technology and member of Jawbreaker.

■ Amir . . . . Arab-American member of Jawbreaker who was sent to work with Afghan warlord ███████ ████████████.

■ Bilal . . . . Arab-American former Marine who deployed with me to ███████ in 1999 and later joined Team Juliet in Tora Bora.

Cofer Black . . . . Very capable and aggressive Director of CTC, 1998–2004.

■ Breen . . . . My young team leader in Taloqan, assigned to work with warlord Berryelah Khan.

■ Brock . . . . No-nonsense team leader of Jawbreaker 2000.

■ Coleman . . . . Chief ███████████ in Dar es Salaam, Tanzania, at the time of the U.S. Embassy bombing.

■ Craig . . . . CIA team leader assigned to work with Hamid Karzai in southern Afghanistan near Kandahar.

■ Davis . . . . Blond-haired, blue-eyed former Marine Recon and CIA Case Officer who became my right-hand man in the Panshir and Kabul.

❑ Dawson . . . . CIA analyst and Uzbek speaker who was sent into Qala-i Jangi fortress with Mike Spann.

■ Donna . . . . Bin Laden expert who was part of the Emergency Deployment Team to Tanzania.

■ Dusty . . . . CIA contractor and former JSOC soldier who joined Juliet Forward in Tora Bora and directed air strikes on the al-Qaeda camp at Milawa.

■ Halsey . . . . Case officer serving in Uzbekistan who became a member of Jawbreaker 2000 deployment and had been a student of mine at the Farm.

■ Hamid . . . . Ivy League law school graduate and Muslim-American member of Jawbreaker 2001 used on the Shomali Plains as the primary translator.

Hank . . . . Hard-as-nails director of CTC/█████ (CTC/██) formed after 9/11/01.

■ Harold . . . . Former U.S. Special Forces Sergeant and my deputy in the Hezbollah element of CTC.

■ Hoss . . . . CIA Special Activities Division officer and former SEAL who deployed with Billy Waugh.

■ Johann . . . . East European-born ████████ officer who inspected al-Qaeda training, chemical and weapons facilities.

John . . . . Hank's deputy at CTC/██, who was scheduled to retire after 9/11.

■ Adam Khan . . . . Muslim-American and Pushtun speaker who played a key role with Team Juliet in Tora Bora, December 2001.

■ Klesko . . . . Aggressive Special Activities Division officer and member of Agency Team Delta who captured the number-two and number-three Taliban intel officials.

■ Lance . . . . JSOC soldier assigned to Juliet Forward who directed air strikes on the al-Qaeda camp at Milawa.

■ Lawrence . . . . Chief in Uzbekistan, who helped abort Jawbreaker 2000.

■ Marlowe . . . . Science and Technology expert and former Navy Seal who was a member of Jawbreakers 2000 and 2001.

■ Mary . . . . Chief of CIA Career Service Training Program (Recruitment).

■ McQueen . . . . Emergency Deployment Team leader from Special Operations who was with me in Tanzania.

■ Nelson . . . . Muscular African-American ███████ officer who inspected al-Qaeda training, chemical and weapons facilities.

Jeff O'Connell . . . . Director of the Counter Terrorism Center (CTC) in 1997–99.

■ Parker . . . . CIA officer and former SF officer who entered Kabul with Bismullah Khan's men and later joined Juliet Forward in Tora Bora to direct air strikes on the al-Qaeda camp at Milawa.

Jim Pavitt . . . . CIA Deputy Director of Operations, 1998–2004.

■ Phillip . . . . CIA Directorate of Intelligence South Asia expert who worked with Special Representative James Dobbins.

■ Reno . . . . Air Force Combat Controller assigned to JSOC who joined Juliet Forward in Tora Bora and directed air strikes on the al-Qaeda camp at Milawa.

Rich . . . . Chief of the Bin Laden Group who succeeded me in late December 2001.

■ R.J. . . . . Chief of CIA Team in Mazar-e Sharif who worked with General Dostum.

Mike Spann . . . . CIA first-tour officer killed at Qala-i Jangi fortress.

■ Stan . . . . Russian-speaking case officer who originally deployed on the Shomali Plains with Gary Schroen.

■ Storm . . . . Big, red-bearded Special Activities Division officer and member of Jawbreakers 2000 and 2001, who led the effect to free the SNI hostages.

■ Ted (aka FBI Ted) . . . . FBI detailee to the Hezbollah working group who led Emergency Deployment Team to Nairobi, Kenya, in August 1998.

George Tenet . . . . Director of the CIA, 1998–2004.

■ Todd . . . . Loyal Hooters customer and commo officer of Jawbreakers 2000 and 2001.

Billy Waugh . . . . Legendary seventy-two-year-old Special Forces Sergeant Major and CIA Special Activities Division contractor, joined Jawbreaker in late November 2001, later deployed south with Team Romeo.

■ Yale . . . . Workaholic first tour officer and member of Jawbreaker 2001.

U.S. MILITARY

■ Colonel Al Alexander . . . . . . ████-American SF officer detailed to CIA Special Activities Division, who led SF team into Tora Bora.

Master Sergeant John Bolduc . . Leader of Special Forces A Team 585 deployed in Taloqan.

Major General Dell Dailey . . . . . Head of Joint Special Operations Command (Delta Force) and highest-ranking U.S. military officer in Afghanistan during the fighting in Tora Bora.

Chief Warrant Officer David Diaz Leader of the Triple Nickel (555) Special Forces A Team members deployed on the Shomali Plains.

General Tommy Franks . . . . Commander in Chief of CENTCOM.

Lt. Colonel Chris Haas . . . . Commander of Special Forces A Team 555 (Triple Nickel) assigned to the Panshir and Shomali Plains, and later entered Kabul.

Brigadier General Gary Harrell . . Former commander of Delta Force and CENTCOM'S Director of Security, sent by General Franks to direct humanitarian effort in Afghanistan.

Colonel John Mulholland . . . . . 5th Special Forces Group Commander in charge of all Special Forces teams in Afghanistan.

■ Lt. Colonel Mark Sutter . . . . . Leader of three-man JSOC advance team sent to Afghanistan in late November 2001.

NORTHERN ALLIANCE

Dr. Abdullah Abdullah . . . . Northern Alliance Foreign Minister; met with U.S. Special Representative James Dobbins in Uzbekistan.

Engineer Aref . . . . Dapper, suspicious and canny head of Northern Alliance intelligence (aka, the Director).

Mohammad Atta . . . . Tajik Northern Alliance military commander in northern Afghanistan who helped liberate Mazar-e Sharif.

General Babajan . . . . Portly Northern Alliance subcommander on the Shomali Plains, under Bismullah Khan.

❏ Babrak . . . . Pashai warlord who joined the Eastern Alliance and fought in Tora Bora.

Abdul Rashid Dostum . . . . Hard-nosed Uzbek warlord who led an army in northern Afghanistan that liberated the Uzbek city of Mazar-e Sharif.

Mohammed Qasim Fahim . . . . . Massoud's successor as the military leader of the Northern Alliance.

Hamid Karzai . . . . Pushtun leader who led a small army in southern Afghanistan and was named leader of the interim government in December 2001.

Dr. Karim Khalili . . . . Hazara leader and Northern Alliance commander.

Berryelah Khan . . . . Northern Alliance commander in the north near Taloqan.

Bismullah Khan . . . . Commander of Northern Alliance forces on the Shomali Plains.

Ismail Khan . . . . Northern Alliance military commander in western Afghanistan, near the city of Herat.

❏ Majid . . . . Massoud's protégée and my main liason with the Northern Alliance; worked for both the foreign ministry and NA intel.

Ahmad Shah Massoud . . . . Tough, inspirational leader of the Northern Alliance, killed by an al-Qaeda bomb on September 10, 2001.

Jan Mohammad . . . . Northern Alliance chief of protocol.

General Mohammad Mohaqqeq . Hazara commander of the Hizb-e Wahadat forces who helped liberate the northern city of Mazar-e Sharif.

❏ Nuruddin . . . . Pushtun warlord who had been living in exile in France, returned to Afghanistan and joined the Eastern Alliance in Tora Bora.

Burhanuddin Rabbani . . . . Ex-President of Afghanistan and political leader of the Northern Alliance.

Abdurabab Rasul Sayyaf . . . . . . Pushtun warlord and original sponsor of bin Laden in Afghanistan who joined the Northern Alliance and was implicated in the assassination of Massoud.

General Sharifi . . . . Russian-speaking military subcommander on the Shomali Plains under Bismullah Khan.

❏ Ustad . . . . Engineer Aref's intel deputy on the Shomali Plains.

Haji Mohammed Zahir . . . . Older brother of Pushtun warlord Abdul Haq who was captured by the Taliban and hung in October 2001; became part of the Eastern Alliance that fought in Tora Bora.

TALIBAN AND AL-QAEDA

Qari Amadullah . . . . Chief of Taliban intelligence.

Mohammad Atef . . . . Former Egyptian policeman and military commander of al-Qaeda, killed by U.S. airstrikes outside of Gardez, Afghanistan, in November 2001.

Osama bin Laden . . . . Saudi-born leader and founder of al-Qaeda.

Mullah Mohammed Omar . . . . . One-eyed spiritual leader of the Taliban.

Ayman al-Zawahiri . . . . Egyptian militant and second in command of al-Qaeda; planned attacks on U.S. Embassies in Kenya and Tanzania.

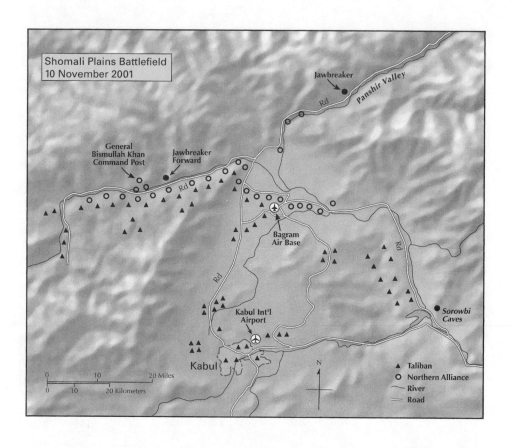

Shomali Plains Battlefield
10 November 2001

Jawbreaker

Panshir Valley

Rd

General
Bismullah Khan
Command Post

Jawbreaker
Forward

Rd

Bagram
Air Base

Rd

Kabul Int'l
Airport

Sorowbi
Caves

Kabul

N

▲ Taliban
○ Northern Alliance
River
Road

0   10   20 Miles
0   10   20 Kilometers

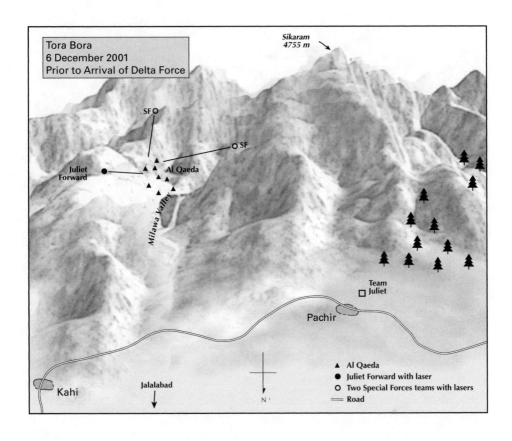

Tora Bora
6 December 2001
Prior to Arrival of Delta Force

Sikaram
4755 m

SF

SF

Juliet
Forward

Al Qaeda

Milawa Valley

Team
Juliet

Pachir

Kahi

Jalalabad

N

▲ Al Qaeda
● Juliet Forward with laser
○ Two Special Forces teams with lasers
═══ Road

JAWBREAKER

1

THE ATTACK—7 AUGUST 1998

"Dawn comes not twice to awaken a man."
—*an Arab proverb*

* * * * * *

jumped out of bed by the second ring and grabbed the STU-III secure telephone from the waist-high dresser. The digital clock read 4:23 A.M. in the dark bedroom of our Reston, Virginia, townhouse. My wife, Rebecca, sat up, rubbing her eyes.

"Hello."

A voice on the other end said, "Gary, it's Dorothy in the watch office."

I recognized her voice immediately. Dorothy was one of ███████ officers assigned to my staff in the CIA's Counterterrorism Center. Our job was to identify, penetrate and disrupt the activities of Islamic Jihad Organization (IJO)—the Hezbollah's terrorist arm and the most deadly organization of its kind up to that time.

"One second," I said, removing the top of a ███████ by the phone, extracting a ███████ key ███████ and inserting the key into the phone. "I'm going secure."

"Ready."

After pushing the "secure voice" button, a small horizontal panel lit up indicating that the encryption sequence was underway. It took fifteen seconds before the screen on the phone read "TOP SECRET."

Dorothy said: "I have you TS."

"I have you TS," I echoed back.

"Thirty-five minutes ago the U.S. Embassy in Nairobi was attacked with a large explosive device," Dorothy began. "Ten minutes later our Embassy in Dar es Salaam was also attacked with an explosive device. I just talked to Chief CTC O'Connell [CTC is the CIA's Counterterrorism Center]. He wants you to come in."

"Do you have numbers on casualties? Did we lose any of our people?" I asked.

Hearing the word "casualties," my wife gasped.

"There have been large-scale casualties, including some of our people," Dorothy answered.

"Thanks," I said. "I'm on my way in."

I turned the key, extracted it, ████████████████, carefully reset the top and stood for a moment in the darkness. I was one of our country's most experienced clandestine counterterrorism officers, but news like this still filled me with cold, seething anger. Pictures of the carnage from bombings I'd witnessed in places like Sri Lanka and Nepal flashed in my head.

My wife understood instinctively that something terrible had happened. "Where?" she asked.

Being an intense, aggressive guy, I imagined myself rushing to the scene immediately and grabbing the bombers. But I managed to remain outwardly calm. "Nairobi and Dar es Salaam," I answered. "We've just had two Embassies bombed within thirty minutes."

After nineteen years married to a CIA officer, my wife knew the drill. "Should I pack a bag for you now?" she asked.

I thought of practicalities for a second. "I have to go into the building first. If I fly out I'll come back first and get some things. Why don't you go back to bed?"

"Go back to bed?" she asked, incredulously. "I can't go back to bed now. I'll make you some coffee and start getting your stuff ready."

Using the encrypted phone, I called one of my branch chiefs, Ted—an FBI agent assigned to CTC. The CIA and the FBI, in the spirit of cooperation, had begun placing officers in each other's counterterrorism units, and Ted was one of the first FBI detailees.

Ted was one tough guy. Prior to joining the FBI, he'd been a Maryland State Police officer. While working undercover, he infiltrated a motorcycle gang suspected of major criminal activity. One night, they got suspicious, dragged him into a deserted field on Maryland's Eastern Shore and stuck a gun to his head. Ted didn't lose his cool. Not only did he talk the gang out of killing him, he eventually locked up sixty of them for crimes varying from grand theft, to drug trafficking, to murder. At the Bureau, he played a lead role in a number of important counterterrorism investigations, including the Iraqi attempt to assassinate former President George Herbert Walker Bush after the Gulf War.

He was the kind of officer I wanted at my side in a crisis. I quickly filled him in.

Then I jumped in the shower, skipped shaving and got dressed, foregoing a jacket because it was going to be a hot, humid August day. Exiting the bedroom, I ran into my seventeen-year-old daughter, Alexis, on the landing. The sound of my moving around had roused her.

She asked, "Dad, what's going on? Why are you guys up so early?"

There was no point trying to hide the truth. Alexis already knew that I was one of the CIA's senior counterterrorism officers, but her thirteen-year-old brother, Thomas, thought I had a desk job at the ████████████.

"There were some attacks on our Embassies in Africa so I need to go in early," I told her.

"Are you going to Africa?"

"Maybe, sweetheart, but not right now."

After a quick cup of coffee and kisses for my wife and daughter, I started out the door. Over my shoulder, the first reports of the bombings aired over CNN.

Standing outside our townhouse was my maroon 1987 Chrysler K station wagon—the car my son and daughter teasingly called "the red rocket." No, it wasn't an Aston Martin or a Land Rover equipped with surface-to-air rockets, but it got me where I wanted to go. My wife and daughter got the new wheels.

I'd taken this route so many times I could drive it in my sleep: down the Dulles toll road, onto route 123, a sharp turn into CIA headquarters twenty minutes later. At this hour of the morning the vast parking area was almost empty, except for vehicles belonging to members of the watch office and Directorate of Intelligence personnel who worked on the President's Daily Brief.

Passing through the CIA entrance, I swiped my badge over an optical reader and punched in my security code. My watch read 5:05 A.M. as I entered an elevator of the oldest wing of the three-building complex and hit five.

The Crisis Center consisted of two large rooms—one packed with communications racks with radios and multiple workstations to monitor Counterterrorism Center (CTC) developments around the world. The second room housed a large conference table and chairs.

CTC is part of the CIA's Directorate of Operations. The rest of the CIA's ███████ employees are organized under three other directorates: Science & Technology, Intelligence and Administration. Most of them are analysts, scientists and administrators.

The Directorate of Operations (DO) is the place that employs clandestine case officers like myself. Back in the mid-'90s the Clinton administration had reduced the number of operations officers by twenty-five percent. The DO is responsible for collecting human intelligence and running operations against 6 billion people and governments around the globe who want to harm the United States.

The FBI, for purposes of comparison, has approximately 10,000 field officers (special agents) covering the United States. There are one thousand FBI officers assigned to New York City alone.

You could say that working for Operations is challenging. Most of my closest colleagues are type-A individuals who won't back down from anyone or anything. We accept the fact that we live in a hard world and deal with that reality. It's dangerous work.

In the past, I've stopped dozens of bombings and assassinations overseas. I've also hunted down and captured terrorists from various groups. These are CIA successes that were never reported in the news.

When we're portrayed in the media, ninety-five percent of what's said or written is dead wrong. Books like Tom Clancy's *Clear and Present Danger* where the Deputy Director of the CIA personally hunts down terrorists—ridiculous. Movies like *Three Days of the Condor* where CIA operatives assassinate members of the American Literacy Historical Society—disgusting!

*   *   *

I felt a jolt of energy as I entered the Crisis Center. Chief CTC Jeff O'Connell stood in the dimly lit conference room speaking on a secure phone directly to the White House. Especially at that early hour of the morning, it was an intensely focused group. Ted (my FBI deputy) as well as the top officers in CTC were already there. News reports from CNN were being projected on the wall behind the head of the table.

O'Connell was around fifty, with slightly thinning reddish blond hair, five-foot-ten and fit. An excellent Arabist, O'Connell had served with distinction in multiple Middle East posts fighting Palestinian terrorist groups like Black September and Abu Nidal. Every time I saw him I was reminded of William Buckley and my early days in the Directorate of Operations.

I'd met both men in 1984 when—fresh out of training—I received my first assignment in NE Division (Directorate of Operations Near East and South Asian Division) working on Iraqi issues. It was a hell of a time to cut one's teeth. Two days before my assignment, on April 18, 1983, a van packed with two thousand pounds of explosives blew off the front of the U.S. Embassy in Beirut, collapsing the front portion of the seven-story structure and killing sixty-three people including the ███████. In one fell swoop, the crème de la crème of the United States' Middle East intelligence had been wiped out. A single CIA officer, who happened to be out of the building buying a carpet, survived.

The attack was the work of Hezbollah, Lebanon's Shiite Muslim political party (Party of God), under the banner of the Islamic Jihad Organization (IJO). Led by the Shiite cleric Fadallah, Hezbollah was closely tied to the Islamic regime in Iran.

I'd entered NE Division during its darkest hour. The darkness grew thicker a few months later when the man dispatched as the new chief in Beruit, William Buckley, was kidnapped by Hezbollah. Hezbollah wanted the government of Kuwait to release Mustafa Badr al-Din (the brother-in-law of Imad Mughniyad, Hezbollah's IJO terror chief), who was responsible for the 1983 bombing of the U.S. Embassy in Kuwait City. But the United States would not allow itself to be blackmailed by terrorists.

Despite the heroic efforts of many brave men and women to try to rescue Buckley, he was tortured and maltreated and eventually died in captivity. One of my last tasks before being deployed in the field was to review tapes of Buckley sent to the CIA by Hezbollah. As long as I live, I'll never erase the heartbreaking image of that tired, broken man, dressed in a sweat suit and holding up a newspaper to confirm the date, forced to read Hezbollah propaganda.

I promised myself right then and there that I'd do absolutely everything in my power to guard against myself or any of my people getting kidnapped by terrorists. Out of the Buckley experience, I derived two important lessons: focus on those groups that pose an immediate threat and strike them quickly; understand that the risks cannot be removed even though CIA and political leadership will always gravitate towards risk-free solutions.

Most of the officers in the Crisis Center conference room had lost a friend or colleague in the '83 Beirut bombing. O'Connell lowered the sound on CNN so that it played like a silent horror movie on the wall behind him. I watched as shocked, injured people climbed out of the rubble of the U.S. Embassies. O'Connell pointed out that initial estimates indicated that casualties were higher in Nairobi than in Dar es Salaam. When he mentioned the name of a young ███████ assigned to the U.S. Embassy in Kenya, found among the confirmed dead, I felt like I'd been kicked in the chest. ████████████████ ████████████████.

O'Connell wasted no time. "I think all of us probably sense Hezbollah fingerprints on both these bombings," he said. "But let's keep an open mind." Then he reviewed the bombing report for the Khobar Towers in Dhahran, Saudi Arabia. In 1996, after years of not attacking the U.S., the Hezbollah and the Iranian Government set off a gigantic bomb in a fuel truck that killed nineteen U.S. servicemen in Dhahran, Saudi Arabia.

O'Connell looked directly at me. "Gary will lead an Emergency Deployment Team (EDT) to Dar es Salaam, Tanzania. Ted will lead a second team to Nairobi. Both of you understand Hezbollah, but I'm going to cover my bets. I'm going to give each of you an officer out of the bin Laden shop in the event bin Laden has decided to go big."

The CTC Chief of Operations gave us our air deployments. I would leave that afternoon on a ████████ jet. Ted would travel with a big contingent of FBI special agents out of Andrews Air Force Base at noon.

Ted raised his hand. "Given that initial reports indicated larger loss of life and damage in Nairobi, I recommend that Gary lead the Nairobi team. I can serve as his deputy and you can insert someone else into Tanzania."

██

██

████████████████████████████████

O'Connell said, "We're going to have a massive deployment of the FBI in Nairobi. Ted, I need you to ensure that we do not get off track with the FBI. Any more questions?"

O'Connell dismissed the group. The Chief of Operations (who was my immediate supervisor), Ted and I waited until the others filed out. The Chief of Operations, a former Marine and experienced Near East veteran, turned to me and said, "Your assuming command of the EDT teams has not been coordinated with the CIA Special Missions folks. I'll smooth it over. They already have established teams. You'll be layered on top of the existing structure."

"Don't worry," I said with a grin. "We'll work like one big happy family."

The three of us left at 6:00 A.M.—the Chief of Operations for his office in CTC; FBI Ted and I in search of Africa's Chief of Operations. With twenty years' experience in the field, the Chief of Operations/Africa quickly described the size of the missions in Nairobi and Dar es Salaam, approximate number of employees.

"Who's the CIA Chief in Nairobi?" I asked.

" J.T. He's an intelligence analyst."

"An intelligence analyst?" I blurted out. "What the hell's the matter with you guys sending a DI [Directorate of Intelligence] type to Nairobi?"

The Chief of Operations/Africa tried to explain: "Dave Cohen [the former Deputy Director of Operations and an Intelligence Officer himself] felt that analysts are Intelligence Officers, too, and should have a chance to lead in the field."

"Come on," I said. "That's like putting the mayor of a small city in charge of an Aircraft Carrier Battle Group."

"J.T.'s a smart guy, but he's not in-country."

"Where is he?"

"On leave somewhere in the Midwest."

"Great."

Under former CIA Director John Deutsch (a President Clinton appointee who served from 1994 to 1997), intelligence analysts—whose job was to study open and clandestine source material and write reports—were put through the ops course and sent into the field to run CIA offices. The fact that they had no real experience running agents or managing operations didn't seem to matter. It's one of many things instituted by former Director Deutsch and his deputy and successor George Tenet that I felt undermined the Agency.

By 0700 Ted and I headed down to our offices in CTC. Standing in the doorway was my deputy, Harold—a former U.S. Army Special Forces Sergeant who had entered CTC as an analyst. He looked pissed. "I should kick your ass for not calling me in," he said. "Do I have typhoid or something?"

I said, "You do almost everything around here. You have to let me do something now and then."

"What kind of bullshit answer is that?" Harold asked. "Now I'm definitely going to kick your ass."

"Cool off," I said. "Ted and I are both leading Emergency Deployment Teams. I need you to run the show here while I'm gone."

"Oh, you're leaving me here to mind the store. Thanks." Harold quickly changed gears. "Anyone claim responsibility?"

"Not yet."

"I'll call everyone together for a skull session. I wonder if we've seen any movement from Mustapha Badr al-Din."

As usual, Harold was right on the money. Badr al-Din was the guy who built the bomb that killed 242 U.S. Marines in Beirut on October 23, 1983. He also constructed the bomb that destroyed the U.S. Embassy in Kuwait. He'd been captured in Kuwait as part of a group known as the Dawa-17, but was released after the Iraqis invaded Kuwait and opened the prisons. [He's the man Hezbollah wanted exchanged for William Buckley.]

Instead of fleeing back to Lebanon after his incarceration, Badr al-Din stayed to fight alongside the Kuwaitis against Iraq. It was a strange way for showing his appreciation for being freed from prison, but this was the Middle East.

The rest of the morning passed in a flash: a quick meeting with McQueen (the regular EDT leader from Special Missions) to assure him we would work in tandem and a final one-on-one with O'Connell in his office. O'Connell again stressed the importance of cooperating with the FBI. "They don't have the overseas experience you have," he told me. "But since these were attacks on U.S. installations, they have to treat them as criminal investigations. For purposes of a prosecution they have the lead. In relation to other intelligence issues, it's your show. But do your best to help them."

"No problem," I said. "I've worked closely with the Bureau in the past."

It was noon. Rebecca, who had taken the day off, met me with a packed bag and drove me to the airport. Our family had spent a good number of years living overseas in places like the Persian Gulf and South Asia. She said: "My mind's on the Embassy families in Nairobi and Dar es Salaam and the suffering they are going through."

"Mine, too."

"I'm glad you can help," she said kissing me on the lips. "Be safe."

A sleek ▇▇▇▇▇▇▇▇▇ jet waited on the runway. In addition to McQueen (from CIA Special Missions) and myself, the Emergency Deployment Team included a communications officer, bomb technician, computer specialist, military specialist assigned to CTC and the bin Laden intelligence analyst Donna.

As the jet zipped across the Atlantic at six hundred miles per hour, piloted by a man who lost his leg in Vietnam, I tried to remember what I knew about East Africa. It had been part of the vast Oman Empire, which included the islands of Zanzibar and Pemba off the Tanzanian coast. Until 1963, the ruler of Zanzibar was an Arab sultan and cousin of the current Sultan of Oman, Sultan Qaboos.

For some reason an image of Humphrey Bogart kept coming to

mind. Then I remembered that the film *African Queen* was supposed to take place in Tanzania during World War I. That's when it was a German colony. After World War I, German East Africa was transferred to the dominion of Great Britain under the name Tanganyika. In 1964 it gained its independence and, merging with Zanzibar, became Tanzania.

Despite the fact that it was home to Mount Kilimanjaro and the largest wild animal population in the world—safari groups called attention to its spectacular wildebeest, monkey, antelope, lion, cheetah, crocodile, gazelle and flamingo populations—Tanzania remained one of the poorest countries on the planet. It is largely rural, with eighty percent of the workforce involved in agriculture, even though a mere five percent of the land is suitable for cultivation. Its citizens come primarily from various branches of the Bantu tribe. Most speak Swahili, but English is widely used.

After its independence, Tanzania had been led by Julius Nyerere, who instituted a unique form of African Socialism tied to community farming, which proved to be an economic disaster. At the height of the Cold War, Nyerere had been a close ally of the Communist Chinese, which put a severe strain on his relationship with the U.S. ████████████████████████

After stops to refuel in Scotland and Athens, the ██████ jet started to descend.

On the ground in Dar es Salaam, I saw nothing. No terminal. Only a single-story building with a few dim lights. As we deplaned, two very determined women strode towards us. One was a light-skinned black woman, the other white. The black woman spoke in perfect American English: "Good evening. Welcome to Dar es Salaam. We're from the Embassy. Coleman, our chief, is waiting for you at your hotel."

During the thirty-minute drive into the city, the African-American woman informed us that ten Tanzanians had died in the bomb attack. Thanks to an Embassy staff meeting that was taking place on the opposite side of the building to where the car bomb exploded, there had been no American casualties. Most of the dead were Tanzanian visa applicants and local Tanzanian guards. "We were real lucky," she said.

It was 10 P.M., August 9, when we arrived at the hotel. A six-foot-tall American with salt-and-pepper hair stood waiting with a very tall black woman sporting dreadlocks. The pair introduced themselves as Coleman (the Chief) and his deputy, Patricia. I'd never met either of them before.

"I'm glad you're here," Coleman said. He was from Alabama and spoke with a thick southern accent.

"Thanks," I replied, studying Coleman's face. I knew from experience that people react differently to bombings, murder and unexpected crises. Coleman seemed intensely angry—not sad, not doubting, not questioning himself. *That's good*, I thought.

Coleman said, "I want one thing and one thing only: Find and capture the bastards responsible. I won't shed any tears if they're killed."

"Understood."

As we entered the elevator, a third, light-haired man squeezed in. "Are you part of the State Department Response Team?" he asked me.

Coleman pegged him right away as a journalist. "Fuck off, asshole."

The journalist, shocked by the vigor of Coleman's response, quickly got off at the third floor. My team rode up to five and six.

After dropping off my bag, Patricia drove me to the Embassy for a firsthand look. It was dark, but the devastated building and surrounding area were lit with special lights. The bomb had taken a big, savage bite out of the three-story white structure so that a large piece of one side was missing. In its place, directly to the right of the entrance where a concrete guardhouse had previously stood, was a deep, smoldering crater. Charred vehicles littered the property. The bomb had blown open the hoods of every vehicle in the Embassy parking lot.

Behind yards of yellow plastic police tape Tanzanian soldiers, sporting jaunty berets and automatic rifles, stood watch. A pretty petite blond-haired woman with a big camera around her neck appeared behind us. She said she was an American journalist and wanted to enter the Embassy to shoot photos.

"I don't think so, honey," dreadlocked Patricia said.

The journalist didn't want to leave and the Tanzanians didn't want to let me in because they didn't know who I was. Patricia pulled out a radio and called for someone. Two minutes later a young ███████ Officer wearing a baseball cap, khakis and a T-shirt emerged from the damaged building carrying a shotgun. Patricia explained that I needed entry and that the blonde needed to go. The young officer turned to the journalist and said, "You get your skinny ass out of here."

The journalist didn't move. "The American people have a right to know what happened," she said.

He leveled the shotgun at her. "I said, get the hell out of here, bitch!"

I entered, thinking, *These Africa Division people are tough.*

But the journalist wasn't giving up. She stood behind the yellow tape screaming at the Tanzanian guards: "This is no way to treat an American citizen. I'm going to come back."

I surveyed the destruction with an analytical eye. Having served as a firefighter in the Air Force, I was no stranger to the nauseating smell of burnt fuel and human flesh. Before me stood shredded vehicles and a six-foot-deep crater. I figured it had been produced with several hundred pounds of explosives. I'd seen worse in the late '80s during my assignment to Sri Lanka, where explosive devices of several thousand pounds had left twenty- and thirty-foot craters and hundreds dead.

Patricia and I stepped around burned-out vehicles and walked through the main entrance. The blast had passed through much of the building and blown out the hardened bulletproof glass structure of Post One—always manned by a U.S. Marine security guard who controlled entry and exit to the Mission.

"What happened to the Marine on guard inside the building?" I asked.

Patricia replied: "He's fine; bit of a headache. Tough fellow."

Patricia had been one of a few people who hadn't attended the staff meeting on the opposite side of the Embassy. When the bomb went off, she and another officer were with the Deputy Chief of Mission in his office on the second floor, toward the center of the building. They were literally launched off the sofa they were sitting on and smashed headfirst into the opposite wall.

We moved through the downstairs corridor, which looked like it had been struck by a tornado. The blast had thrown furniture into hallways and through walls. It was a miracle that no one inside the structure had died or was critically injured.

Coleman sat amid the rubble with a laptop hooked to a communications package and antenna and was typing out messages.

"What's going on?" I asked.

Coleman quickly narrated events of the previous morning. "At 0940, a white pickup truck parked approximately one hundred yards down along the side of the road. It was there only momentarily. A fifteen-hundred gallon water tanker was turning around just inside the entrance preparing to exit the Embassy compound. At the side Embassy entrance, the guards initiated the switch to open the gate. The white pickup truck, with covered cargo in its bay, drove rapidly down the road and tried to enter through the entrance. The delta barrier, which is a steel structure that comes up from the ground like a steel flap facing the driver, was up and the white pickup truck could not get in.

"Inside the pickup were a driver and one passenger. The passenger got out, and started yelling at the guard to let them in. The guard, sensing something was wrong, ran back into the concrete steel security structure alongside the gate to shut the gate. At that moment, the white pickup detonated. The large chassis that you see sitting there next to the building was the water truck. Luckily, it was full of water and absorbed a lot of the blast. Probably saved a lot of lives.

"The pickup truck is in a thousand pieces. Several of the guards in the guard shack died. The one who refused them entry and ran back to the shack survived. Tanzanian visa applicants waiting in line outside the Embassy were killed outright or terribly maimed."

The building across the street from the Embassy had been completely destroyed. It housed the Embassy's kindergarten and child-care center, which were fortunately closed because of a Tanzanian holiday.

"I have a lot to do," Coleman said. "I have to ████████████, pursue those who have perpetrated the blast and simultaneously deal with a massive FBI investigative element that's on its way."

I understood that he was angry and facing an enormous number of tasks, but the destruction and chaos of the previous day wasn't going to be neutralized in a day or even a month. I said, "Why don't you let me get the Tanzanian side of things up and running. Let my team deal with the FBI."

"Fine."

That's when the State Department's Regional Security Officer (RSO) appeared to tell me that his senior Tanzanian local investigator was waiting in front of the Embassy. The local investigator, a former Tanzanian Police Officer, was an acquaintance of the Chief of the Tanzanian Intelligence Service.

██

From midnight until 4 A.M., Patricia and I pored over maps looking at land routes for escape. We studied airline manifests of flights several days proceeding and the day of the attack. I knew that Hezbollah frequently sent a senior member to oversee the planning of an operation, who would then flee before the attack.

"We've got to start casting a net," I said. ████████████████

██

██

██

██

████████████████████████████████████

Back at my hotel at 5:30 A.M., I took a two-hour nap, showered, shaved, then went up to the fifth floor to see how my buddy McQueen and the EDT were making out. Laptops, cameras and scanning devices covered several tables. "We've got our communications up," McQueen reported. He said he planned to rent a helicopter to get overhead photos of the Embassy and blast site.

As we talked, scenes of the chaos in Nairobi were broadcast over CNN. Uncontrolled crowds swarmed over the bombsite. Bodies were being dragged without stretchers and tossed about.

"What the hell are the Kenyans doing?" I asked, cringing.

"The team for Nairobi got stuck in England," McQueen said. "There's still no one running the site."

From CNN we learned that a building next to the Embassy—the Ufundi building—had completely collapsed. Ambassador Prudence Bushnell, with a bloody bandage on her head, addressed the press.

I was on my way down to the restaurant, which looked out on an exuberantly green garden. Big game photos lined the walls. My breakfast was interrupted by a tall man in a zebra-striped safari suit. I looked up and smiled at my old friend Nelson.

"Nice to see you again, Gary," he said.

Nelson was an African version of the Harvey Keitel character in the movie *Pulp Fiction*. Born in Uganda, he spoke fluent English, Swahili and German. If you wanted a revolt started or stopped, an air drop of humanitarian relief or, even, the purchase of a ████████ mini-sub, Nelson was the guy to see. ████████████████████████████

I said, "Thank you for traveling here on such short notice to help us."

"It's always a pleasure to help out my American friends," he replied with a big grin.

"I'm looking for what I suspect are Islamic extremists who fled just before the bombing or immediately after."

Nelson said, "I have many useful contacts here. A man named

Phillip will meet you at two P.M. ███████████████████████████
████████████████████████████████████

At 2 P.M. I returned to the hotel restaurant. Waiting was a man who looked like a clerk. "Mr. Gary Berntsen," he said, "I am Phillip. I will be your working contact." Phillip was ████████████████████████████. He struck me as low-key and optimistic.

Phillip listened intently as I told him who I was and the nature of my mission. Then I handed him a list of what we needed: ███████████
██
██
██
█████████████████████████████████

Phillip said, "These tasks will require a great deal of time and work. When do you need the information?"

"Now," I answered.

The laid-back Tanzanian screwed up his face. "Sometime tomorrow or the next day maybe?"

I was firm. "Each hour that passes allows the terrorists to put more time between us and them."

After swapping cell phone numbers, we agreed to meet in my room at 7 P.M. Upstairs in the Emergency Deployment Team suite, McQueen had just returned from a nearby airfield. Using a computer, he displayed digital photos taken from a rented helicopter. They showed damage to the buildings around the Embassy. Roofs had been blown off; others were missing beams and tiles.

At 7 P.M. Phillip knocked on my door. ████████████████████████
██
██████████████████████████████

████████████████████████ "Given the fact that the attack was conducted via truck bomb they would have needed to assemble the device in a secure location," I said, thinking out loud. "It's likely, therefore, that they rented a house somewhere."

██

████████████ ████████ There was a good chance that the FBI would dig pieces of the engine block out of the blast pit and find the vehicle identification number (VIN), which would allow them to track the vehicle from its original owner through purchases to the bomber. But that could take weeks.

Back in the EDT room, McQueen, Donna (the bin Laden expert) and I dug through the ██████████████████████████████ (material provided by Phillip). I was looking for Lebanese and Jordanian names.

Donna interrupted me at one point. "Have you asked your contacts for a list of non-governmental organizations (NGOs)? Say it's not Hezbollah. Say instead we're looking at Sunni extremists like Osama bin Laden. If so, they very likely used NGOs for cover to plan and execute the operation." Terrorist groups often used NGOs to transfer money and explain their presence in countries other than their own.

"That's a good idea. ████████████████."

"The Sunni Jihadists in Pakistan and Afghanistan under the famous Palestinian Sheikh Azzam began their anti-Soviet activities out of NGOs," Donna added. "One NGO of particular importance is Al-Haramain. "

I'd never heard of Al-Haramain, but Donna was the bin Laden expert. So I added NGOs to our list of priorities.

*　　*　　*

It wasn't until dawn of August 10 when four hundred miles northwest Ted and his team arrived at Nairobi International Airport. A bright, hot African sun rose as they dragged their gear from the C-141 aircraft. Dozens of U.S. Embassy vehicles and trucks waited on the tarmac to transport them to hotels. Ted grabbed a car and directed the driver to take him to the U.S. Embassy.

Leaving the airport, they entered a strip of shantytowns. As Ted looked out on roads clogged with taxis, buses and tens of thousands of people, he noticed something else. Every third person seemed to be wearing some type of bandage on their head, neck, shoulder, arms or legs. "Are those a result of the blast?" Ted asked the driver.

"Lots of flying glass shards. Lots of injuries. Yes, sir."

Closer to the city center, the ratio grew to one of every two people. In addition to the estimated death toll of more than two hundred, more than five thousand people had been injured.

Unlike the bombing in Dar es Salaam, which took place in a wide-open suburban area with space and trees between buildings, the attack in Nairobi occurred in highly congested narrow streets and alleys. The full force of the blast had literally been trapped. Drivers, pedestrians, street vendors, etc., found themselves assaulted from all sides by pieces of flying concrete, steel, aluminum and glass.

Ted finally arrived at U.S. Embassy grounds, now protected by Embassy guards and Kenyan police who had gradually established order. A massive rescue effort was still underway at the Ufundi building next to the Embassy. Within the first forty-eight hours one hundred bodies had been removed. At least another hundred were still missing. Anxious, red-eyed family members ringed the area waiting for news of missing loved ones.

Ted used his credentials to access the perimeter of the U.S. Embassy and found the Assistant Regional Security Officer.

"I need to get inside the building," Ted said.

"Not a good idea. We've got to test the structure first."

"The thing is, I can't wait. I need to get on to the fourth floor."

"They lost a couple of people up there."

"Let's go."

The two men climbed through the wreckage at the entrance and worked their way up a stairwell to the ███████. The office space was a mess of broken glass, furniture and partially collapsed walls. Ted couldn't help but notice large patches of half-dried blood where several Americans had spent the last moments of their lives.

He saw classified documents scattered among the rubble on the floor. Grabbing a trash can with a plastic liner, he dumped the can's content and began filling the plastic bag with classified documents. He extracted a classified hard drive from a computer and stashed it inside. He knew that the only reason those ███████████████ officers had left without securing the space completely was because they were busy dragging out their injured and dead.

From the shattered fourth-floor window Ted watched what appeared to be a never-ending extraction of dead from the Ufundi building next door. Generator engines ripped the air; floodlights lit the pile of rubble and twisted beams. Hundreds of Kenyan workers, many in street clothes, dug through chunks of concrete with their bare hands, only a few feet away from heavy machinery. Rescue dogs and their American handlers searched frantically for signs of life.

Looking directly below, he saw white rectangles floating in the wind like big snowflakes.

Realizing they were more documents from the Embassy, he hurried down the stairs. The first two crumpled documents he picked off the ground were Secret ██████████.

*   *   *

FBI Special Agent Ken Piernik finally arrived with his team in Dar es Salaam late in the morning of the tenth, after the other FBI team got off the C-141 in Kenya. Piernik was a big, aggressive take-charge kind of guy. A former U.S. Army helicopter pilot in Vietnam and twenty-year Bureau veteran of the FBI, Piernik had recently run an FBI gang task force in Chicago.

His specialty was hunting down criminals. The fact that he'd never led an overseas deployment and had never set foot in East Africa didn't bother him. He was ready to take action and wasn't surprised by the bombings. He felt that as the world became more crowded and violent, the U.S. should expect more terrorist attacks.

Piernik and his team were staying at the handsome Sea Cliffs Hotel a few miles down the coast. Its center lobby was piled high with gray weapons cases. Swarms of FBI agents in short-sleeved shirts with FBI logos were busy dragging the crates to designated rooms. All wore khaki or green tactical-looking pants and boots. Gradually, they became aware of the strange American standing in their midst. The first to make eye contact with me was a dark-haired Special Agent of about thirty years of age.

I pulled out my ██████████ passport and approached him. "Excuse me," I said, "my name is Gary Berntsen, and I'm a U.S. official. I need to speak to whoever is leading this FBI deployment."

The young man examined the ████████ passport and dialed a cell phone. "Is Piernik available?" he asked in the phone. "This is Donnelly. I have an American official who wants to speak to him."

Satisfied with himself, the young FBI officer handed me the cell. I heard a voice say, "This is Ken Piernik."

"Hello, Mr. Piernik, this is Gary Berntsen. I was sent by Jeff O'Connell and told to make contact with you on your arrival."

Piernik immediately knew who I was. "Great! Let's meet tonight. I'm conferring with a group of people at the moment so I can't come down."

"Agent Piernik, I have an important meeting with ██████████ in less than an hour and would like to have one of your officers accompany me."

"Who do you want?" Piernik asked.

"This young fellow standing here with me will do just fine."

"He's yours. Let me speak to him for a second."

The confused-looking young FBI agent (Donnelly) took the phone. Piernik instructed him to accompany the man standing in front of him to a meeting, then return with him as soon as possible.

"What if he doesn't want to come back?" Donnelly asked.

"Club him, cuff him and drag him back. See you then." Piernik hung up.

The young agent looked even more perplexed. "What is this?"

"Welcome to the world of intelligence," I said. "I'm the CIA team leader. You're coming with me now."

"What the hell are you talking about? I'm with you . . . for what?"

"I'll brief you in the car."

Back at my hotel, we met with Phillip, who handed over more manifests, maps, names of NGOs and hotel registries. When the meeting ended, I took Donnelly upstairs to meet the rest of the Emergency Deployment Team.

The fifth-floor suite was a beehive of activity with people huddled over computer screens, sifting through documents, scouring maps. I said, "Good evening, everyone. I want you all to meet FBI Donnelly. He's part of the team now, just a little shy and not sure he wants to work with us."

The entire team read the suspicion on Donnelly's face. "Nice to have you aboard," McQueen said, cheerfully.

Donna chimed in: " Good to have you on the team."

The bomb technician, a former Marine, stood up: "Hey, Donnelly, since you're the new man, go downstairs and get me a cup of coffee. Black."

Everyone broke out laughing.

Donnelly wasn't amused. "This is just for tonight," he stammered. Then, realizing that the ex-Marine was pulling his leg, turned to me and asked, "Don't we have to see Piernik?"

For the next week, FBI Donnelly would be attached to me almost every waking minute. He would attend meetings with me, read my reports, host meetings for me in a crunch and become fully integrated into the team.

Donnelly liked the informal way the EDT functioned. He was also amazed at my latitude regarding resources.

*   *   *

On the fourteenth of August—one week after the bombings—an Egyptian named Mustapha ███ entered the embassy of a close ally of the United States and said he had information to sell regarding the U.S. Embassy attacks. The friendly government alerted the CIA.

It turned out that Mustapha, a man in his early fifties who had spent a considerable amount of time in East Africa and currently managed ███████████ Corporation in Dar es Salaam, was known to the Agency. A year before, Mustapha had visited the U.S. Embassy and tried to sell information about a planned attack on the U.S. Embassy. Mustapha ████████ provided data, some of which was confirmed, but part of which was proven to be false. He was branded a fabricator and sent on his way. Unfortunately, the tip he gave about the bombing of the U.S. Embassy in Nairobi proved to be correct.

On August 15, Mustapha ████████ went to the friendly government's Embassy in Dar es Salaam for a follow-up visit, only to be shown the door. I stood waiting outside with an Arabic-speaking FBI agent named Joseph.

███

██████████████████████████████████

[*NOTE TO READER:* CIA censors redacted the investigation of Mustapha ███████ that later led to this arrest.]

* * *

On the morning of August 15, a CIA officer in Karachi, Pakistan, noticed a small article in a side column of a Karachi newspaper. It said that on August 8 (the day after the bombings), an Arab traveling on a false Pakistani passport was arrested at Karachi's International Airport.

███

███

███

███

███

█████████████████████████████████

[*NOTE TO READER:* CIA censors redacted this account of al-Qaeda terrorist Saddiq Odeh's arrest in Pakistan.]

Seated toward the front of Pakistan's version of ████████████████, on the Karachi runway. I watched five Pakistani Security Agents escort a scrawny, pathetic-looking figure onto the aircraft. Saddiq Odeh was shackled, wearing handcuffs attached to a belt fastened around his waist, and what looked like twenty feet of tape wrapped around his head and eyes.

I had to resist the impulse to clobber him. Instead, I watched him take a seat at the back of the jet, between several Pakistani Security Agents. Then the plane took off.

███

███

███

███

████████████████████

The significance of Saddiq Odeh's confession was profound. It meant that Lebanese Hezbollah was no longer the only terrorist group conducting large-scale bombings of U.S. targets. Osama bin Laden had graduated into the group. I quickly drafted a detailed report that was sent to President Clinton.

At some point during the three-hour flight, Saddiq Odeh began to realize that he was not being returned to Afghanistan as promised. He started to shake, first gently, then uncontrollably.

When the aircraft landed, Pakistani escorts led a trembling Saddiq Odeh down the stairs. Waiting on the tarmac was a contingent of smartly dressed Kenyan Police officials. One of them stepped forward and said in perfect English, "Welcome back to Nairobi, Mr. Odeh. We have been waiting for you."

Odeh's knees almost gave out. The FBI wanted immediate custody of Saddiq. But I didn't doubt that the Kenyans would get him to talk.

Two Kenyans replaced the Pakistani escorts and Saddiq Odeh was placed in a car and whisked off. He would have a very bad time, and would share everything he knew about Osama bin Laden and the al-Qaeda organization.

*　　*　　*

Earlier that same day, a twenty-four-year-old Saudi citizen named Mohammed Rasheed Daoud al-Owahali was taken into custody for the Nairobi bombing. On August 7, 1998, the day of the bombing, Mohammed Rasheed Daoud al-Owahali was the only passenger in a white pickup truck that stopped at the entrance of the U.S. Embassy in Nairobi. He got out and approached one of the Embassy's guarded entrances, with the intention of pressuring the guard to open the gate. But he was so nervous that he had left his gun in the truck. When screaming at the guard didn't work, he tossed a grenade. The driver of the pickup, seeing that the gate to the U.S. Embassy compound was not going to open, backed up the vehicle and positioned it alongside the Embassy.

As the driver got ready to detonate his truck bomb, Mohammed Rasheed had a change of heart. He didn't want to be a martyr. He turned and ran as fast as he could from the truck. The blast blew him off his feet and forward, leaving lacerations and cuts from the back of his head down to his ankles. Returning to his hotel with blood running down his back, he entered and exited several times, acting like a person in shock. Hotel management called the police, who, together with the FBI, tracked his movements to a local hospital. During a search of Mohammed Rasheed's hospital room, the FBI found bullets in the pockets of his pants. They belonged to the gun he had forgotten in the pickup. Mohammed Rasheed was placed under arrest.

*   *   *

In the weeks that followed, FBI teams in Nairobi and Dar es Salaam tirelessly dug through blast pits, extracted pieces of engines, identified VIN numbers and ran down the owners of the vehicles. Piernik's men also hunted down other attackers, including a twenty-seven-year-old Tanzanian named Khalfan Khamis Mohammed, who had rented the safe house for the Dar es Salaam team and helped build the bomb. They nabbed him in Cape Town, South Africa.

Another terrorist captured was a naturalized U.S. citizen named Wadih El Hage, who had been bin Laden's personal secretary and a principal planner of the East Africa bombings under the cover of a non-governmental organization called Help Africa People.

Donna had been correct. Al-Qaeda had used charititable organizations to tranfer money, build and transport bombs and move personnel. Instead of feeding starving children and building hospitals, Help Africa People had murdered a total of 12 Americans and 242 Africans and injured at least 5,000 Kenyans and Tanzanians.

All of the men captured would be convicted of terrorism charges in a New York City Federal Court. They would receive life sentences without parole. Federal prosecutors asked the judge to withhold capital punishment so the terrorists couldn't become martyrs.

* * *

I spent my last afternoon in Dar es Salaam on the terrace of Sea Cliffs Hotel, enjoying the view and sipping a gin and tonic. A cool breeze blew in across the water from Zanzibar. They were my first minutes of leisure in many weeks.

The juxtaposition of smoldering bombsites to gentle tranquility was jarring. It reminded me that life was like that, filled with surprises, terrifying one minute, indescribably beautiful the next.

One hundred feet away, framed against the aqua sea, stood a single Masai warrior, dressed in a red tunic carrying a spear. I said to myself, *I wish I brought my camera. Two different hunters in two different worlds.*

2

THE DECLARATION

"We are now at war with al-Qaeda."
—CIA *Director George Tenet, August 1998*

*   *   *   *   *   *

I was a bad kid growing up on Smithtown, Long Island—a blue-collar suburb of New York City. My friends and I drank, got into fights and caused all sorts of trouble.

The only thing I studied with any passion was horses. Roosevelt Raceway was only a forty-five minute drive from my house, so I would hitch-hike there and put down bets for myself and my buddies from school.

This was the mid-1970s. The Vietnam War was winding down. Bachman Turner Overdrive blared from our eight-track cassette players. The social changes of the '60s were shaking up everyone around us. I wasn't as big or as tough as my friends were. I was just trying to hang on and survive. Dope wasn't my thing, but I drank beer by the six-pack every weekend from the age of thirteen.

The night before my sixteenth birthday I was bussing tables at the Fontana di Trevi Restaurant on Jericho Turnpike when some buddies stopped by. My friend Terry had "borrowed" his Dad's '69 Cadillac. I stood in the parking lot in my white shirt, black tie and short red jacket as they guzzled beer and tried to convince me to join them. "I can't," I said. "I've got to work all damn night."

They drove off yelling at arriving customers: "The food sucks. Don't go in!"

Several hours later they slammed the Caddie into a tree at seventy miles an hour. One of my best friends, Ben, severed his aorta and died.

A few months later, another close friend got caught hijacking an eighteen-wheeler. I used to visit him at prison in Riverhead, Attica and Elmira.

Out of a Hauppauge High School class of around 300, I graduated one from the bottom—a functional illiterate with a 65.6 grade point average.

But I had secret ambitions and wanted to escape my confined, drab, negative life. I tried to join the Army my junior year, but my father, an engineer for Fairchild Republic Aircraft, wouldn't sign the papers. He said President Nixon was a liar and was afraid that I would fall victim of a failed war in Vietnam. Even though my mother loved me, she wanted me out of the house. She knew that I needed to leave to make something of myself.

So I waited until my eighteenth birthday and signed up myself. First, I talked a Marine Corps recruiter on Long Island into giving me the answers to the Armed Forces Aptitude Exam. Then I took the train into Manhattan, walked into the Armed Forces Recruitment center in Times Square and joined the Air Force.

I'll never forget January 30, 1976, my first day of basic training at Lackland Air Force Base, Texas. I stood in line for early morning roll call, feeling lousy because my body was craving alcohol. All of a sudden, a consciousness came over me that I'd never experienced before. It was as though a veil had been lifted from my eyes and I was seeing things clearly for the first time. I realized in that moment that I'd misused my life. I'd squandered opportunities and failed myself and those around me. I decided right then and there: I was going to change.

I stopped drinking immediately and decided to make something of myself. The first Monday of my first Air Force assignment as a crash firefighter in Osan, South Korea, I went to the Base Education Center and signed up for self-studies. After reviewing the high school subjects I'd slept or cheated my way through, I started tackling college courses. I aced the first five, and continued.

I tore through biographies of famous people: Lord Kitchener, Teddy Roosevelt, Golda Meir, Harry Truman, Albert Schweitzer, Mustapha Kemal Ataturk, Winston Churchill, the German Lutheran Minister Dietrich Bonhoeffer, who studied in the U.S. and returned to Germany to confront the Nazis.

My thirst for knowledge became insatiable. When I wasn't working or studying, I was skydiving or hitting the gym. I was totally committed to improving myself.

Good things followed. At Kirtland Air Force Base in New Mexico I met and married my wife, Rebecca. The day after my discharge from the Air Force, I signed into the Marine Corps Platoon Leader Class program and attended two very tough summers of Officer Candidate training, majoring in political science with a minor in Russian studies. But before I received my Marine Corps commission, I was recruited into the CIA.

The Agency liked the fact that I'd completed four years of Air Force service and Marine Corps officer candidate training, had studied Russian and was a sport parachutist. They put me through two years of training including the operations course, small arms qualifications, air operations, parachuting, explosives training, small unit operations and a survival course. In 1984, just shy of twenty-seven, I became a clandestine case officer and a member of the Agency's paramilitary reserve cadre.

For the next seventeen years, my career was centered in the Directorate of Operations Near East and South Asia Division, known as NE/Division. I completed multiyear assignments in the Persian Gulf, Sri Lanka and a special ███████ Operational Element based in Europe, served as an instructor at the Farm (the Directorate of Operations training facility) and then became Chief ███████████.

My assignment as Chief of Hezbollah was the direct result of my leading a number of very successful counterterrorism operations in South Asia. I stopped an assassination attempt against a major world leader, thwarted a series of bombings by Islamic militants, and hunted down and captured terrorist ██████████████.

While most CIA Case Officers advanced their careers by recruiting sources and producing intelligence, I took a more grab-them-by-the-neck approach. Instead of writing pithy intelligence reports, I focused on recruiting sources and using them to hunt and capture terrorists and explosives. I wanted my reports to read: "Target captured and rendered to justice." I was to be my own consumer of intelligence.

Up until August 1998, my unorthodox approach had worked. I operated on the principle that it was easier to seek forgiveness than ask for approval. Take risks, but make sure you're successful. Success, not good intentions, would determine my fate.

*   *   *

When I returned from Tanzania, people throughout Washington were applauding the achievements of our Emergency Deployment Team. Greeting me on the wall outside my office in CTC was a framed 8 X 10 photo that showed a small white pickup truck, like those driven by the al-Qaeda members who attacked the U.S. Embassies in Nairobi and Dar es Salaam, with my head superimposed behind the wheel and Ted next to me. A caption coming from FBI Ted's mouth read, "Are you sure you know what you're doing?"

Posted on the walls of CTC's conference rooms were a series of articles in the press lauding the cooperation between the FBI and CIA in the investigations of the East Africa bombings. Our team's mission had been a success. Not only did we break new ground in terms of CIA-FBI coordination, we also captured a good number of the bombers.

The question that burned in all our minds was: *Now that we know that Osama bin Laden is responsible for the bombings, how is the Clinton administration going to respond?*

The answer came on August 20 in the form of a Tomahawk cruise missile attack on several al-Qaeda training camps in Afghanistan and a pharmaceutical factory in Sudan. The plan was to hit bin Laden during a large meeting of terrorist leaders and to destroy a factory in Sudan that was allegedly producing chemical weapons. Both failed. Bin Laden was not at any of the three camps that were hit and the Clinton administration quickly backed away from their claim that the pharmaceutical factory in Sudan produced anything more than analgesics and aspirin.

When I met with Mike Scheuer, the career intelligence analyst who led the CIA Bin Laden Group, a few days after the U.S. reprisal attacks, he was pissed. Here was a guy who studied bin Laden eighteen hours a day and knew him better than anyone in the U.S. government. He said categorically that the destruction of bin Laden and his forces in Afghanistan could be accomplished only with the direct intervention of some type of force on the ground.

I said: "Mike, that won't happen. President Clinton doesn't have it in his DNA to act that boldly."

Mike agreed. He pointed out parenthetically that the public's attention was more focused on Monica Lewinsky and a stain on her dark blue dress.

"Clinton's contempt for military action coupled with risk aversion on the seventh floor [the DCI's office] makes it a nonstarter," I concluded.

None of us in Operations had come to expect strong leadership from DCI George Tenet. A former Senate staffer, Tenet had been brought in by President Clinton in 1995 as Deputy Director under John Deutsch and later promoted after Deutsch resigned in December 1996. Tenet seemed hell-bent on downsizing Operations and tying what was left of it in red tape.

Operations officers who conceived of clandestine operations usually saw their plans second-guessed to death by Division Chiefs. These Division Chiefs—equal in rank to four-star generals—were responsible for managing CIA stations in a particular region of the world. Europe Division (EUR/Division), for example, was notoriously bad. It had a reputation for creating so many impediments that officers from the aggressive divisions—like CTC—would look to other regions of the world to conduct their operations.

It was a frustrating time to be an aggressive officer. I knew that Hezbollah terrorists with active U.S. warrants were hiding in Beirut, but Clinton administration policy forbade captures and renditions within Lebanon. Did this make sense? Individuals who had blown up the U.S. Embassy in Beirut, killed 241 Marines in another bombing, kidnapped and killed CIA Chief of Station William F. Buckley and as recently as 1996 supported the bombing of Khobar Towers in Saudi Arabia, killing 17 U.S. Air Force personnel, could not be seized from the very place were they planned and trained for these operations.

Several days after I returned to headquarters, I attended a weekly CTC staff meeting. Speaking in the crowded first-floor conference, Chief CTC Jeff O'Connell said that the CIA Director Tenet wanted us all to know that we were now at war with al-Qaeda. He repeated, "The Director wants you all to know that we're now at war with al-Qaeda."

No one said a thing. Instead, we looked at one another in stunned silence. I saw FBI Ted across the large conference table and mouthed the words: "We are at war."

Ted mouthed back, "Thanks for sharing."

Looking at the thirty or so senior CTC officers gathered in the room, I realized something else. There were only two of us who spoke Middle Eastern languages. I spoke decent Farsi and CTC Chief O'Connell was fluent in Arabic. During the past three years Director George Tenet had given hundreds of Operations officers early outs so the Agency could save money.

I thought, *Great, let's get rid of our most senior and qualified officers, tie those who are left in red tape, and then declare war.*

*   *   *

The bureaucratic conundrum I was dealing with hit home three months later during the ███████████ case, which showed how I had to bend the rules to effectively do my job. One afternoon I was seated at my desk reviewing hundreds of intelligence reports and operational messages that came into CTC from CIA Stations around the world when I heard a knock on my door. "Come in."

A large, well-built man of forty entered—clean-shaven with ethnic Arab features and a military bearing.

"Excuse me," he said. "My name's Bilal. I'm a former Master Sergeant in the U.S. Marine Corps. Special Missions said you might need someone like me."

We shook hands. "Tell me about yourself, Bilal."

"I'm a Marine."

"Lee Harvey Oswald was a Marine, too. I'd like a little bit more detail."

Bilal laughed. "I grew up in Detroit, not Dallas." Then continued: "I'm a Shiite Muslim. I was born in West Beirut and immigrated to the United States when I was seven. I didn't speak a word of English. In Beirut, our whole family lived together in two rooms. When I arrived in the U.S. I had my own room. I remember being so happy that I jumped up and down on my bed like it was a trampoline. But in school no one could understand me. Within a few months I learned to speak in English.

"My mom and dad were strict and insisted we speak Arabic at home and stick to our family. But because of school and friends I became a hundred percent American. My parents had plans for me to go to college and work near home. They weren't happy when I told them I planned to join the Marine Corps.

"When I finished Basic Training I went home to Detroit. For a week my father insisted I wear my dress blues and go with him to visit all our friends and family in the community. I'd become the final validation of the family's decision to come to America. I was proud, too."

At that point my deputy, Harold, walked in carrying a sheaf of ops messages. Seeing Bilal, whom he had met already, Harold wise-cracked: "Bilal wanted to go into Special Forces, but since we don't let men hold hands he had to join the Marines."

Bilal responded with a four-word burst of Arabic and they both broke out laughing. "I guess you know one another," I said. As they continued trading insults, I sat thinking, *Bilal is exactly the kind of guy we need in Operations, but given the recent cutbacks I'm going to have a hard time getting him in.* Then, noticing the papers in my deputy's hand, I asked, "What have you got?"

Harold turned serious. ██████████████████████

██

██

██

██

██

██

██

██

██

██

██

██

██

██

██

██

██

██

██

██████████████████████████████████

[*NOTE TO READER:* This redacted section, which runs several pages, deals with the arrest of a Hezbollah terrorist and bomber in another country south of the Equator.]

I was taken to task by my superiors for bending the rules. Luckily, I was supported by Chief CTC Jeff O'Connell, who reminded me that, "No good deed goes unpunished."

To my mind, the ███████ case was a glaring example of the red tape you had to hack through to get anything done. It also showed the complex legal and governmental terrain we had to negotiate in order to bring known terrorists to justice.

*　*　*

After CIA Director George Tenet declared war on al-Qaeda, we were told that a large number of new officers would be assigned to CTC to do work in the field. That number was soon reduced again, and again, and again, until it became meaningless. I watched in frustration as officers who sat in safe staff jobs were promoted faster than ops officers who risked their lives in the field. In George Tenet's CIA the conduct of operations was less important than Beltway politics and networking on the seventh floor.

So when my two-year tenure as operations leader against Hezbollah came to an end in July 1999, I thought long and hard about getting out. I had heard that the Senate Select Committee on Intelligence (SSCI) was looking for a Senior Operations Officer to join its staff. I conveyed my interest in the SSCI job to Chief CTC O'Connell, who said that while he didn't want to lose good officers, he understood that the Agency desperately needed greater congressional support.

But the man who succeeded him, Cofer Black, didn't want me to go. A career Africa/Division officer, Cofer had fought his way through the ranks in Third World hardship posts and was famous for orchestrating the capture of ███████████████████ while serving as ████████. He was tall, balding and charismatic.

When I sat down with him in early July 1999, days after O'Connell's departure, he got down to brass tracks. "Gary," he said, "I know you have been considering taking a job on the Hill, but we cannot afford to have strong officers like you leave."

As I poured out my frustration with the bureaucratic malaise, the cutbacks and the lack of recruitment of native Arabs, Cofer nodded his head. "Good."

"What do you mean, good?"

"These are some important things you can do for me," Cofer said. "First off, go to the recruitment center for a couple months to kickstart a program of bringing native Arabic and Persian speakers into CTC."

"I'd like that."

"Once you get that started, I want to move you into a couple of tough field assignments I'm envisioning."

"Sounds good."

He wasn't finished. "Over the past few years the Directorate of Operations has, because of political concerns and fear of losses, closed down CIA offices in Somalia, Tajikistan, Sudan and Afghanistan. I recognize that none of these governments are friendly, and they are chock-full of folks who would like to kill us, but we have to go back in one way or the other."

Cofer's predecessor, O'Connell, had used the less direct FBI tactic known as double tap. It was a strategy of disruptions, arrests and renditions against the infrastructure that numerous terrorist groups had created around the world. Double tap had been productive. Something like ███████ men and women, responsible for planting bombs and murdering indiscriminately around the globe, had been captured by CTC and put into prisons around the world. Thousands of lives had been saved without a whisper to the public.

But Cofer was talking about a more aggressive approach. He said, "Gary, give me a year of your time, a couple of months at the recruitment center, some special assignments inside terrorist sanctuaries, and I will get you another Chief of Station post."

"You've got a deal."

After two weeks of leave, I reported to the recruitment center on September 1, 1999. There I met Mary, the Chief of the Career Service Trainee program—an accomplished Operations Officer whose husband, also a highly regarded ops officer, had been killed in the line of duty in the early '90s. She continued her career after his death and raised their three children on her own.

Mary wanted to be helpful and was willing to recruit officers directly into CTC, which had never been done before. She introduced me to one of her staff officers, who outlined a new recruitment strategy complete with handsome-looking ads in high-end foreign affairs magazines. Within weeks, résumés started pouring in and I was flying all over the country interviewing applicants in Los Angeles, Miami, Detroit, Chicago, Houston, Boston and New York.

One of the first candidates I met was a young Arab-American who had been interviewed months earlier and rejected. After four years in the U.S. Navy as a communications specialist, he'd received an honorable discharge and enrolled in a good U.S. university where he received a bachelor's degree. The officer who interviewed him wrote that the candidate was too much of an introvert and probably didn't possess the interpersonal skills needed.

I thought, *Native Arabic speaker, ex-military, already possesses a Top Secret clearance, good grade point average at college.* Seemed like a winner to me.

Within three days I was on a plane to the Midwest to interview Amir. We met in the lobby of a Holiday Inn.

"Tell me about your previous interview," I said.

Amir responded in perfect American English: "I was asked to role-play in two different scenarios. I didn't think it went that well."

"Why?"

"Honestly, I was caught off guard. I had spent all my time preparing for questions on current affairs and memorizing the structure of the Agency. I was never asked about the Agency. It clearly would have helped had I taken drama classes in college."

"We're not going to do any role-playing today."

Amir laughed. "I practiced with my wife last night. Are you sure?"

I said, "I came here from Washington, D.C., to see and speak only to you. I want you to take the next two hours and tell me the story of your life. I'm all ears."

Amir was born in to a Sunni Muslim family living in ▮▮▮▮▮▮. His father was a professional; his mother, an educated woman who attended university, had stayed home to raise Amir and his brothers and sisters. His father had a brother in the United States who was a doctor and talked incessantly about America's freedoms and opportunity.

They moved to the States when Amir was eleven. At that point he had already studied English for three years, which helped a lot. Still, school was difficult. The kids were rough and fought a lot.

His mother and father continued to speak Arabic at home, but Amir and his siblings spoke English among themselves. They watched American cartoons and, later, sitcoms. Amir began to straddle two cultures. His parents were stricter and more controlling than the parents of his native-born American friends.

After graduating from high school, Amir enlisted in the U.S. Navy even though his parents said they were willing to pay for college. In the Navy, he had to prove himself again to be one of the boys. He accepted the fact that he was Muslim in a dominantly Christian country. After the Navy, he went to college and married an ▮▮▮▮▮▮ American girl. America might not be a perfect place, he thought, but it was still the greatest country in the world.

We talked about politics, history and culture. When the interview ended, Amir asked if he had done better this time.

"Are you ready to take a plane ride?" I asked him.

Amir responded with the Arabic "*Aywa,*" which means, "Yes."

*   *   *

I hadn't forgotten about Bilal, who had contacted me during the ▮▮▮▮▮▮ case. In addition to being an excellent candidate himself, Bilal provided me with the names of several Arabic and Persian speakers he had met in the military.

One of these was a former Marine and native-born ▮▮▮▮▮▮

named Adam Khan. Khan, who held a masters degree in history, was now living in Washington, D.C., and working as senior officer with another agency of the U.S. government. He was thirty-seven and my height, six-feet tall, with a full head of jet black hair and dark skin.

[*NOTE TO READER:* CIA censors have redacted the story of Adam Khan's background.]

Once in the U.S., Adam Khan and his siblings adapted quickly. He studied English and found work as an auto mechanic. One day Adam was in a restaurant when he struck up a conversation with three men in U.S. Marine Corps uniforms. They spoke proudly about the Corps' traditions and bought Adam a drink.

Within two weeks, Adam Khan enlisted. ████████████████████, Adam fit right in. His unit participated in evacuating U.S. Embassy staff from Sierra Leone during a bloody civil war.

While in the Marines, Khan became fascinated with history and technology. He used his GI Bill benefits to get a masters degree.

I had no doubt that Adam Khan could be a huge asset to the Agency. He spoke Pushtun and Dari (the Afghan version of Persian) and was fluent in the culture, history and politics of South Asia.

I interviewed a number of other Muslim candidates. Many were Arab men in their mid-thirties with no college degrees. What they shared was fluency in their native language, a love of the United States and a willingness to serve their new country.

Before Christmas, I met with Cofer to review my progress. He was pleased, but understood that identifying good candidates was half the battle. Getting them trained, cleared and up to speed was the hardest part. Staffing CTC with the native-speaking Middle Eastern officers needed would take a decade of work.

As the meeting ended, Cofer mentioned that he was moving forward with his plan to infiltrate terrorist sanctuaries.

I said, "I'm ready to travel whenever you need me."

"Bring your shot records in after New Year's," he answered. "You're going overseas."

3

DEPLOYMENTS

"You make promises and abandon us.
I will never understand your country."
—*an aide to General Ahmad Shah Massoud*
of the Afghan Northern Alliance, February 2000

* * * * * *

███

███

███

████████████████████████████████████

[*NOTE TO READER:* This redacted section, which runs several pages, is about an operation against al-Qaeda terrorists that Bilal and I undertook in late 1999 in a Balkan country.]

* * *

Late February 2000 I was back at Langley beginning a month of intensive Farsi language review. Chief CTC Cofer Black and his deputy, Hank, had asked me to put together a small team to go into ██████████, which could serve as a springboard for establishing a semipermanent presence in Afghanistan.

One morning in early March, I was sitting at the breakfast table getting ready to leave for class when the phone rang. It was Mike Scheuer's deputy from the bin Laden shop.

"How's your Farsi?" he asked.

"Not bad. I've been doing a full-time one-on-one review for the last three weeks."

He said, "We have a problem. We need you to skip class this morning and come into the building."

My wife, Rebecca, who was leaving for work, reminded me that I had to take our son, Thomas, to get fitted for a back brace. Thomas had pulled his back muscles while jumping into a swimming pool. I found him sitting up in bed in his room watching TV.

I said, "Relax, son. I'll be back in an hour."

Entering the bin Laden unit I was quickly ushered into Scheuer's deputy's office. He wasted no time: "Gary," he said, "for the past three months we've been preparing to deploy a six-man team into Afghanistan's Panshir Valley to undertake several missions. Our team has been off for specialized training and is being led by Brock, a former Army Special Forces major who has worked with Ahmad Shah Massoud's

Northern Alliance in the past. The team had one Farsi-speaking case officer whom we just found out can't travel. The Afghans have one guy who speaks English. But that's not enough to handle the missions that have to be done in country."

"This is all very interesting," I said. "But when does the team deploy?"

"Early this evening," he answered. "And we expect them to remain in Afghanistan for at least two months."

"Are Cofer and Hank aware that you want to send me off on this op?"

"Hank says this takes precedence. But you need to know that even though you outrank Brock, he's the one who put this program together, so we want you to serve as his deputy."

"That's not a problem," I replied. "You need a linguist, you got one. I just have to take my son to a medical appointment at one, then break the news to my wife."

Scheuer's deputy laughed. "You're a good sport, Gary. We knew we could count on you."

I met briefly with Brock, the team leader—a hard-as-nails case officer who had a reputation for being the worst-dressed guy in the Agency. He favored jeans and cowboy boots and basically didn't give a damn what people thought.

Brock expressed his gratitude, then arranged for one of CTC's finance officers to give me ███████████████ to buy gear. We would be traveling commercially from Washington to Frankfurt, Germany, and then into Tashkent, Uzbekistan, for two or three days before traveling on to Dushanbe, Tajikistan. We would be ferried into Afghanistan via a Northern Alliance helicopter. He explained that the weather was frequently clouded over between Tajikistan and Afghanistan, which made helicopter flights over the Pamir mountains impossible. "The last team that tried to enter sat in Dushanbe for three weeks and was then told to abandon the mission and return to D.C.," Brock said.

Before I left, he told me that the code name for the CTC deployments was Jawbreaker and that our communications would be under that name. He also said that ██████████ Lawrence, had responsibility for ████████ because the ████████ was still closed. According to Brock, our current relations with both ████████ and the Northern Alliance were somewhat strained because of Lawrence's erratic behavior. I'd worked for Lawrence in the past and understood.

With ██████████ in my pocket, I headed home and called Rebecca, who wasn't pleased.

"Please tell me you're taking Thomas to his medical appointment this afternoon," she said.

"Of course."

I watched Thomas being fitted for a back brace and bravely fighting back tears. It wasn't the best time to tell him that I was leaving on a trip that could last several months.

"Can't someone else go?" he asked.

My daughter, Alexis, gave a similar response when she returned from school. "Oh no, Dad!"

The one person who was pleased that I was traveling was the young sales clerk at the local sporting goods store, who worked on commission. He happily helped me pick out three and half thousand dollars worth of cold-weather gear. I told him I was moving to Alaska.

That evening, Rebecca drove me to Dulles International Airport. She understood the importance of my job and my commitment to my country, but she was still seething inside. "It isn't fair," she complained. "Why does it always have to be you? Why don't you tell them 'no'?"

I didn't even try to answer. It wouldn't have done any good.

Inside the terminal, no-nonsense Brock introduced me to three other members of the team. They included Storm, a former Army Special Forces Captain from Special Activities Division; Marlowe, a former Navy Seal Lieutenant who was with the Directorate of Science and Technology; and Todd, a former Marine and the team communicator. The final member was a case officer named Halsey who was a former U.S. Army paratrooper who participated in the invasion of Panama and had been a student of mine six years earlier at the Farm.

Halsey greeted me the next morning after we arrived in Tashkent. "Aren't you going to thank me for getting you a seat on this one?" He asked with a big smile on his face.

"What are you talking about?" I asked back.

"I remembered you were a Farsi speaker and heard you had just returned from the Balkans. Lawrence, the chief, hates Brock, the team leader, who has no respect for people in authority who don't know what they're talking about, and we thought you would be good to have on the team. We sent back channel messages to headquarters requesting your presence."

"Thanks."

"You know Lawrence, right?"

"Oh, yes."

"He's a nightmare," Halsey said. "Since we have no ▒▒▒▒▒▒ in ▒▒▒▒▒▒ and no presence in Afghanistan, Lawrence has a lot of say regarding what goes on in ▒▒▒▒▒▒ and our relations with the Northern Alliance."

I shook my head and said, "He needs professional help." During Lawrence's first Chief of Station tour, all his assets were caught and most of them were executed. Every single person in the CIA Station was declared persona non grata and expelled from the country. He was later involved as a minor player in the Iran-Contra scandal. Despite these major screwups he had managed to get himself promoted.

Halsey said that Lawrence was less than thrilled to have a CTC team on his turf. All this led to the unpleasant conclusion: We couldn't count on Lawrence for support.

The plan called for Brock, Marlowe, Halsey, and Todd to fly over the mountains to Dushanbe. Since they were taking a commercial flight that couldn't accommodate all our gear and weapons, Storm and I would make the dangerous seven-hour drive by truck. We set out the next morning at 5 A.M.—me in the first vehicle with an ████████ driver; Storm in the second.

It turned out to be an enlightening journey since our driver, Zayd, was a native of the ancient Uzbek city of Bhukara with a degree in history. For the next six hours he lectured me on Uzbekistan, beginning with the ancient Silk Road trading route between China and the West. He covered Alexander the Great's conquest of the region and the invasions of the Huns and Turks, who brought Islam and, later, Genghis Khan. Zayd explained in colorful detail how Timur (also known as Tamerlaine and a descendant of Genghis Khan) conquered Persia, captured Baghdad and then led expeditions into what is modern-day Turkey and India.

He talked proudly about how the Uzbeks fiercely resisted the Russians both in the 19th century and after the First World War. When he smiled he flashed two rows of Soviet-made silver teeth.

The countryside we rumbled through was desperately poor. Zayd said that the average Uzbek family made the equivalent of one hundred and forty U.S. dollars a month.

We reached the Tajik border an hour early and found no ████████ escort, just a group of hostile-looking armed men looking for trouble. The Tajik soldiers on the other side of the border looked equally menacing. The front tire of Storm's vehicle was very low and needed air.

I said, "If we stay here too long, one of these guys is going to draw down on us and we'll have a shootout."

So instead of unloading the truck to get at the spare, we filled the tire with a small compressor and pressed on. The roads on the Tajik side of the border were even worse. If Uzbekistan was poor, then Tajikistan was a basket case. Not only was it a nexus of narco-trafficking with heroin coming in from Afghanistan and moving on to Russia, it was also teeming with Islamic extremists who had their hands in the Tajik government.

Entering the capital at high speed, we passed a massive industrial complex on our right. Zayd claimed that it was the largest aluminum factory in the world and had been built by the Soviets.

The next morning at a safehouse a few blocks from the U.S. Embassy, Brock sat down with me and explained our mission. We would enter the Panshir Valley just north of Kabul, Afghanistan, and work with General Ahmad Shah Massoud's Northern Alliance to gather intelligence on bin Laden and his training camps. Our chief liaison would be Engineer Aref, the Chief of Northern Alliance Intelligence, and an English-speaking aide named Majid.

Brock said that we needed to work fast because the Taliban was scheduled to launch an offensive against the Northern Alliance in ten days. ██
██
██
██
██

After the East Africa bombings, the U.S. had put a three-million-dollar bounty on bin Laden's head. Bin Laden, aware that CIA officers had entered Afghanistan and worked there from time to time, retaliated with a three-million-dollar bounty on any CIA officer brought to him dead or alive.

I had read enough history to know that Afghans could be treacherous. Back in the 17th century the famous Pushtun poet Khushal Khah Kattan had written about feuding Afghan warlords:

> *They place before them the Koran*
> *They read aloud from it*
> *But their actions not a one*
> *Conforms with the Koran.*

Over the centuries, Afghan tribal leaders had accepted bribes and changed sides when it suited them. The Taliban's rise to power in the mid- to late 1990s was accomplished in large part with Saudi money that was used to buy off opposing warlords, some of whom allowed their men to be outflanked and slaughtered on the battlefield.

Majid, Engineer Aref's deputy and close advisor to Ahmad Shah Massoud, arrived to tell us in perfect English that the cloud cover over the Pamir mountains was expected to break in two days.

Majid ███████████████████████████████ was well-educated, knowledgeable and determined to free his country from the Taliban—all of which made me glad to have him on our side.

In the afternoon Brock and I met with the U.S. Embassy Political Officer who said that the Tajiks were aware of our mission into Northern Afghanistan and, therefore, the Russians knew, as well. Even though Massoud had been a deadly enemy of the Soviets during the Afghan Jihad, they now saw him as the lesser of two evils.

The Embassy Political Officer told us what we already knew: Iran's ruthless Ministry of Intelligence and Security (MOIS) was also on the ground with the Northern Alliance in the Panshir Valley and maintained relations with Massoud. I'd spent years working against MOIS and considered them the equivalent of Middle Eastern Nazis. Either directly or indirectly, they had been responsible for deaths of many U.S. citizens since the Islamic Iranian Revolution.

MOIS was helping Massoud because Shia Iran hated the Sunni Taliban. On the eighth of August, 1998, the day I'd arrived in Dar es Salaam to investigate the East Africa bombings, the Taliban seized the northern Afghan city of Mazar-e Sharif and murdered eleven Iranian diplomats at the Iranian consulate. The Taliban then executed thousands of Afghanistan's Shia Hazara tribesmen. The Iranians were still incensed.

Bright and early on our third day in Dushanbe, Majid announced that the weather was clear and it was time to insert. We'd be traveling in a Northern Alliance Russian-made MI-17 helicopter. The first flight would carry several Northern Alliance commanders and some of our equipment. The helicopter would then return for the Jawbreaker team and the rest of our gear.

No sooner were we on the road in a small caravan of SUVs than a seven-series BMW followed by a pack of SUVs sped past. Through the open windows of the SUV, I saw assault rifles sticking up in the air.

"What the hell's that?" I asked Halsey, sitting beside me. "A government official?"

"They're narco-traffickers," answered Halsey. "It's very common for them to move around the city like that, armed to protect themselves against attacks by rival groups. Half the guys riding in the SUVs are probably off-duty police or military."

When we arrived at the airport, a Tajik ████████ officer escorted us onto the flight line past several Russian MIG-27 fighters and a mangled assortment of military helicopters. All were Soviet or Eastern European built. Many of the helicopters looked like they hadn't been flown in years. We stopped next to a large Northern Alliance MI-17 with faded camouflage paint interspersed with dozens of painted over patches to fill holes that were probably produced by ground fire. Its tires were completely bald and covered with fifty-cent-sized bubbles. The blades were full of nicks.

I climbed in to inspect the fuselage. Lying smack in the middle was an internal fuel tank the size of a single bed. The heavy smell of fuel indicated a serious leak.

Having served as a U.S. Air Force firefighter, I knew an aviation accident waiting to happen. I said to Halsey, "We'll all be asphyxiated before we clear the field."

"Don't worry," Halsey replied. "We ride with the windows open." Halsey had participated in two previous Jawbreaker deployments and returned in one piece.

I overheard Majid say to our team leader, Brock, "We had a little problem on the first trip this morning. A Taliban MIG-19 was tracking us, but our pilot was able to fly low enough in mountainous territory to avoid us getting shot down."

"Who is flying the MIG-19s for the Taliban?" I asked.

"Russian mercenaries," Brock answered.

Halsey broke in with a laugh, "Nothing like a little free enterprise on the part of Russian pilots to make our day interesting."

As we loaded the helicopter, an old Russian sedan pulled up. Out climbed several Afghans—some in suits, others in worn army surplus fatigue jackets with oily blue jeans and torn sneakers. They looked like homeless people. The one who wasn't wearing socks was introduced as the pilot.

I greeted him in Farsi. He said his name was Behzad. He told me that he'd been flying for more than ten years and had been taught by Russian instructors. When I asked what the most dangerous part of flying over the Pamirs was, he said, bad fuel.

Half of us took seats along the fuselage; the others sat on gear. Then the engines started with a roar. Since several of the round portal windows were already open, we started pulling on gloves and hats to stay warm. The helicopter lifted up, took a sharp turn, and drove forward low and fast with its head down.

Heading south toward the Afghan border, we quickly cleared the city of Dushanbe and were over farmland. Even though we were flying at an altitude of only five hundred feet, the air was cool and clear. After ten minutes the paved roads stopped and all we could see below were dirt roads cut deep into the terrain.

Within another ten minutes we were over grassland following trails that could only be traveled by camels. The trails were too rutted for even a jeep and carved at least five feet into the ground. Majid said they had been in use for hundreds, if not thousands, of years.

The pilot dropped even lower, running at full throttle along a giant dried-out river or *wadi*. Suddenly, the bucket of bolts we were riding in began a rapid ascent. The Pamirs grew closer and closer, until we entered a dramatic gap with walls of stone on both sides. Continuing to climb through snow-filled passes surrounded by magnificent peaks, we reached the top—a vast snow-filled expanse of impassable territory.

If we ever go down, I thought to myself, *it will take us three months to hump out.* I remembered the great British Antarctic Explorer Ernest Shackleton and the story of how he and his men survived in Antarctica after their ship had been crushed by the ice.

But I wasn't unnerved. Nor did I want to turn back. This was the type of experience I'd been craving since I was a little boy growing up in Smithtown, Long Island. I considered myself lucky to be living this great adventure in the company of brave men.

We were flying at close to 18,000 feet. From the cockpit it looked like the snow and ice continued forever. With fuel fumes burning my nostrils, I asked Majid, seated between the pilots, how much longer it would be until we landed. "An hour and a half," he responded.

A week earlier, I'd made a deal with my son. I'd choose a book for him to read and he would pick one for me. I'd given him *Black Hawk Down* by Marc Bowden; he handed me *Harry Potter and the Sorcerer's Stone* by J.K. Rowling. To the amusement of my five Jawbreaker team members, I opened *Harry Potter* and started to read.

Ninety minutes later we began our slow descent. We passed over lower, less jagged mountains to avoid detection by Taliban MIG-19s, then entered the long Panshir Valley—known as Death Valley to the Soviets. Clay-colored mud houses clustered in villages clung to the banks of the river, which were covered with grass and mulberry trees. The rest of the valley was brown and barren. We banked and set down along the river. A half a dozen jeeps and pickup trucks with three-dozen Afghans were approached.

We passed our gear to the Afghans as the rotors continued to turn. I stood holding on to the roll bar in the back of a Toyota pickup next to two smiling bearded Afghans as the helicopter took off, spraying us with sand as groups of children waved.

We were in a valley surrounded by towering mountains of gray stone with very sparse vegetation. The highest peaks were covered with snow. It was beautiful, but forbidding. I thought to myself, *You wouldn't want to try to come in and take this valley by force.*

A mile down the road we made a sharp left into a walled compound that contained a very large three-story building. This was the guesthouse of Ahmad Shah Massoud and would serve as our headquarters. The first floor was made up of a dining room, a kitchen and a large carpeted parlor. The second floor had five bedrooms. One would serve as our workspace/communications center. Todd, our commo officer, would sleep in this room. Brock, Halsey, Storm, Marlowe and I spread out into the other bedrooms. The living room was on the third floor.

I started giving orders to the Afghans, none of whom spoke English, telling them where to put our gear. We dragged boxes of military MREs (Meals Ready to Eat) and two dozen cases of water up to the second floor. The bedrooms on the side of the house that faced the river had plastic taped over the windows instead of glass. Jan Mohammad, who maintained Massoud's guesthouses, explained that the Taliban had dropped a five-hundred-pound bomb about a month ago that'd blown out all the glass.

I thought it might be a good idea to check the basement in case we had to defend the house against attack. Downstairs, I found an Afghan man, his wife and two daughters living in two rooms. The rest of the rooms were packed full with one-hundred-pound burlap bags of wheat. I explained to the head of the family that in case of an air attack they should expect six armed *ferangis* (foreigners) to join them, prepared to defend the building. He proudly showed me his three AK-47 rifles.

Our compound was in a village of about fifty structures with a small bazaar. White-bearded Jan Mohammad took me outside to meet the guards who lived in a two-room hut near the front gate. I introduced myself in Farsi as Agha Gary (Mr. Gary) and explained that I would be checking on them every night. They were all young men in their late twenties with beards, flat wool Afghan hats known as *pakols, shalwar kameez* knee-length shirts and pajama-type pants. Two of them wore combat boots; the others, sandals.

I set them up in two shifts of three that rotated every twelve hours.

In addition to the two men in the compound, I wanted a third man every shift to patrol the village so that Taliban and al-Qaeda intruders could be identified and dealt with before they launched an attack. An armed American would stand watch on the second floor. No vehicles other than those belonging to Majid, Engineer Aref or those designated for use by the team would be allowed inside the compound to guard against a car bomb attack.

I told them that I knew they were proud Massoud fighters, but would give them a fifty-dollar bonus each week for guarding us. They seemed very pleased.

Within an hour Todd had the commo up and Brock was sending out messages on a laptop confirming our arrival. That night the six of us sat down with Jan Mohammad for a dinner of meat, potatoes, hot soup and a pile of flat bread called naan. Jan Mohammad knew Brock and Halsey from their previous trips to the Panshir.

Brock said in English, "Jan Mohammad. No firing guns inside cars, right?" And used both hands to mime the pump action of a shotgun.

Jan Mohammad smiled and responded, "*Nakher*" (which means "no").

I asked, "What are you talking about?"

"Last time I was here Jan Mohammad got in a four-by-four with us holding a shotgun," Brock explained. "Thank God it was pointed up, because he accidentally pulled the trigger firing a round through the roof and nearly blowing out our eardrums."

"Shotgun," Jan Mohammad said, sharing his only word of English. We had a good laugh.

After dinner, Brock broke out the maps and showed which faction controlled what pieces of territory. Then he went through our missions. Halsey would handle the first round of debriefings with Engineer Aref and drive the intel process. Marlowe would begin the radio intercept training. Storm and I would survey the Panshir Valley, then work with Northern Alliance teams to identify, track and capture a bin

Laden lieutenant. Since I spoke Farsi, I was going to be involved in all elements of the deployment, which was fine with me.

The following morning, after a breakfast of fried eggs, thin strips of steak, bread and tea, Chief of Northern Alliance Intel Engineer Aref arrived with Majid. Engineer Aref was in his late forties with slightly thinning black hair and a short beard. He wore Western clothing, not a *shalwar kameez*, better he said for blending in when he visited his second office in Dushanbe, Tajikistan. According to Afghan custom any individual with a degree in engineering was addressed as "engineer."

The cooks arrived with tea and crackers and we settled in for a full morning of briefings. About an hour in, antiaircraft fire rang out from two different mountaintops and echoed through the valley. After several minutes of nonstop firing, I interrupted Aref to ask, "Why are those guns going off?"

"Maybe they are practicing, or maybe not," he answered.

We broke out laughing, because none of us thought to stop the meeting and take cover.

With a map in front of him Engineer Aref explained in a soft, even voice how the Taliban was moving large forces from the North and West for a massive assault on Taloqan. This northern city was important for a number of reasons. First, it was the Northern Alliance capital. Second, Taliban control of Taloqan would cut off vital supplies from Tajikistan and would pin the Northern Alliance in Badakshan province and the Panshir Valley. Finally, Engineer Aref said that the fall of Taloqan would produce at least 100,000 refugees.

Next he spoke about the plight of the Hizb-e-Wahadat Hazara, who were trapped with their backs to the Hindu Kush mountains and starving to death. Commanded by Dr. Karim Khalili, the Hazara were one of three main tribes that made up the Northern Alliance. The other two were Massoud's Tajiks and the Uzbeks led by General Rashid Dostum.

The Hazara were shorter and stockier than the other two, with distinctive Mongul features—the result of Genghis Khan and his army of 150,000 horsemen who swept through Afghanistan in the 13th century. The only Shia tribe in the predominantly Sunni country, they populated the central province of Bamiyan to the west and had been fighting the Taliban since 1998. Their capital, Bamiyan, had been the spiritual center of Buddhism in Central Asia until the 11th century, when it was conquered and converted to Islam. The Buddhists had built two giant hundred-plus-foot statues of Buddha that were considered among the wonders of the ancient world. In 1999, Bamiyan fell to the Taliban, who, despite the pleas from around the world, fired hundreds of rounds of artillery at the giant statues of Buddha and destroyed them.

Engineer Aref next spoke about General Pervez Musharef of Pakistan. He stated categorically that the Pakistanis still provided crucial support to the Taliban. And he did not believe that the UN Security Council Sanctions of October 15, 1999, had much effect on the Taliban.

Finally, Engineer Aref sketched out military positions on the Shomali Plains just south of the opening of the Panshir Valley, twenty miles north of Kabul. He said the Northern Alliance needed resources to feed and arm their forces in order to resist the slow, steady loss of territory to the Taliban, which was being aggressively funded by Pakistan and Saudi Arabia. He was pleased to welcome our team, but frustrated that the United States had not helped them in a meaningful way.

We knew the Northern Alliance were no angels. Like every other Afghan group, they had engaged in drug smuggling and committed human rights abuses. The Taliban, however, were strict religious fundamentalists who reminded me of the Grand Inquisition. They routinely chopped off people's arms for theft and hung them on ropes for public display. They dragged large steel shipping containers into the desert packed with hundreds of their enemies and left them to bake. They butchered Hazaras, Uzbeks and Tajiks and took their wives as concubines. They treated women like animals, denying them the right to work and get an education and stoning war widows to death for so much as going to a local store to buy bread.

After Engineer Aref left, Marlowe (from Science and Technology) and I donned local Afghan clothes borrowed from our guards and went with Majid to a Northern Alliance SIGNIT collection facility a mile north. It was in a normal-looking concrete house with a corrugated tin roof and two antennas that were carefully concealed from view.

We passed through a living room decorated with tribal rugs and entered a back room crammed with radio equipment piled on two tables. The only light came from a single bare bulb because the windows had been blocked with plywood. Two young Northern Alliance soldiers in civilian clothes wore headphones and jotted down notes. One had jet black hair and a beard that seemed to start just below his eyes. The other looked like a fair-skinned, blue-eyed descendant of Alexander the Great.

Their radio equipment, which resembled a crazy high school experiment, was a mixture of old French and Russian components wired together. Majid explained that their position allowed them to monitor enemy messages from the Shomali Plains to the south all the way north to Taloqan. Marlowe watched the men work, then told them he was pleased with their level of technical competence. Both men said they had studied engineering in Tajikistan.

Over the next several days, Marlowe and I trained them in the third floor of the guesthouse. ███████████████████████ ███████████████████████ We also gave them uninterrupted power supplies to help regulate the electricity and more sophisticated ███████ to capture signals.

With the ███████████████ instruction taken care of, Brock, Storm and I began to survey the Panshir Valley. We did this by traveling south onto the Shomali Plains then north. Throughout the length and width of the valley we used Global Position Systems to identify and mark significant structures, possible landing sites for fixed-wing aircraft, Northern Alliance military camps, prisons that held captured Taliban and other landmarks.

The Panshir is no ordinary valley. It starts off steep and narrow at its southern entrance just above the Shomali Plains where it's dissected into tiny wheat fields and a complex system of irrigation canals. Then it widens as big rivers including the Panshir River slam through it and the fields become sparser and the land rockier. The single-lane road winds along massive boulders with the river on one side and mountain cliffs thousands of feet high on the other. Passing through a gorge of jaw-dropping awesomeness, you enter the main valley of villages and tiny fields worked by oxen.

It was incredible to think that the Soviets had tried to occupy this valley with heavy machinery and tanks. We passed the rusted remains of many of them pushed haphazardly along the side of the road or dumped into the riverbed. Massoud had lost thousands of men directing raids from the Hindu Kush mountains, but managed to drive the Soviets out.

Along the western bank of the river ahead, Storm and I spotted a large gathering of men.

I noticed that some appeared to be standing in the water. Through my binoculars, I made out four on the periphery holding rifles.

"*Zendanian,*" our driver said, which means "prisoners" in Farsi. He explained that the men were Taliban soldiers who had been captured by the Northern Alliance in August when they retook Bagram Airbase.

Storm remarked, "Not a lot of guards down there for a group that size."

"Yeah," I responded. "Looks like an accident waiting to happen."

I soon learned that Afghans individually could fight and bear up under staggering hardship. They could also operate a multitude of individual and crew-served weapons systems. But they knew next to nothing about safety and were often the victims of treacherous behavior.

The following day, Storm, Marlowe and I drove to the position of the Northern Alliance's southernmost antiaircraft guns, directly above the mouth of the Panshir. To complete the two-hour drive I had to pay eighty Tajik villagers three hundred dollars to clear a two-hundred-yard stretch of mountain road covered with four feet of snow. I told them I was a European filmmaker.

From the mountaintop antiaircraft gun position, we saw the battlefront spread below across the Shomali Plains. Through binoculars, we could make out Kabul thirty miles in the distance.

The bunker held a single antiaircraft gun manned by two men. I asked the Afghans if we could climb down the face of the mountain into the Shomali Plains. They warned us that the area was full of mines and they had no way of knowing which parts were safe.

From our perspective, our first ten days in the Panshir had gone well. But, to our surprise, it wasn't perceived that way at headquarters. Part of the reason is that Lawrence (the ████ in ██████████) had been sending back a stream of messages complaining about us. He said our Jawbreaker team had, against his orders, left the capital without an escort. He claimed that a vehicle we had borrowed in ███████████ had blown a piston.

At the same time a bogus source in Eastern Europe reported that bin Laden knew that a CIA team was in Afghanistan and he was planning to bomb their position. Brock responded immediately, stating, correctly, that there had been constant rumors of CIA teams in Afghanistan, even when there weren't. If headquarters was concerned, he suggested we simply move our team to another location.

Chief CTC Cofer Black and his deputy, Hank, remained calm. But members of Director Tenet's seventh-floor staff panicked. Initially, we found all this amusing and dismissed ██████████ Lawrence as a fool. But in one secure telephone call after another, we heard our mission slipping away.

Rich, who had replaced Mike Scheuer as leader of the bin Laden unit, called from Langley to inform us that the DDO Jim Pavitt was telling his staff that he didn't want to attend funerals for his officers in the Agency auditorium. Brock, our team leader, responded prophetically: "One day we will all have to attend many more funerals in the U.S. if we leave."

Months of preparation, training and deployment were going down the drain because of one bogus source and lack of courage on the part of CIA leadership. We were just beginning to plan the operation to capture a bin Laden lieutenant when Brock was ordered: "Bring your men out."

I got on the STU-III and explained that our location was secure, that I, too, had led deployments and as a former COS believed ending the mission was totally unnecessary. Cofer and Hank were sympathetic, but said: orders are orders.

Brock, not a man to be easily dissuaded, told headquarters, "We will leave, but the weather is overcast and we can't fly out at the moment." The sky outside was clear blue.

I seconded him. "We should delay in order to buy time for a change of decision back home," I said.

"In the event we are called out," Marlowe added, "we need to complete whatever we can now."

Halsey jumped in: "Engineer Aref said yesterday that they expect that the Taliban spring offensive will begin in two days. Today is March twenty-fifth. We need to get ██████████ equipment close to the front lines."

Brock nodded. "Let's do it tomorrow night."

The next morning, Brock and I met with Engineer Aref to tell him that we might be ordered out. He was stunned. "But we agreed to help you kidnap a senior al-Qaeda member," he said. "We have started the planning. Have you lost interest?"

When Brock tried to diplomatically explain that Washington was concerned with the threats against us, Aref shook his head in disbelief.

That evening we traded our Gortex jackets for Afghan garb and deployed in two vehicles over some of the most dangerous roads in the world. The group consisted of Storm, Marlowe, Majid, the two Northern Alliance SIGNIT officers and myself. Driving south we passed though the Panshir onto the Shomali Plains. Sloped below us, dug into the rocky soil, were the Taliban positions.

Around midnight we pulled into a compound that looked as if it was on the moon. Twenty years of conflict had obliterated every vestige of plant life. Majid ducked inside. When he didn't reappear after five minutes, I went in to see what happened.

The room was pitch black. I asked: "*Majid, koja hastid?*" (Majid, where are you?)

A voice answered: "*Majid, inja nist.*" (Majid, is not here.)

As my eyes adjusted to the darkness, I realized I was standing in a roomful of Northern Alliance soldiers. They got up from the floor and grabbed blankets and weapons. I said, "*Bebabsid,*" which means "excuse me" in Farsi as they pushed past me to the door. Would one of them, stunned by the presence of a *ferangi* (foreigner) in their sleeping quarters, open fire? I wasn't sure.

After the twenty or so men left, Majid reappeared from an inside room and we started turning the space into a ███████ site. While Marlowe and I worked with the Afghans, Storm climbed onto the roof with a rifle and level-four night vision goggles. We wanted to be prepared in case of attack.

Later, I climbed on the roof to join him. Using the night vision goggles we looked out over a landscape of half-destroyed buildings and craters for as far as the eye could see. It reminded me of old World War II films I'd seen of the bombed-out Dresden. But people were still living here. I felt deep sadness for the Afghans and their children.

By four in the morning, the equipment was in place ███████. ███████ Taliban communications revealed continuous activity on their side of the lines. Northern Alliance commanders started readying their troops. We climbed into our two vehicles and drove back into

the mouth of the Panshir, leaving thousands of soldiers, tanks and artillery poised for a fight.

The secure phone was ringing when we got back to the guesthouse. It was the seventh floor demanding that we leave immediately.
They had checked on the weather in Afghanistan and figured out that
we were stalling.

Majid was incensed. He said, "This is common for America. You
make promises and abandon us. You ask for our commitment to fight
an enemy that wants to kill our children and then you walk away. I will
never understand your country."

We were too ashamed to argue. All we could do was direct profani-
ties at DDO Jim Pavitt and DCI George Tenet thousands of miles away.

On arrival in Tajikistan we found out that Lawrence, the lunatic
████████ from ████████, had been telling anyone who would listen
that we had disobeyed his orders. As a result, Brock was treated to a
tongue-lashing from the U.S. Ambassador. Then Brock and I were
yelled at by the State Department Regional Security Officer. It was unusual to say the least.

Prior to our departure from Dushanbe, Halsey and I went to visit
Shah Ahmad Massoud, who was in town for a day of meetings. He was
in his fifties and worn by years of fighting.

Surprisingly, Massoud expressed no emotion about our sudden
withdrawal, despite the fact that our deployment had been planned
months in advance. Instead he provided calm, sober analysis of the
political and military situation. He underlined that it was important
for Washington to understand that the relationship between the Taliban and bin Laden and his al-Qaeda organization was symbiotic. Each
side benefited from the relationship and was strengthened by it. He
said that the U.S. should get it out of its mind that the Taliban would
ever be convinced to expel bin Laden. They would both have to be destroyed together.

Massoud was a charismatic and wise man with dark intense eyes.
He'd won great battles, but had also let his men participate in the

murder of thousands of Hazaras in Kabul during the mid-'90s. He was loved by the international community, but had also participated in narco-trafficking. At various times, he had accepted money from the Russians, Iranians, Indians and Americans.

Before we left, I pulled a copy of Peter Hopkirk's *The Great Game* from my backpack. My Jawbreaker team member, Marlowe, had lent me this excellent book about the struggle between the British and Russians for control of Central Asia in the 18th and 19th centuries. I asked Massoud if he would sign the cover, which he did. Marlowe was thrilled when I gave it back.

*　　*　　*

When we returned to Washington, I did something I'd never done before. I drafted a letter to the DDO calling for Lawrence's dismissal as ████████████. Both Cofer Black and Hank co-signed my recommendation. Brock followed with a letter of his own.

None of our letters was ever answered despite the fact that Lawrence had repeatedly tried to undercut our mission, ultimately to the great detriment of his country. Lawrence had friends on the seventh floor.

A few weeks later, Storm resigned and moved to North Carolina. When Halsey's assignment in ███████ ended, he resigned, too. Marlowe returned to his job in the Directorate of Science and Technology. After I was turned down for a number of Chief of Station positions, Cofer went to bat for me and got me a Chief of Station assignment in Latin America.

But the aborted mission to the Panshir continued to leave a sick, empty feeling inside me. As leaders of CTC, Cofer and Hank had shown a willingness to plan and execute risky missions. But neither CIA Director George Tenet nor President Bill Clinton had the will to wage a real fight against terrorists who were killing U.S. citizens.

Several weeks later I learned that the Northern Alliance did in fact beat back the Taliban offensive to dislodge them from the Shomali

Plains. There was no doubt in my mind that Brock's decision to delay and insert the ▮▮▮▮▮▮ equipment had helped.

I also learned that the helicopter that we'd used, piloted by the Afghans in old, tattered clothes, had crashed in the mountains between Dushanbe and the Panshir Valley. All on board had died. I can't say I was surprised. It was the price of waging war in Afghanistan.

4

CTC/████████

"Is it in any way rational to expect that after America has attacked us for more than half a century that we will leave her to live in security and peace?"
—*Osama bin Laden, Letter to America*

*   *   *   *   *   *

On Thursday, October 12, 2000, I was in Virginia studying Spanish when, on the other side of the globe, two Arabs in a motorized rubber Zodiac boat loaded with five hundred pounds of explosives conducted a suicide attack on a U.S. Navy destroyer. The resulting blast to the USS *Cole* produced a forty-by-forty foot hole in the ship's hull, killing seventeen U.S. sailors and injuring thirty-nine others.

The USS *Cole* was a billion-dollar command-and-attack ship that had stopped in the Republic of Yemen port of Aden to refuel. Seconds after the blast, the captain issued orders to seal the ship's engineering compartments, which kept the vessel from sinking. But the ship's crew had been told not to use fire hoses, which is standard procedure for keeping smaller vessels away. Nor had they fired on the unidentified Zodiac as it moved alongside the hull.

The press reported weeks later that, according to Pentagon-approved rules of engagement, sentries on the deck of the *Cole* carried unloaded weapons. *Cole* Petty Officer John Washsak said that right after the blast he was ordered to turn the M-60 machine gun he was manning away as a second small boat approached. "With blood still on my face," he said, he was told, "That's the rules of engagement, no shooting unless shot at." Fear of provoking a diplomatic incident took precedent over the ship's security. U.S. sailors had paid with their lives.

As I watched the story on CNN, there was little doubt in my mind that this was another al-Qaeda attack. I also knew that Yemen wouldn't be as cooperative to the subsequent FBI-CIA investigation as the Kenyans and Tanzanians were in '98.

Yemen was a backward, dangerous place. In the '91 Gulf War its government supported Saddam Hussein, despite the fact that the rest of the Arab world had supplied troops to fight against Iraq. North Yemen had a reputation for being the only part of the Arab world that had never been conquered by an outside power. South Yemen had fought a brutal war for independence from Britain in the 1960s, which turned so bloody that British Marines left without so much as a peace treaty as their band played "Things Ain't What They Used to Be."

Yemen was also the ancestral home of the bin Laden clan. Osama bin Laden's one-eyed father Mohammed bin Laden had emigrated from Yemen to Saudi Arabia in the 1930s. There he founded the Bin Laden Construction Group; fathered fifty-six children; built houses, roads, office buildings and hotels and fostered ties to the Saudi royal family to amass a tremendous fortune.

His seventeenth son, Osama, was born in 1957 to a young Syrian woman named Hamida al-Attas. As a teenager and young man, the six-foot-five Osama was reported to be a bit of a playboy who used family money to travel, educate himself in Beirut and Saudi Arabia and have fun. He received an engineering degree from the King Abdul Aziz University in Jeddah in 1979 and prepared to take over part of his father's construction and civil engineering business.

But the Soviet invasion of Afghanistan in 1979 changed him. Like many young devout Sunni Islamists, he rushed to Afghanistan to join the jihad. He used some of the millions he'd inherited from his father to fund Maktab al-Khidimat (MAK), an organization which helped recruit Muslim fighters from around the war and funnel arms and money into the mujahideen. In 1989, as the Soviet occupation faltered, bin Laden widened his political focus and founded a group called al-Qaeda (the base) with Mohammad Atef. Al-Qaeda was conceived as an international network of militants who would defend Islam from Western domination.

After the Gulf War and the establishment of permanent U.S. military bases on Saudi Arabian soil, bin Laden became an increasingly strident critic of the Saudi monarchy. In 1994, the Saudi Arabian government stripped him of his citizenry and forced him to leave. After a two-year stop in Sudan, he returned to Afghanistan and teamed up with Egyptian militant Ayman al-Zawahiri to plan for war. In 1998 the two men co-signed a *fatwa* (religious edict) in the name of the International Islamic Front for Jihad Against Jews and Crusaders declaring: "The ruling is to kill the Americans and their allies, civilians and military. It is an individual duty for every Muslim in any country to liberate the al-Aqsa Mosque [in Jerusalem] and the holy mosque in Makka [in Saudi Arabia] from their grip and for their armies to move out of all the land of Islam, defeated and unable to threaten any Muslim."

By the year 2000, al-Qaeda had established terrorist cells in as many as sixty countries around the world and had attracted thousands of young jihadists to its terrorist training camps and bases in eastern Afghanistan.

*   *   *

I found out days after the *Cole* bombing that DC/CTC Hank and FBI Special Agent John O'Neill would lead their organization's respective teams to Yemen. Because they were both high-level, competent men, I had no doubt that the investigation would be thorough.

The problem would be the response. President Clinton and his advisors would repeat a pattern that started with the 1996 Khobar Tower attack in Saudi Arabia that left nineteen U.S. Air Force personnel dead. They would demand evidence beyond a shadow of a doubt, and even when it was incontrovertible, respond weakly or not at all. What they needed to do was launch an immediate U.S. Special Operations raid into Afghanistan to destroy bin Laden and his chief lieutenants.

In between my study of Spanish verb tenses, I stopped in to visit Mary at the recruitment center.

"How are my boys doing?" I asked her.

"Amir is good. He just passed his polygraph."

"What about Adam Khan?"

"Hank was able to get the seventh floor to sign off on bringing him on as a GS-15, but Adam has decided to turn us down."

"You're kidding."

"Since his father was assassinated years ago and his sisters, mother and other members of his family rely on him for support, he did not want to spend the rest of his life back in the Middle East when they are all here."

"How are the others doing?" I asked.

"We have several Arab Americans with associate degrees, but they are being blocked by Human Resources, which does not want them brought in as GS-12s and GS-13s. HRS wants to bring them in as GS-8s and GS-9s."

"That's insulting."

Mary said, "I know. But not even Cofer Black can move this little old lady who manages the gateway process for bringing people into the Directorate of Operations. She says that our Arabic and Farsi speakers lack college degrees and will do poorly under the HRS system."

I complained bitterly: "We desperately need officers with native skills. We'll get them degrees later. Doesn't she understand?"

I knew that Mary would do anything she could. Still the bureaucratic proclivity to preserve outdated rules and protect turf was frustrating as hell. I witnessed yet another example of this disturbing phenomenon when I met with the new Division Chief for Latin America. He greeted me by saying that he had heard about my successful record of conducting counterterrorism operations, but that would not, *repeat not*, be my primary mission as a Chief of Station in South America. He stated categorically that he wanted me to conduct normal foreign intelligence collection against traditional targets and no, *repeat no*, counterterrorism.

I was stunned. Had this man been living in a cave the last two years? Had he listened to the news and read the intel reports? Didn't he know that recent intelligence showed that al-Qaeda had established terrorist cells in sixty countries and was planning operations throughout the world?

*   *   *

████████ is a charming country in South America. Its capital, ████████, features spectacular beaches, fine food and top-flight cultural events. It's the kind of post where you can kick back and enjoy yourself.

But I was still red hot. I'd been there two months with Rebecca and Thomas. Alexis was in her second year at the University of Virginia and planning to join us for Christmas.

Three mornings a week Thomas and I got up at 6:15 and headed to the nearby ████ Boxing Club, where we sparred with the owner—a former national middleweight champ—and his son. Once at the office I booted up my computer, logged into the system and read the daily intel reports. The news of the previous day (9/10/01) still made me feel sick to my stomach. The *National Intelligence Daily* (NID) had reported the death of Ahmad Shah Massoud in the Panshir Valley. According to preliminary reports, Massoud had been assassinated by two al-Qaeda terrorists posing as journalists.

I figured this was the end of the Northern Alliance. Massoud, the Lion of the Panshir, had been the glue that held together the tribes opposing the Taliban. The Taliban would most likely pay off wavering Northern Alliance commanders and launch a final military offensive while Massoud's troops were in disarray. The man likely to replace Massoud was one of his lieutenants, Mohammed Qasim Fahim.

As Chief ██████ I had to quickly prepare for the weekly country team meeting that would be chaired by the Embassy Deputy Chief of Mission (DCM). Gathered in the conference room were officers representing all agencies of the ██████. It was a few minutes after 9 A.M. when our DCM entered looking unsettled. Remaining standing, she said, "I'm sorry to inform you that minutes ago what appeared to be a large passenger jet crashed into the World Trade Center in New York."

A meeting that normally lasted half an hour was over in five minutes. We ran out quickly in search of television sets broadcasting CNN. Back in my office, I learned that a second commercial aircraft had just hit the second tower of the World Trade Center. Plumes of thick black smoke rose from the two structures that dominated the skyline of Manhattan.

As a former U.S. Air Force Crash Fire Fighter I knew that the massive quantities of fuel carried by the planes did not simply combust on impact. Tens of thousands of gallons of JP-4 jet fuel were now dispersing throughout multiple floors of the building. I thought about the hundreds of firefighters climbing the staircases in full equipment with Scott Pack self-contained breathers.

At the age of twenty, I'd fought structural fires, aircraft crash fires, and had been sent to rescue the crew of a burning barge in Alaska. With acetylene tanks exploding around me, I carried out a trapped man who was already dead. But the courage of the big-city firefighters climbing the steps of the World Trade Center surpassed anything I could imagine.

I sat thousands of miles away unable to help. At 9:45 a third hijacked airliner crashed into the Pentagon. At 10:05, the South Tower of the WTC collapsed, followed by the North Tower at 10:28. Later that morning we learned that a fourth hijacked commercial aircraft crashed in a field in Pennsylvania.

Thousands of Americans had died. Others had fought valiantly to save family members, colleagues, friends, neighbors and total strangers.

I called Rebecca, who'd been watching at home on TV. She said, "Gary, it's almost too incredible to believe." Then she asked the question that every other rational person was thinking, "How could this have happened?"

In my gut, I knew the answer. That evening when I returned home, Thomas was in the den watching rescue workers search for survivors. Turning to me, he asked: "When will you be leaving?"

"I don't know, son."

He looked at me with concern and said, "I love you, Dad."

"I love you, too."

Almost immediately Osama bin Laden and al-Qaeda were named as the prime suspects. Within days I received a worldwide message from the Deputy Director of Operations (DDO) Jim Pavitt stating that Operations would be playing an important role in the upcoming conflict and asking those with requisite skills to communicate with CTC. That same day, I got an e-mail from the Chief of LA/Division instructing me and all other Chiefs of Station not to volunteer for the coming conflict.

I didn't understand. Our Division Chief was junior to the DDO and actually under his authority, yet he was ordering me and other highly skilled officers in Latin America *not* to step forward? Had this guy taken leave of his senses? In a time of national tragedy was he still thinking of how to protect his Division? Taking a deep breath and trying to sound diplomatic, I drafted a polite reply that said despite his instructions, I would be volunteering because I had the needed language skills and I had been a member of the last team on the ground in Afghanistan.

The word from headquarters was that CTC would be creating a

new unit within CTC to handle the war. Hank, the former Deputy Chief of CTC, would be in charge. I said to myself, *Thank God they chose someone who knows the business.*

Within days, I received instructions to return to headquarters and report to CTC on September 30. Rebecca and Thomas drove me to the airport. I felt bad leaving them in ██████████, but Rebecca had taken an administrative job at the U.S. Embassy and Thomas had just started tenth grade. I told them that I would be gone for a minimum of five to six months and wasn't sure if they would keep me at headquarters or deploy me in the field.

Rebecca said, "Don't worry about us, Gary. You do what you have to do."

On the flight to Miami, my mind raced to the challenges ahead. Afghanistan was a landlocked country of rugged mountains and barren, dusty plains slightly smaller than Texas. Its twenty million people spoke over thirty languages and were made up of Pushtuns, Tajiks, Hazaras, Uzbeks, Aimaks, Turkmen, Balock and other tribes. The British, Soviets and others had been humiliated in this desperately poor country with the highest infant mortality rate in the world.

Then there was the bureaucratic minefield in Washington and headquarters. Would the White House and Congress give us the resources to get the job done? Would senior officers at headquarters put aside their petty jealousies over turf in favor of the greater good?

*   *   *

A retired Secret Service Officer, who had worked for me when I handled Hezbollah led me downstairs to the basement where the new CTC unit had set up shop. I entered a large rectangular room with a forty-foot table in the center. Lining each side were fifteen computer workstations. An attractive young woman in her mid-twenties blocked my way.

"Who are you?" she asked. "Are you cleared to be in this area?"

Laughter erupted from the people at the table, most of whom were old hands at CTC.

"You better let him enter," my Jawbreaker buddy Storm called out. "He bites."

I said, "I'm Gary Berntsen. I'm looking for Hank."

I shook hands with Storm and other people at the table. I recognized one of them as a Farsi-speaking Muslim American named Hamid who had just finished the ops course at the Farm. Seconds later I was in Hank's office being introduced to his deputy, John.

John, a former U.S. Navy officer and highly distinguished Case Officer, was in headquarters on September 11 to sign his retirement papers. Once the attacks began, he changed his mind.

Hank said, "Gary, it's good to see you. Where's your family?"

"They're remaining at post in ████████. LA/Division has someone sitting in for me for the next four to six months."

"Good," Hank said. "I, too, came back from overseas. I just pulled my sons out of school for the year. Our focus has just got to be on the work right now. You understand?"

"Absolutely." Hank was one of the most organized and disciplined men I'd ever met. He was tough and compact and reminded me of the actor Scott Glenn.

"We're getting ready to do something that hasn't been done since World War II and the days of the OSS," he said. "We here at CTC/██ are assembling teams of case officers and paramilitary officers to drive the fight into Afghanistan. Cofer has the support of the seventh floor and the President. The rules have finally changed, which means we get a full shot at bin Laden and al-Qaeda. Gary Schroen is out with a Jawbreaker team laying the groundwork with the Northern Alliance. Without Massoud they could be crushed. I just don't know how effective General Mohammed Fahim will be."

"Will I be staying here or be deployed?" I asked.

"You're being deployed to take Gary Schroen's place and lead the Jawbreaker team in a few weeks," John answered.

Hank jumped back in: "For now, you'll build CTC/██'s internal staff, which will be responsible for receiving and answering all the incoming cable traffic from the Jawbreaker team. Also, you will select, assemble and prepare those officers who will be deployed on the teams to be inserted."

I said, "I'll start with a list of all the Farsi speakers in the organization. We're also going to need Arabic speakers to interrogate al-Qaeda prisoners."

Hank was emphatic. "No one comes into this group or is placed on any of the teams without my personal approval. We have to have the very best and can't afford personnel problems either here or in the field. Is that clear?"

"Perfectly," I answered.

"You just missed your buddy R.J. He left with a team for Uzbekistan yesterday and will be moving into Central Afghanistan to link up with Dostum."

General Abdul Rashid Dostum was an Afghan Uzbek general who had a penchant for changing sides. First, he sided with the Russians, then joined the mujahideen, which eventually became the Rabbani Government. Then, he did a switcheroo and joined Gulbuddin Hekmatyar to attack the Rabbani Government. He was later betrayed by his own deputy, which led to the fall of the Uzbek capital Mazar-e Sharif to the Taliban, and caused Dostum to flee Afghanistan. Now he was back fighting with the Northern Alliance.

R.J., who'd be working with Dostum, was a tall, imposing former U.S. Army Ranger who spoke the Afghan dialect of Farsi known as Dari and had served multiple tours in South Asia.

Hank explained his vision of how the CTC/█████ teams would work. Separate teams would deploy in different parts of Afghanistan to work with Northern Alliance and other allied Afghan field commanders. A Farsi- or Dari-speaking case officer would head each team, with a Special Activities Division paramilitary officer as his deputy. The teams would be filled out with a combination of case officers (most with previous military training) and SAD officers, who had served as combat soldiers with the U.S. Special Forces, Navy Seals, or Marine Corps Force Recon.

Working alongside the Afghans, the teams would produce intelligence on enemy positions and capabilities that CTC headquarters would use to drive and coordinate the war. CTC would be the point of interface with U.S. Armed Forces Central Command (CENTCOM) and General Frank's staff as they, first, managed the air campaign and, then, moved U.S. military forces into theater to eventually assume a larger role on the ground.*

Each CTC team on the ground would have a Special Forces team attached to it with an air combat controller who would direct close air support. I understood immediately that the coordination process within our building and between us and the military would be complex. Hank was blunt. "What do you think about sharing everything, I mean, everything with the military on this op, which means sources, the entire ball of wax?"

"If we want to win in this tough place, we'd better be ready to do a lot of things differently," I answered. "Sharing one hundred percent with the military makes sense."

Hank smiled. "Good. We already made the decision to do that. You are going to have to make your military counterparts your full partners in the field."

"Okay."

"You need to remember that even though you work for me, any time General Franks tells you he needs something or wants something done, you do it immediately and then inform me. We have to be married to CENTCOM."

"We fight together, or die separately," I said.

---

*Henry A. Crumpton, "Intelligence and War 2001–2," in *Transforming U.S. Intelligence* (Georgetown University Press, 2005), Jennifer E. Sims and Burton Gerber, editors. In this CIA-approved article, Mr. Crumpton describes in detail the strategy of the Afghan War, the deployment of CIA and U.S. military personnel, and the use of money to buy the allegiance of Afghan warlords.

*   *   *

I had two immediate tasks. First, bring in officers to CTC/███ 's internal office to handle incoming messages and requests from our Jawbreaker teams in Afghanistan. Second, find Farsi and Dari speakers to
staff the upcoming paramilitary deployments in Afghanistan.

Time was of the essence. Within a week, the five officers we had in
Internal grew to thirteen. We were putting in sixteen, eighteen, sometimes twenty-four-hour days. Some nights I caught a few hours rest on
an inflatable mattress in a nearby conference room, then dashed to
my hotel room for a quick shower and shave.

The Gary Schroen–led Jawbreaker team in the Panshir Valley
was already bombarding us with a steady stream of intelligence—
battlefield positions, troop-strength assessments, the names and char-
acteristics of friendly and enemy commanders. It became clear right
away that the Taliban had a massive strength advantage over the
Northern Alliance. The Taliban was telling anyone who would listen
that they were itching for a chance to humiliate the Americans like
the Soviets had been in the 1980s.

I had a woman on my staff named Diane. On September 11, 2001,
her father, a retired CIA case officer, had died from a heart attack
while he watched the World Trade Center collapse. Diane, a mother
of two, buried her father and reported back to headquarters the next
day.

Having worked in the Bin Laden Group for years, Diane knew
Afghanistan, the various tribes and our sources on the ground. She
briefed me in detail about how to deal with a whole assortment of
Afghan warlords. She told me which Taliban commanders I would be
able to turn and which ones I had to kill. I made sure every single
piece of message traffic from the Jawbreaker team was routed through
her to provide valuable historical context. Every time I looked over
and saw her at her terminal I said to myself, *Thank God she's here.*

Staff meetings began at 7 P.M. sharp. Hank was tough. Those who hadn't completed an assigned task on time were dressed down. I was hit with his first salvo.

That particular evening, I'd completed twenty-seven action items on a list of twenty-eight. The twenty-eighth assignment called for me to track down a senior analyst and ask about the potential regional impact of our providing large quantities of weapons to the Northern Alliance. I phoned the analyst twice and sent a junior officer to his office. He wasn't in and didn't return his messages.

In front of the twenty most senior officers in our seventy-five-person group, I received the worst chewing-out of my life. There was no time for excuses, soft-soaping or discussions of time management. I took both barrels and soldiered on.

The talent on our side was impressive. Cofer Black very convincingly built political support for CTC/██ on the seventh floor and at the White House. John, Hank's deputy, deftly managed the disparate elements of CTC/██ and provided expert advice. But Hank was the key. It was his job to conceive the strategy for the upcoming conflict in which intelligence, technology and irregular forces would be used in an unprecedented way. He was, in effect, creating the template for a new intelligence and technology-driven kind of warfare.

A week after my arrival, the actual shooting war broke out. On October 7, 2001—nearly a month after the attacks in Washington D.C. and New York—fifteen land-based bombers, twenty-five strike aircraft from carriers and fifty Tomahawk cruise missiles from U.S. and British warships and submarines hit al-Qaeda and Taliban targets in Afghanistan. In order to avoid antiaircraft artillery, Soviet SA-7 and SA-17 portable antiaircraft missiles and 200-300 Stinger missiles believed to be part of the Taliban and al-Qaeda arsenal, aircraft flew no lower than 10,000 feet. Initial attacks successfully destroyed large physical assets such as radar, aircraft and command and control facilities. But we didn't have the capacity to clearly define the front lines, because the U.S. Army Special Forces team with Special Operations Forces Laser Acquisition Markers (SOFLAMs) had been unable to deploy because of the severe weather.

Once our teams were on the ground, we could use our Northern Alliance intelligence counterparts to identify targets with hand-held Global Positioning System (GPS) technology. We'd send them into enemy territory to capture the exact geo-cords on enemy positions that could be forwarded to CTC and the military for targeting. But I was worried that the Afghans might find all the scrolling and changing of programs confusing. So I asked our technicians: Can you insert simple Dari language commands on a hand-held GPS? They went to work.

On October 19, the first U.S. Army Special Forces twelve-man team, A-Team 555, landed on the Shomali Plains. A day later, Special Forces A-Team 595 joined R.J.'s team in Central Afghanistan directly south of Mazar-e Sharif, where they linked up with General Abdul Rashid Dostum. When I spoke to R.J. on a secure satellite phone he sounded focused and optimistic.

The cooperation I had initially received from Divisions Chiefs and officers in DO in terms of identifying officers needed to fill the Jawbreaker teams started to fade. As I moved through headquarters, talking to prospective candidates, hate mail started to arrive at CTC/▮▮ . One e-mail sent by a senior officer stated that I was an embarrassment to Cofer Black and should be relieved. I was told by several Division Chiefs that some officers were too valuable to spare. Hank ordered me to soldier on.

I found Amir, the Arab-American I'd recruited, working in my old Hezbollah branch. He'd just finished ops training and wanted to join the team I was leading into Afghanistan.

"What does your wife think about the fact that you want to deploy?" I asked.

"As Arab-Americans we have to make this fight," he answered. "I need to do this for me, and my entire family." Hank asked me to prepare a paper on the Pushtun tribes of southern Afghanistan and wanted it on his desk in twenty-four hours. So I went up to the Directorate of Intelligence offices on the fifth floor to ask for help. Within minutes, four different Afghan analysts appeared with finished intel pieces, Ambassador Jim Spain's book on the Pushtuns, and incredible, three-dimensional maps of Kabul, the Shomali Plains, Mazar-e Sharif and Kandahar.

One analyst gave me a quick twenty-minute lecture during which I learned that the Pushtuns (also known as the Pathans) are a race of warriors who live in sixty separate tribes throughout southeastern Afghanistan and Pakistan. Although their origins are unclear, they are likely descended from ancient Aryans who intermingled with subsequent invaders. Pathans live by an ethical code called *pushtanwali*. *Pushtanwali* includes the practices of *melmastia* (extending hospitality and protection to every guest), *nanawati* (the right of a fugitive to seek refuge within the tribe), *badal* (the right to extend blood feuds and extract revenge), *turch* (bravery), *mamus* (the right to defend one's woman); and other principles.

Another analyst, a young woman in her early thirties, said to forget about the Taliban giving up.

Heading back down a hallway, I walked straight into Adam Khan, the Pushtun-speaking former U.S. Marine whom we'd tried to recruit. He was walking with the Deputy Chief of Translation.

Stopping them, I said, "Adam, it's great to see you. Thank goodness you're here."

He said: "I asked my home agency to allow me to come over for several months to help you out."

"Listen," I said to the Deputy Chief of Translation, "we have no other Pushtun speakers. Hank will want to talk to him immediately. Let me borrow Adam and I'll return him to your office in an hour."

The guy from Translation was too surprised to say no.

I ushered Adam Khan straight into Hank's office, where Adam announced, "I'm ready to deploy and do whatever you need while the ground conflict gears up."

Within minutes he was working with one of our young case officers on the Pushtun piece.

I later learned that the deputy from Translation went to the newly arrived Deputy Chief of CTC and complained that I had stolen one of his linguists. Though Hank had wide-reaching authority, he couldn't stop CTC from ordering Adam Khan back to Translation. So while we were preparing for an important mission, Adam, a Pushtun-speaking former Marine and probably the single most important man I could have with me, sat in a Washington, D.C., cubicle translating Pushtun wedding certificates, drivers licenses and other legal documents. I hated the bureaucracy. Even in the most critical times, people couldn't set aside petty issues of turf and control in the interest of the greater good.

By hook and by crook, Hank and I assembled five more teams of six to eight officers. My team would relieve Gary Schroen and become the new Jawbreaker team leader with the Northern Alliance in the Panshir. We could cover Taloqan in the north and the Shomali Plains just above Kabul. R.J., leading Team Alpha, would continue liaison with General Dostum in the north. A young Farsi-speaking officer in his midthirties would lead the team in Western Afghanistan with ███████. Team Delta would go into Bamyan province in the center of the country to join the Hazara tribe and Dr. Karim Khalili. A former Marine Corps officer from the Special Activities Division would lead Team Echo in the south near Kandahar.

Prior to the commencement of training, I was sitting with John (Hank's deputy) in his office when he received a satellite phone from Pakistan. It was the famous Pushtun mujahideen commander Abdul Haq, who had gotten John's name and number from a member of the White House staff.

Abdul Haq was a legend in Afghanistan. He had lost part of his lower leg during his ferocious fight against the Soviets. Disgusted with the intertribal warfare and disarray in Afghanistan following the Soviet defeat, he had moved to Pakistan, where his wife and eleven-year-old son were murdered.

Haq was now telling anyone who would listen that he could convince Taliban commanders to defect and fight against their spiritual leader, Mullah Omar. He told us that he'd won the support of former Reagan administration National Security Adviser Robert (Bud) Mc-Farlane and the Chicago millionaire commodity trading brothers Joe and Jim Richie.

We at CTC/████ were focused on linking our teams with the Northern Alliance tribes in the North. Southern Afghanistan presented a much more daunting challenge since it was the Pushtun-controlled stronghold of the Taliban. John told Haq categorically, "Do not enter Afghanistan across its southern border. We do not have the resources in place to help you. If you enter now with a small force you are likely to be captured or killed."

Undaunted, Haq entered southern Afghanistan a few days later with a force of twenty men, was quickly surrounded by the Taliban and radioed for help. According to the Associated Press, an unmanned Predator was directed to Haq's location and fired a Hellfire missile at Taliban troops. It wasn't enough. Haq was captured and hung.

Within days we learned that another Afghan named Hamid Karzai was raising a force to invade Afghanistan from the South. Hamid Karzai was the highly cultured son of Abdul Ahad Karzai, an Afghan political leader and Deputy Speaker of the Afghan Parliament. Born a Pushtun and fluent in Pushtun, Dari, Urdu, English and French, the younger Karzai had worked for the royalist mujahideen doing press and humanitarian work during the jihad of the '80's. After the withdrawal of Soviet forces, he was appointed Deputy Foreign Minister.

In the early '90's, during a time of political instability, Hamid Karzai was accused of spying for Pakistan and arrested. During his interrogation by Mohammed Fahim (who was now the new military leader of the Northern Alliance) a rocket-propelled grenade hit the building in which he was being held and Karzai escaped. He briefly supported the Taliban only to turn against them when they started to impose their extreme fundamentalist beliefs. In August 2000, Taliban agents assassinated his father in Quetta, Pakistan.

Shortly after September 11, Hamid Karzai appeared at the U.S. Embassy in Islamabad, Pakistan, and announced that he was ready to take up arms against the Taliban. True to his word, he entered southern Afghanistan on a motorbike, raised a force of men and seized an airfield in the town of Tarin Kowt. ███████████████████ ██████████████████

Using satellite resources we confirmed that he was in control of the small Tarin Kowt airfield. Instead of the five thousand soldiers he claimed, we counted about five hundred. Team Echo was assigned to insert alongside him. But nothing could be done overnight.

On the night of October 19, Hank, myself and the rest of CTC/ ███ crowded around video monitors to watch two hundred Rangers from the Army's 75th Ranger Regiment being parachuted onto an isolated airstrip (code name "Rhino") seventy-five miles south of the Taliban stronghold of Kandahar. As we watched, Rangers with night vision scopes killed forty Taliban defenders and captured the airstrip. That same night a squadron of U.S. Delta Force soldiers conducted a helicopter raid on a compound at the edge of the city that belonged to Taliban leader Mullah Mohammed Omar. As they left the house without Mullah Omar, who wasn't there, but carrying Taliban documents and messages, the Delta Force soldiers were hit hard by RPG rockets. A dozen of them were badly injured. An AC-130 Spectre gunship was called in to pound the Taliban resistance. Thirty of them were mowed down by dense machine gun and cannon fire and the Delta Forces were pulled out, but not before an MH-60 Penetrator helicopter taking off on a rescue mission from Pakistan rolled over, killing two Rangers.

This was the first salvo in the ground component of the war, which we'd been feverishly planning and preparing for day and night. The next morning, I sat down with two officers who worked in CIA's Special Activities Division and were responsible for coordinating targets between the military and the Agency. They explained that there would be two separate components of the air war in Afghanistan—air interdiction and close air support. Air interdiction, which would comprise about eighty-five percent of the sorties, would hit targets at the front and deep inside the country from CIA reporting and satellite photography. Geographic coordinates would be transmitted to pilots for precision bombing.

Close air support (CAS) would be infinitely more dangerous but very effective in eliminating evolving threats during battle. U.S. Special Forces and Air Force combat controllers on the ground would develop targets using GPS systems and laser designators (SOFLAMs) for either GPS-guided or laser-guided weapons. GPS-guided weapons had the advantage of being effective in all weather conditions, while laser-guided bombs required the ability to see a laser spot and lock onto its beam.

The geographic location of Afghanistan posed logistical problems for CENTCOM. In the Gulf War of 1991, our aircraft carriers had been able to station themselves close to the theater of conflict in the Persian Gulf. Afghanistan, on the other hand, was set back deeply into Central Asia. B-52s and B-1s from Air Force bases in the U.S. were required to make a sixteen-hour flight before they could release their bombs. Fighter aircraft were also required to fly long sorties from aircraft carriers or from bases in neighboring countries. Instead of three to four hundred sorties a day in the Gulf War, we were getting thirty or forty. We also believed the Taliban would be a very stubborn foe.

On October 21, 2001, two weeks after the commencement of bombing, Hank, his deputy John and I met to assess our progress. As we studied satellite photographs we noticed something unusual. We expected to see Afghans clogging trade and drug routes on their way out of the country. Instead, we observed hundreds of volunteers with weapons on their way in. They crossed from Pakistan in the east, from Iran into Nimruz province in the far west and from Kashmir in the northeast across to Konar province. We'd heard from human intelligence sources that mosques and Islamic NGOs throughout the region were busy recruiting faithful to fight the Americans in a defensive jihad.

Hank turned to John and asked, "What do you think?"

"I recommend that we do everything possible to allow these volunteers to reach the front lines," John responded dryly.

"Good idea," Hank said. "We can then destroy them in mass. What do you think, Gary?"

"That works for me. Better to fight them there than closer to home."

While all this was going on, I stole time to read Ahmed Rashid's book *Taliban*. Not only did I find it to be a fascinating history of the rise of the Taliban, but a virtual who's who of Taliban officials. I ordered thirty copies and made it mandatory reading for all officers who were about to be deployed.

Those selected for deployment were sent to the Farm for a week of map reading, communications training, and weapons training focusing on Soviet-made arms. Both the Taliban and our Afghan allies were equipped with AK-47 assault rifles, RPK and RPD machine guns and the Soviet version of bazookas known as RPG-7s.

The week of training also gave me an opportunity to get to know individual members of my team. I considered myself lucky. In addition to Storm (the former SF captain), Marlowe (the only former Navy Seal) and Todd (the communication officer), who had been with me on the 2000 deployment into the Panshir Valley, my team consisted of: George, a former Marine Infantry Officer and Texan who would serve as my deputy; A.C., a tech expert from Science and Technology; two new ███████████ paramilitary officers, Parker and Yale; Hamid and Amir, the two native Farsi and Arabic speakers I had recruited and recent graduates of the ops course; and a case officer who had been a former Force Recon Marine named Davis. Half of my team members had never been in the field on an Agency deployment or assignment of any kind.

As the senior officer and someone with considerable experience conducting CT operations, I was asked to speak to the teams collectively. I told them that our intel showed that the Taliban had dug in for a long, tough fight. They were no doubt praying for an early winter. Military experts were predicting prolonged trench warfare not unlike that of World War I.

Our enemies would be ruthless, I told them. Anyone captured would likely be tortured to death on video, which would be aired to the world for the purpose of shocking the country and our families. Therefore, at no time should anyone in any position of authority surrender himself or any force under his command.

My Jawbreaker team was scheduled to deploy in seventy-two hours. Hank would accompany us into the Panshir Valley for several days to get a firsthand look at the battlefield. He explained that unlike other operations the senior officer on the ground (myself), would not be calling all the shots. Since I was going to supervise two major battlefields—the Shomali Plains (with twenty thousand combatants) and Taloqan (with fifteen thousand)—Hank at CTC/■■■ would handle the rest of the teams directly from headquarters.* ■■■■■■■■■ ■■■■■■■■■■■■■■■■■■■■■■■■■■■■■■■■■■■■■■■. Teams would communicate between themselves via encrypted radio net and satellite phones.

I had been running on adrenaline for weeks. Every couple of days, I called my wife and son in ■■■■■■■■■. Two nights before I left, my sisters Susan and Barbara and Barbara's husband drove down from New York to collect on a bet. Several years earlier, I had wagered that President Clinton would not only be impeached, but found guilty and removed from office. I had lost. Now I had to take them to dinner at the most expensive restaurant of their choice. They picked Morton's in Tysons Corner and feasted on expensive steaks, desserts, cognac by the glass and fifteen-dollar cigars. The tab came to a whopping four hundred dollars!

---

*Henry A. Crumpton, "Intelligence and War 2001–2," in *Transforming U.S. Intelligence.*

The next day I was called by LA/Division to meet with the Group Chief who handled the ████████ of South America. I figured he was going to update me on developments at my Station in my absence. Instead, he informed me that Latin America's Division Chief had co-ordinated with Human Resources to have me removed from my post in ████████████ . Even worse, my wife and son would have to return to the States two months into the school year while I was fighting in the Panshir.

I was livid and stormed down to CTC in search of Hank and Cofer Black. Usually, the CIA took pride in taking care of the families of its officers who are out on deployment, but apparently that had changed. Cofer and Hank got on the phone and straightened it out. For the next two days, Chief LA/Division called CTC/████ trying to get me on the line. When I finally took the call, he said it had all been a misunderstanding.

"Do not move my family in my absence!" I insisted.

"Don't worry," he said. "Everything has been fixed."

On the day before departure, Cofer Black called me into his office and shut the door. "Before Gary Schroen deployed, I told him I wanted bin Laden's head in a box," he said. "I want that, and more from you. The current Jawbreaker team has done great work on establishing our relationship and defining the battlefields. It's now your time to make war.

"Gary, I want you killing the enemy immediately. I know how aggressive you are in everything you do. That's why I approved you to lead this team. It is difficult to say how long this thing may last or how ugly it's going to get. I believe you will probably lose at least one third of your men. You need to be prepared for that. The modern battlefield is a terrible place. Bad things happen and our Afghan allies are less than fully reliable. Don't let anything deter you. Am I clear?"

"Perfectly."

"We're taking the lead in this phase. Your military counterparts in the Army Special Forces teams don't technically work for you.

███

██████████████████████████ You have access to all of our intel and the intel you develop on the ground. You speak the language. And you know the Afghans. They have none of this. Help them. The SF soldiers on the ground will be looking for you to lead."

"I completely understand," I said. "The senior SF officer attached to me will be my brother. I'll include him in everything."

"Take it to them," Cofer said, standing, taking my hand and looking me in the eye.

"Yes, sir."

When I arrived back in CTC, I found out that Hank was calling all the teams that were about to be deployed into a conference room on the fifth floor. Entering, I found twenty men sitting in chairs around the table and another dozen or so standing along the walls.

Hank said, "Not since World War II have we in the CIA been called upon to conduct armed conflict with such great importance to our nation. It's a privilege for me to be in the company of men like yourselves. I want to go around the room and have each man speak his name, the name of his team and his position."

It was solemn to say the least. I thought to myself, *If some of us are killed in action at least we've had this moment to acknowledge one another.*

I left CTC/███ at 6 P.M. to meet my daughter who had driven up from Charlottesville. Alexis was twenty-one but possessed the intellectual and emotional maturity of someone in her thirties. After dinner we went back to my hotel room and called my wife and Thomas in South America. Rebecca was calm and concealed her anxiety.

As my daughter prepared to leave, she hugged me and said, "Take care of your men, Dad."

Given the circumstances, that was the best thing she could have said.

5

NEGOTIATIONS

"I gave the Taliban leaders a series of clear and specific demands: close terrorist camps, hand over leaders of the al-Qaeda network, and return all foreign nationals, including American citizens, unjustly detained in your country. None of these demands have been met. Now the Taliban will pay the price."

—President George W. Bush, Address to the Nation, October 7, 2001

*   *   *   *   *   *

At dusk our small convoy of vehicles pulled onto the tarmac of Dushanbe, Tajikistan's International airport. Chief CTC/█ Hank sat beside me; Hamid was in the passenger seat. The unmarked aircraft that had flown us south from Tashkent, Uzbekistan, was gone. In its place sat a USAF C-17 belonging to Commander CENTCOM General Tommy Franks.

In the distance, past Russian-made fighter jets, I saw another convoy of vehicles led by a dusty Mercedes speeding towards us. I assumed they brought with them General Mohammed Qasim Khan, Ahmad Shah Massoud's successor and the new military leader of the Northern Alliance. As Hank, Hamid and I approached the C-17, a very large man stepped out.

We could barely make out General Franks' face as he called out, "You ready to take care of business tonight, Hank?"

"Yes, we are, General," Hank responded. He then introduced me as the new commander of the Jawbreaker team and Hamid as a translator for the upcoming meeting.

"Good to meet you, Gary, and you, too, Hamid," General Franks said, shaking our hands. That's when the four-vehicle convoy pulled up and General Fahim, a short squat, stocky and balding man, stepped out of a black four-by-four with Engineer Aref, his Chief of Intelligence.

I put my hand on Hamid's shoulder and said, "Get next to General Franks and begin."

General Fahim and Engineer Aref both welcomed me in Farsi, and greetings were exchanged all around. Then we stepped inside the aircraft where military aides showed us a third of the way back to a large, open conference area. We sat around the table—General Franks, Hank and myself on one side; General Fahim, Engineer Aref and Hamid facing us. Approximately twenty-five members of General Franks' staff formed a circle behind us.

General Franks' C-17 was packed with state-of-the-art communications and guidance systems and military personnel. General Fahim and Engineer Aref looked around with awe in their eyes. I was reminded of myself as a young Air Force recruit touring the Boeing 747 that served as the flying command post for the President of the United States. General Franks' aircraft was less plush and probably more sophisticated, but conveyed a clear message: "I am the Commander of CENTCOM, the premier war fighting component of the United States of America. I am big; I am bad; and I will kick anyone's ass that I so choose."

Franks began in his Texas accent stating that he was a simple country boy and a soldier.

Nothing could have been further from the truth. Franks was a brilliant four-star general with three Bronze Stars, three Purple Hearts, three Defense Distinguished Service Medals and four Legion Service Awards. He'd led troops into battle in Vietnam and Desert Storm.

Franks explained that the United States wanted to achieve a rapid and efficient victory against al-Qaeda and their hosts, the Taliban. He said he'd prefer a rapid Taliban defeat in order to spare large numbers of Afghan casualties, but was prepared to annihilate Taliban forces if they didn't yield.

General Fahim commanded about fifteen thousand fighters, many of whom were badly equipped. Latest intelligence put the Taliban at three times that number or more. The enemy also had several thousand heavily armed al-Qaeda allies backing them up.

Gnome-faced General Fahim stated emphatically that the Taliban would not surrender. What he didn't say is that the Northern Alliance didn't want the Taliban to turn over Osama bin Laden to the U.S. in return for the survivability of what they saw as the Taliban's evil regime. He also pointed out that his men badly needed food, fuel, weapons and uniforms.

[*NOTE TO READER:* CIA censors redacted this discussion of resources for the Northern Alliance.]

With that taken care of, General Franks moved to a discussion of strategy. He explained that given the issues of geography and the impending winter, it was critical that we collectively seize the northern Afghan city of Mazar-e Sharif as soon as possible. The capture of Mazar-e Sharif, he argued, would provide a land supply route to combined U.S.–Northern Alliance forces and serve as a staging area for a subsequent move against Taloqan. "With control of the north," he concluded, "we will defeat the Taliban and al-Qaeda on the Shomali Plains." With a smile on his craggy face, General Franks proposed to meet General Fahim at Bagram Airbase outside Kabul before Christmas to discuss the next steps.

I'd been thoroughly briefed about the strategy that had been previously laid out by Hank and General Franks with their staffs. With the support of U.S. airpower, the plan called for General Dostum, in the center/north of the country, to drive his Uzbek forces into Mazar-e Sharif. Once the city was secured, Dostum's forces would then take a hard right and march east to support Northern Alliance Tajik forces, commanded by Berryelah Khan, for an all-out assault on Taloqan. General Fahim's army, farther south on the Shomali Plains, would manuever westward to cut off retreating Taliban troops and trap them in a large kill box. Once trapped, the Taliban army of the North could either surrender or be decimated by massive U.S. bombing runs.

Fahim thanked General Franks for U.S. support, then launched into a detailed argument of why the capital city of Kabul needed to be seized first. He explained that Afghanistan was a nation of tribes and competing factions with Kabul as the center of power. Once Kabul was in Northern Alliance hands, he reasoned, the rest of the country could be subdued over time.

It was clear to me that General Fahim had set his sights on seizing political control of the country. We, on the other hand, were focused on defeating the Taliban and destroying al-Qaeda. General Franks was not going to be dissuaded by the political aims of one individual warlord. He stated simply, "This is how we're going to proceed: Mazar-e Sharif first, Taloqan second, Shomali Plains third." He explained again why this was sound militarily. His tone was respectful, but communicated clearly, This is not open to negotiation.

As Hamid translated, Engineer Aref whispered into General Fahim's ear. *If General Fahim has any sense,* I said to myself, *he will simply thank General Franks and move on.* He didn't, and, once again, argued that we should focus first on the Shomali Plains.

General Franks cut him off. "General," he said, "we will proceed with Mazar-e Sharif."

Fahim finally got the message. General Franks next told General Fahim that he should immediately start launching offensive ground operations against the Taliban in all sectors.

General Fahim's response took our breath away. He said that he'd require an additional ████████████████████ a month to fight. The ██████████████ a month he had requested earlier was needed to maintain his forces. Offensive operations would cost an additional ██████████████ a month on top of that.

I knew from experience that Persians and their Afghan cousins are all carpet salesman at heart. In their culture, everything is open to negotiation in an endless search for advantage. General Franks, a Texan, a U.S. Army General, prided himself on being direct and to the point. To his way of thinking, this is not how allied warriors should be conducting themselves.

General Franks uttered the word "bullshit" and stood up straight, so that from our perspective he looked ten feet tall. Without saying another word, he walked off. Dead silence passed. Hank sat rigid, his face stone cold. I leaned across the table and said, "*Chaneh nazanid,*" which translated literally means "do not hit chins" in Farsi, or, "Do not negotiate like this."

Hamid looked at me in horror because of the hostile tone I had used to address the Military Chief of the Northern Alliance. Engineer Aref turned pale.

The seven or eight minutes that passed felt like an hour. Hank glared across the table and said sternly, "This is not the way we do business."

Both General Fahim and Engineer Aref were visibly nervous. I learned later that General Franks had gone to the john, then outside the aircraft to smoke a cigarette.

██
██
██
██
██████████████████████

The remainder of the meeting addressed specific needs regarding logistical support and the disposition of enemy forces. Colonel John Mulholland, Commander of the 5th Special Forces Group, joined us to talk about the SF teams that would deploy into Afghanistan. At the conclusion, General Franks offered to take General Fahim on a tour of his C-17. As they went off together, Hank introduced me to Brigadier General Kimmons, the CENTCOM J-2 (Chief of Intelligence), and Vice Admiral Albert Calland of Special Operations Command (SOCOM) and the only officer out of uniform. Admiral Calland, who was the senior ranking SEAL in the U.S. Navy, said he would be accompanying Hank and my team into the Panshir to survey the battlefield.

Hank and I zipped up our Gortex jackets as we stepped from the aircraft into the cool evening air. When Engineer Aref approached, I shook my head from side to side as if to say, Poorly handled meeting. He explained in Farsi that Hamid had made some mistakes in translation. I had used the language for years and followed the translation completely. There had been no errors.

I translated Engineer Aref's statement to Hank. In a deadpan, Hank replied, "Sure, conduct yourself like crap, then blame the translator." All the careful chief of NA intel could do was grit his teeth.

Hamid translated General Franks's final words to General Fahim: "I'll see you at Bagram in mid-December." Then Hank, Hamid and I climbed back in the SUV and speed off. Hamid looked exhausted. As a brand new officer on his first deployment, he had just played an important role in a historic military meeting.

As we passed through the gate, he asked, "How did I do?"

Hank said, "You did wonderful, but they're blaming you for Fahim's poor performance."

"Oh, no!" Hamid said, looking horrified.

"Don't worry," I added. "If we lose this war, it's all your fault."

We broke out laughing, but left the meeting with serious doubts. General Fahim was going to be difficult. He was already thinking beyond the battle at hand to the postwar alignment of power. In a sense, I couldn't blame him. Afghans had little reason to trust that the United States would stay for the long haul.

More than half of my team had helicoptered into the Panshir earlier in the day. Back at the hotel in Tajikistan, the rest of us waited for the weather to clear. I prepared a written report on the meeting with General Fahim, spoke to R.J. with Team Alpha and General Dostum south of Mazar-e Sharif, then went to the U.S. Embassy with Hank to meet Ambassador Pancho Huddle.

Later that evening we learned that a U.S. Special Forces soldier in the Panshir was ill with meningitis and had to be medivaced out immediately. Since the weather over Tajikistan and Uzbekistan was badly overcast it was impossible to launch helicopters from where we were without the risk of them crashing into the cloud-covered mountains. So the decision was made to send two U.S. Army CH-53 helicopters from southern Pakistan over the heart of the Taliban positions in the South.

We followed intently over the radio as the helicopters crossed the border. And listened with dismay as one helicopter experienced engine problems and was forced to do a hard landing in enemy territory, injuring several crew members. As the second, healthy helicopter circled overhead, soldiers from the bird on the ground exchanged gunfire with members of the Taliban. Some tense minutes passed before everyone was rescued and ferried to safety in Pakistan. Then a U.S. F-16 was called in to obliterate the downed CH-53 so the Taliban couldn't make use of its communications equipment.

Simultaneously, we listened as Team Alpha and Dostum's Uzbek force conducted a night operation to dislodge the Taliban from a small town. Against a backdrop of gunfire and explosions, an Alpha Team member calmly reported the battle's progress. Hank turned to me and asked, "Who's doing the reporting on the radio?"

"It's not R.J.," I answered.

"That's Mike Spann," Hamid inserted. "He was a classmate of mine at the Farm."

*   *   *

The following day as the sun set over Dushanbe, Tajikistan, I helped my team load gun cases, ammo, communications gear, optical equipment and personnel gear into a Russian-made five-ton truck.

In addition to our normal packs, each of us carried a "bug-out bag" containing ammo, food, water, compass, radio, beacon and maps marked with escape routes in case of an emergency escape.

"You guys ready?" Ron asked. Ron was the ▮▮▮▮▮▮ chief in Dushanbe, a city of 600,000 people roughly 170 miles north of the Afghan border.

"I think we're set," I said. Then I instructed the men—my commo officer Todd, Amir, Hamid, Hank and the Admiral—to pile into the convoy of four SUVs.

"Here comes the fun part," Ron said. He explained that while Dushanbe had once been a major stop on the Rome-China silk route, its streets were now controlled at night by criminals and narco-traffickers. "Terrorist groups pay off ministers. It's not a pretty sight."

Neither was Dushanbe from my perspective. Endless tracts of soul-numbing Soviet-style architecture and decaying buildings reminded me of Tirana, Albania—not my favorite spot.

We stopped at a military roadblock. At rifle point, Ron was ordered to roll down his window. He explained in fluent Russian that he was riding in an official U.S. convoy that had been approved by State Security. When the soldier wasn't convinced, Ron handed him the cell phone number of a key colonel in the Tajik ▮▮▮▮▮▮ Service. Appropriate calls were made and we were permitted to pass.

Ron smiled. "A piece of cake."

"Yeah. Right."

Our convoy wormed its way through a forty-five-minute maze of darkened dilapidated apartment buildings, factories, and the occasional Tajik teahouse (*chaikhana*) and entered the back gate of an airfield.

"It's damn cold," Hamid said, shivering.

"This is nothing," I answered. "Bundle up."

I knew from experience the flight over the Pamir mountains into Afghanistan's Panshir Valley would be bone-chilling. Since we would be flying over hostile territory, the large tailgate and side entrances of the helicopters would have to be kept open so machine guns and miniguns could fire back.

As my team strapped on their handguns, Ron approached: "I wish I was going in with you."

"We're going to be hollering for all sorts of support, so I'm real glad you'll be just north of us," I said.

"Don't be shy. Get on the STU-III or the radio and tell me what you want. If you're forced to withdraw don't try to cross back into Tajikistan on the ground without clearance. The Russian Motorized Infantry that guards the border could easily mistake you for bandits or terrorists."

"As soon as we get in, I'll get up on the radio and make contact."

The rest of what I had to say was drowned out by the roar of approaching helicopters. Ron shouted, "Looks like it's showtime."

First one helicopter, then the other, set down without shutting its engines. We piled equipment into the MH-47s, which resembled large flying buses with huge rotary blades front and back. Boarding through the main cargo entry ramp in back, I was struck by the youth of the crew.

"Are any of you over twenty-five?" I yelled in one man's ear.

As the copter roared, the crew member shook his head. At least two of the five appeared to be eighteen or nineteen. They wore flight suits with heavy jackets, Nomex gloves and helmets with third-generation night vision goggles in the snapped-up position.

Todd, Amir and Hamid buckled themselves into the folding aluminum and canvas bench along the side. I waded through knee-high supplies to greet the pilots. "Good evening, gentleman," I said. "We all know where we're going tonight?"

The pilots, both men in their thirties, gave me a thumbs-up. "Have a seat. Our stewardess will be serving drinks after take off." They smiled.

I felt right at home. I'd made my first ten parachute jumps out of an MH-47 while I was a nineteen-year-old soldier stationed in Osan, South Korea, ninety miles south of the DMZ. But a lot had changed since then. A lot.

As soon as we lifted off, I pulled a wool hat over my head and got out my heavy leather gloves. The crew snapped down their night vision equipment as the light inside the cabin was shut. It was going to be a cold, dark flight. As we climbed past 14,000 feet, one of the crew handed me an oxygen mask tethered to a long hard cord. I took a deep breath and passed it down the line to Amir, then Hamid, then the crew member and back. We had to take turns to avoid hypoxia. Todd and the guys sitting opposite passed a second mask.

Approximately thirty minutes into the flight, the engines strained to pass through snow-covered peaks. Some topped 20,000 feet. I figured we had to be flying at an altitude of at least 16,000 feet. I wondered to myself, *How high can this baby go?*

Through a headset, I followed communications between the crews of the two MH-47s. The second one was struggling with the weight of the team's gear. The pilot said he was going to drop some fuel. I knew this wasn't good. The Taliban controlled most of the territory they were flying over and if we had to stop in the event of an emergency, we were screwed.

A year earlier, after a four-week siege, the Taliban had captured the city of Taloqan in Afghanistan's northeastern Takhar province. Taloqan had served as the Northern Alliance's temporary capital. Our now-dead ally, General Ahmad Shah Massoud, had been forced to retreat east over the Khwaja Mohammad Mountains into Badakhshan. More than 150,000 people had been displaced.

I turned to Amir and Hamid, both of whom were new officers and had never been deployed on an operation of any kind. Now they were taking part in one of the most dangerous and important missions in CIA history.

"We're in this fight together," I told Amir, holding up my right fist. The Arab-American responded with the same gesture. So did Hamid. Both men looked nervous. *Once they were on the ground,* I said to myself, *I'm going to pair each man with a paramilitary officer so they don't get killed.*

Out the portal window I saw the other CH-47 with Hank and Vice Admiral Calland flying parallel to us two hundred meters away. Beyond the second helicopter was a backdrop of stars, snow-capped mountains and a half moon.

My mind raced ahead. The brutal Taliban was waiting. I'd seen film footage of how they treated their own people. Women driven in the back of pickups into stadiums packed with cheering Islamic fundamentalists. They were taken out and led by leashes attached to their bound hands. Forced to their knees in the center of the stadium and shot through the back of their heads one by one.

I knew that shortly after the predominantly Pushtun Taliban occupied Kabul in September 1996 they broadcast sixteen decrees over Radio Sharia prohibiting music, shaving, raising of pigeons, narcotics, kite flying, gambling, reproduction of pictures, British- and American-style haircuts, charging interest on loans, washing clothes on riverbanks, dancing at weddings and women leaving their homes without burkas. Their goal was to re-create a society like the one the prophet Mohammed had lived in on the Arab peninsula during the seventh century. According to their fundamentalist worldview, debate was heresy and doubt was sin.

I thought about my wife and kids, my childhood in Long Island and the funerals of the dead from the World Trade Center attacks, some of which took place in the same neighborhood where I grew up. It struck me that there was some irony and a little justice in the fact that as a New Yorker and former firefighter I was going to be one of the leaders of the attack against the Taliban and al-Qaeda terrorists.

I didn't just want to survive: I wanted to annihilate the enemy. And I didn't want to end up like one of my favorite historical characters—Alexander Burns. Alexander Burns, aka Bukhara Burns, had been a British intelligence officer who entered the subcontinent in the late 1830s to negotiate with the so-called one-eyed lion of the Punjab, Sikh leader Ranjit Singh. The second time Burns entered Afghanistan in 1841 was as the intelligence officer for a large British military expedition. He was one of the first of more than fourteen thousand British soldiers to be wiped out by the Afghans in the First Afghan War.

Like Burns before me, I was also an intelligence officer and spoke Persian. This was my second trip into Afghanistan, too. The difference, I told myself, was that Burns had been a gentleman and I would do whatever it took to win.

Afghanistan had been a graveyard for one invader after another. Alexander the Great's army had mutinied. Bukhara Burns and the first British army had been totally wiped out. Lord Roberts, the most successful general of the British Empire, had won a single victory at Kandahar, Afghanistan, before quickly withdrawing. The first British Ambassador, Sir Louis Cavagnari, had been massacred in 1878 along with his one-hundred-man British Indian Army guard. The Soviets, who invaded in 1979, had fought to a standstill and withdrew ten years later battered and bloody.

I had no doubt that a very dangerous and complicated mission lay ahead. Afghan warlords had a habit of selling out to one side or the other. Decisiveness, showing power, establishing and maintaining momentum would all be critical, I told myself. I had to stay aggressive. I couldn't hesitate or show doubt.

The Taliban, on the other hand, would dig in and try to stall us until the first snows of winter, which were only a month or so away.

People back at headquarters had told me to expect six months of World War I–style trench warfare. And as we tried to defeat the Taliban we had the added responsibility of searching for Osama bin Laden and destroying what we could of his terrorist organization.

The helicopters started to descend into the pitch-black night. Looking down at my watch, I figured we had reached the northern end of the Panshir Valley. Northern Alliance headquarters were somewhere in the lower third of the valley. We passed over Tajik villages that clung to the sides of mountains.

The second we touched ground we started moving, dragging cargo to the back ramp. There we were met by Afghans bundled in heavy coats with khafias wrapped around their heads for extra warmth. They took boxes from us and set them on the ground twenty feet away.

A group of men approached with large backpacks. I recognized one of them as the man I was relieving, Gary Schroen. We shook hands as the tail rotor of the helicopter roared over our heads.

"Enjoy your retirement!" I yelled into Schroen's ear. At sixty, Gary Schroen—a legend in the Agency—had reached the age of mandatory retirement.

The light from the back of the helicopter illuminated his smiling face. "Good luck, Gary," he said. "Get it done."

I stepped away from the bird, which took off again with Schroen and his six-man team. There was no time for the usual debriefings. We had to move fast.

Back on the ground, I saw fifty men carrying boxes from the landing field and loading them in trucks. Out of the pitch black came a familiar voice in English, "Welcome back, Mr. Gary."

It was Majid, my prime liaison from the spring 2000 Jawbreaker deployment. He had a turban wrapped around his head to protect him from the freezing cold.

"So here we are, together again."

"It's your fate to be here again," Majid said, somewhat lightheartedly. "Mr. Schroen told me you were coming as his replacement. I told him that this was good."

"I'm sorry about Massoud," who had recently been killed. "He was right about a lot of things," I added.

"Thank you. I know," Majid said.

Back in May 2000 Massoud had explained to us that al-Qaeda and the Taliban were interdependent. If you wanted to kill one, you would have to destroy them both. But parts of the White House, CIA, State and Defense didn't want to hear that then.

Majid and I each picked up a box of equipment and carried it to a Russian-made jeep. Then we joined my team for the drive out of the riverbed, up to a dirt road and into a walled compound five minutes away. This is where we would begin to wage war.

6

PANSHIR VALLEY

"There is a path to the top of even the highest mountain."
—*an Afghan proverb*

* * * * * *

We turned off the main road, up an incline, and parked outside the mud-walled compound that would serve as our headquarters. We were in the dusty little town of Astana on the west bank of the Panshir River. The first person to greet me was my team member Davis with a look of deep frustration. He and four others had inserted two days ago. "The Afghans aren't helping us," he complained, his blond hair slicked back. "We've been virtual prisoners here the last two days."

As we spoke, our breath formed thick little clouds in the dark, frigid air. "Follow me."

The compound contained five separate concrete structures. Climbing up the steps of a building on our right, we filed down a hallway lined with MREs and boxes of bottled water, into a good-sized room with a bare lightbulb hanging from the ceiling.

"Welcome to the Astana Hilton," Davis said.

There was a bed flung in one corner, but no heat. "You have guards?" I asked.

"Four armed men on duty twenty-four hours a day."

"What's your biggest problem?"

"Not enough vehicles," Davis replied. "The Afghans only have a few. Every time we go out, they want to send an escort. Half the time the vehicles never show up. We're too damn far from the front."

"Okay. Do me a favor. Make sure the Admiral and Hank find a place to sleep. Then make arrangements for them to see the front tomorrow. I'll take up the transportation issue with Majid."

Davis took a deep breath and exhaled. "I'm glad you're here."

"Me, too."

In the main building that would serve as our office, I ran into my old friend ████████████████ . His long beard looked even whiter than it did in February 2000. He wrapped me in a bear hug and asked in Persian: "Where have you been, my brother?"

"We are here to destroy the Taliban," I responded.

"*Khali khub. Khali khub,*" he said (Very good. Very good).

It was a spartan structure, but modern by Afghan standards, with concrete floors and a corrugated roof. The toilet was a hole in the floor.

Communications equipment had been set up on one side of the main room. Against the opposite wall sat a large table with eight laptops wired together. Wires ran out a side door to antennae on the patio. In addition to the receivers and transmitters that linked us to Washington we had a HF encrypted radio net, which allowed us to communicate securely with the other teams.

I found Hank at a laptop reviewing incoming messages from headquarters with Vice Admiral Calland reading over this shoulder. "I'm not here to get in your way," Hank said looking up. "Function as if I'm not here."

Sure, I thought to myself, *my boss is here and I'm supposed to ignore him.*

Hank was in the Panshir to absorb the details of our mission, so that he could brief President Bush and his senior staff back in D.C.

I said: "Tomorrow morning, an escort of Northern Alliance soldiers will take you to the front. After about an hour, you'll pass a battalion of old tanks the Northern Alliance keeps up in the valley and the French hospital set up by Doctors Without Borders. After that the valley will get very narrow and drop you out on the Shomali Plains. You can't tell from the maps, but there's a small mountain range midway between the Shomali Plains and Kabul. Both the main roads on the east and west pass through the mountains at low points so they'll block your view of Kabul. If you want to see Kabul, we can get you up on a mountain with optics."

"No," Hank replied. "I want to see enemy positions from the ground. I want to understand how this thing is going to have to be fought and won."

George, my deputy, and I shook hands. The tall, taciturn Texan, who had arrived two days earlier, had conferred with Gary Schroen before he left. I said, "Let's find a place to sit and talk." We had never worked together before.

"The men are anxious to begin," George said, stroking his brown mustache. "Schroen wanted to ensure that no new initiatives were undertaken until you arrived. The Afghans have been hospitable but demand that they accompany us everywhere because they have been ordered not to let any of us get killed. Our man Stan is down at the front lines with Parker and Special Forces Team 555. They call themselves Triple Nickel and inserted about ten days ago. Their leader, Lt. Colonel Chris Haas just arrived. He's in overall command of all the SF units in Eastern Afghanistan including Triple Nickel and SF Team 595 up in Taloqan. Our team in Taloqan is headed by a Special Activities Division officer named Breen, who is a former Marine captain and forward air controller. Both our guys and the SF team are strong."

Stan was Gary Schroen's man at the front. A decade earlier, he'd been a student of mine at the Farm.

"What about Haas?" I asked.

"Fine officer; strong leader. He's in a compound about a hundred meters from here. You and I should go see him first thing tomorrow morning."

"Now, tell me the problems," I said. "There's a sense in D.C. that no progress is being made."

George, wearing a green fleece vest and brown baseball cap, leaned forward. "Schroen was pissed at Washington for not delivering a greater number of air sorties per day. The Afghans have an expectation that because we have committed to providing airpower the sun will be blocked out with the number of planes."

I said, "Here on the Shomali we're going to have to reduce expectations. General Franks just told General Fahim that he's committed to overrunning Mazar-e Sharif and Taloqan before moving on Kabul. That doesn't mean that Fahim won't pursue his own agenda and complain to us on a daily basis. But that's the plan."

"Understood."

"The best we can do is call CENTCOM," I added, "and find what air assets are coming our way, so we can coordinate ground maneuvers to maximize benefits. A friend of mine is the DCI representative at CENTCOM. We can call him direct."

"Sounds good."

"How are the Special Forces guys getting on with the Afghans?" I asked.

"No one on the SF team speaks Farsi or Dari. Our guy Stan speaks Russian as does Afghan General Sharifi. They're the only ones who can communicate."

"The Army sent no linguists?"

"Haas has a little Farsi, but he's at least twenty-five miles from the front lines. They didn't send any native speakers to Taloqan either. "

"That means communication is limited to the top end of the weaker of the two Russian speakers."

"Correct."

"I want Hamid, who is a native Farsi speaker and U.S.-educated attorney, deployed to the front right away," I ordered. "And I want you in charge down there. Keep Stan with General Sharifi. The more communication we have with the Afghans the better."

George cracked a smile. Most deputies were relegated to admin work; he was going to the front.

"One last thing," I added. "Who has the key to the cash box?"

George removed a cord with a key on it from around his head. "It's all yours, chief. Eight million bucks."

"Let's go count the cash."

When we ran into Storm (the SAD officer from the previous Jawbreaker), who was organizing weapons, I slapped him on the shoulder. "You're the keeper of the cash now," I said. "Come with us."

George led us to a RubberMaid trunk the size of a small table filled with eight million dollars ███████████████████████████ ██ ██ Anything over that required approval from Hank.

"Do a cash count and sign for it," I instructed Storm.

The big, red-bearded paramilitary officer asked, "You are sure you want me to watch this money?"

"You bet," I answered. "Because I'm sure you've already seen the inside of Leavenworth Military prison and won't be up for a second stay."

Storm pulled a little spiral notebook out of his pocket. "This will be the book from now on."

"Count it and sign it, Mr. Big Bucks."

With the count underway, Davis arrived to take me to see Majid. At the bottom of the stairs, we took a sharp right and followed a sidewalk to a separate building. This is where our Afghan ███████ counterparts lived and worked.

I greeted Majid with, "I'm not leaving this time until we've won."

"Good!" the clean-shaven Afghan responded as he stood in his socks.

"One thing we need to do immediately is buy more vehicles."

"Vehicles are expensive because journalists are buying and renting them."

"I want six vehicles tomorrow," I said. "How much will it cost?"

"Between ████████████████████ depending on what you get. Pickups cost more than Russian-made jeeps."

"Tomorrow morning I'll give you ████████████████. Buy the trucks immediately."

Majid explained that Engineer Aref had ordered him to have one of his trusted men accompany my officers at all times. "I have strict instructions to make sure none of you are captured or killed." Although this sounded very considerate, the real reason was obvious: General Fahim and Engineer Aref wanted to keep track of our every move.

"I appreciate the concern," I said, "but that won't be necessary."

Majid frowned. "Gary, this will be a problem. I have my instructions."

"With all due respect, tell Engineer Aref that we don't have time to sit around and wait for escorts. My men will be traveling alone when they need to. If they're killed, it'll be their own fault and my responsibility. ████████████████████."

As we left the building, Davis muttered, "Thanks."

"First thing in the morning, tell Storm to give you the money. He's taking responsibility for the cash."

"Why's that?"

"Because George's going to the front."

Davis' blue eyes lit up. "Can I go with him?" he asked.

"I have several other projects in mind for you. Get some sleep."

Back at the office, my mind continued to race. I wanted to press forward immediately and never let up. To do that, I would have to delegate, or drown in a sea of tasks and decisions. I couldn't afford to surround myself with officers like they did in most CIA offices. I had to fire the ones I had forward and make sure they got support.

It was 1 A.M. when ████████████████ arrived to take me on a tour of the compound to inspect the guards. When we returned, he ordered one of the cooks to prepare me a cup of coffee. Sipping it, I said to myself, *This is going to be a war.*

*   *   *

At 0600 hours I rose from the warmth of my sleeping bag and greeted the cook boiling water wearing a Panshiri cap, *shalwar kamiz* and heavy vest for added protection from the cold. He was one of the Afghans who'd listened to me tell the story of the battle of Gettysburg in Farsi during my previous deployment. He handed me a cup of coffee mixed with hot chocolate.

"*Daste shoma dard nakone,*" I said (which means "thank you" in Farsi, or literally "May your hands never ache").

Todd, our commo officer who seemed to be able to function on no sleep, was listening to my young team leader Breen, in Taloqan, give an update on his location, the status of his team and SF Team 595, known on the military network as Tiger 2. They'd received incoming artillery fire from the Taliban the day before.

Todd asked if I wanted to speak with him. I shook my head. "When I have instructions, I'll talk to him. Otherwise maintain scheduled communications."

I had to stay on top of everything 24/7, which meant constantly checking the incoming intel traffic, reading intelligence reports on enemy positions with geographic coordinates, then releasing them for transmission to headquarters. Despite everything we were getting from our Northern Alliance counterparts, there was little reliable information on bin Laden. Some reports put him in Kabul; others put him south in Jalalabad. I thought, *We're going to have to destroy the Taliban first, if we're ever going to get a shot at him and his fighters.*

After a breakfast of scrambled eggs, Afghan flat bread known as *naan*, strips of leftover meat from the previous evening, tea and coffee, Hank and Admiral Calland loaded up into a truck with one of my SAD paramilitary officers and an Afghan driver for a trip to the front. Another vehicle full of armed Afghan fighters led the way.

I put on a baseball cap and gray/black fleece jacket and walked with George to Lieutenant Colonel Haas's SF headquarters. The sun shone bright across the Panshir as we picked our way down a very rocky dirt road and entered a walled compound a little smaller than ours. Haas and his men were in the courtyard trying to start a small generator. They wore a mix of civilian Gortex jackets and tactical pants and boots. Some had grown beards.

George made the introductions. Lt. Colonel Haas was a slightly balding, muscular man in his late thirties. He turned his Ray-Bans my way and said, "There were several things I wanted to address with Schroen before he left but he asked me to wait till you got here."

"Well, here I am and I need to know what you have in the way of men and how I can help."

"I have a full Special Forces twelve-man A-Team, the Triple Nickel, down at the front right now led by a Warrant Officer named Diaz. I have a second A-Team, the 585, commanded by Master Sergeant Bolduc up in Taloqan with your team. Both teams have Air Force combat controllers assigned to them."

"They're not being run by officers?" I asked.

Haas grunted. "My boss, Colonel Mulholland, doesn't give a damn if the teams are led by officers, warrant officers or noncommissioned officers. If they know their stuff they lead. If they don't he relieves them."

"Are you having problems?"

"Transportation is a huge problem. Not enough vehicles. Too much time sitting around waiting for the Afghans."

"What do you have in the way of funds?"

"Five thousand bucks."

I smiled. "I've got a little more than that, so I can help. In fact, I'm buying some vehicles this afternoon. I'll give you two of them."

Haas flashed a big grin. "That works." Quickly, he grew serious: "We also need linguists. It's a major problem not having Farsi speakers down on the front."

I nudged George with my elbow. "I'm moving my deputy here forward. He's an ex-Marine and likes getting shot at. He's taking along a native Farsi speaker named Hamid who I brought in last night. Use him around the clock."

Haas turned to George and asked, "When are you going down?"

"As soon as Gary here gets over his personal issues and doesn't need me to hold his hand."

After we stopped laughing, Lt. Colonel Haas led us on a tour of his compound and pointed out a sand table replica his men had made of the battlefield. He told me that he grew up in Suffolk County, Long Island, like me. We appreciated the fact that two New Yorkers were leading the fight against the terrorists who had directed the attack against the World Trade Center.

Back at our base, I stopped in to see Majid at the Northern Alliance tactical operations center. ████████████████████ "You'll have six trucks in the morning," he told me.

██

██

████████████████████████████████

Here reports from various Northern Alliance sources from within the Taliban and al-Qaeda were assembled, analyzed and passed to us. Five Afghans sat at a table working radios and satellite phones. The wall featured a large map of Afghanistan with colored pins that marked troop positions.

Before we left, I handed over two boxes of the Dari language Global Positioning Systems (GPSs) I had ordered from headquarters. ████████████████████████████████ Hamid carefully explained to the Afghans how they worked.

"First rate," Majid said.

I'd learned that the battlefield was a strange place. When there was no active fighting, individuals on either side would simply walk across the lines to visit with friends and family on the other side. It wasn't uncommon for a Northern Alliance fighter stationed in the Panshir to take a bus up to the front, walk across the Taliban lines and after a rudimentary search continue on to Kabul to spend the weekend with his family. Taliban fighters made the same trip in reverse.

This made it real easy to run spies into one another's territory. Once our Northern Alliance partners got the hang of the Dari language GPSs, we could start sending them into Kabul to mark the geo-cords of Taliban buildings and military units. When they returned, we would debrief our sources, retrieve the geo-cords, then bomb the Taliban targets into oblivion. Pretty sweet.

*　　*　　*

Fortunately for us, the Taliban wasn't aware that the men directing the CIA war against them (Hank and Vice Admiral Calland) were spending the afternoon several hundred yards from their front lines on the Shomali Plains. The view they saw from their position was startling—Taliban tanks, troops and artillery dug into trenches, command posts and ammo bunkers. When Hank and Vice Admiral Calland returned that evening, they described frustrated Northern Alliance commanders who wanted more U.S. air attacks. But Hank had held steadfast and repeated what General Franks had said in Dushanbe: Mazar-e Sharif and Taloqan would be seized first. The NA troops on the Shomali would have to suck it up and wait.

Without airpower, General Fahim's commander in that sector, Bismullah Khan, wasn't going anywhere. He had at most eight thousand men, including regulars and reserves. He knew that the Taliban, on the other side, boasted at least twelve thousand. And that number grew daily as foreign recruits arrived to join the jihad against the Americans.

Part of the reason Bismullah Khan was fixated on U.S. air strikes is that he and his commanders had seen a firsthand demonstration of how effective they could be. The day before Hank's visit, NA Subcommander General Babajan had taken SF Triple Nickel Team leader Warrant Officer Diaz on a tour of Bagram airbase. While they were on top of a twenty-foot tower, the stout, jovial Babajan started pointing out Taliban positions. Using his binoculars, Diaz identified a buried Taliban antiaircraft gun next to a command-and-control shack with a protruding antenna. He radioed his Air Force combat controller to see if there were aircraft in the area that could be redirected to the Shomali. Tech Sergeant Calvin located a couple of F/A-18s from the carrier USS *Theodore Roosevelt* nearby, and Diaz ordered him to hump the thousand meters from their base to the Bagram tower and bring the CAS (close air support) equipment.

Using binoculars, radios, GPSs and laser designators, Sergeant Calvin and his team started lighting up targets and directing bombing runs from the F/A-18s. When the Taliban command-and-control shack was blasted with a direct hit that sent dry mud and metal shards flying three feet in the air, jubilant Afghans cheered and hugged the Americans. "When we saw their bombs for the first time," General Babajan said later, "we were very happy because they were so precise."

The Taliban responded with artillery rounds that whizzed by the tower. Diaz, Calvin and company hit the deck, and called in more strikes. That night, back at the safehouse, the Afghans honored Triple Nickel with a feast.

*　　*　　*

Back at the compound, we worked late. It was impossible to sleep with all the adrenaline coursing through my veins. At 0200 hours I was still reviewing reports from Breen in Taloqan, Stan on the Shomali Plains and Majid's people in the next building. Among the reports was a welcome piece of news: I'd be receiving my own ███████ helicopter and U.S. crew. I hit the sack around three in the morning telling myself that now that I had a U.S.-piloted copter my life expectancy had just increased.

In the morning, Hank, Vice Admiral Calland and I sat down with Engineer Aref* to go over the ████████████ financial commitment made by General Franks. Neatly dressed in pressed black slacks and a white shirt, Engineer Aref* started by telling us that Gary Schroen had promised to ██████ him three helicopters at a cost of ████████ before leaving Afghanistan. Hank's face turned red. "Nonsense," he said. "Schroen would not have made such a decision."

Engineer Aref's* English wasn't perfect, but he understand. The best he could do was act insulted, while I thought, *We're not exactly getting off on the right foot.*

Hank was emphatic, stating that the helicopters were not an option. He said, "We have more important immediate issues to address."

He was referring to eight Shelter Now International (SNI) Christian missionaries who were being held hostage by the Taliban in Kabul. Hank told Engineer Aref* that I would be managing the rescue effort. Aref promised to provide support.

The next morning as the sun rose high above the snow-peaked mountains, I escorted Hank and Vice Admiral Calland to the dusty helicopter landing zone along the river. Before lifting off, Hank said, "Stay aggressive and press this thing with everything you've got."

"I will."

Back at the base, I called my men together. With the sun penetrating the windows of our concrete building, a small number of bearded CIA officers in field clothing gathered. I stood before them and began: "Gentleman, and I use that term very loosely . . ."

A few of them laughed. Others were just becoming familiar with my sense of humor.

"I've been here seventy-two hours and have made some decisions. First off, we need a greater presence at the front. George, Hamid and Commo Sean [our second commo officer] are going to join Stan and Parker down at the front. They will have a complete ability to communicate with us, headquarters and the other teams. But remember the Northern Alliance has their intel here and the intel we receive here will affect the entire country. We can't unhook ourselves from NA intel just because you want to go to the front and start shooting guys in the head. Besides, we're not going to win this war by killing guys one by one. There are only a few of us, so we have to use intel to identify large elements of the enemy and kill in the hundreds. I've reviewed the satellite photos and the enemy is thousands deep at the front. If anyone wants a day off each week to go down to the front line and shoot guys, that's fine. I know some of you live for that shit, but that's not going to win the war."

I turned to big, red-bearded Storm. "I need you to handle the SNI hostage problem and accompany me to all meetings on this issue with the Northern Alliance."

Shelter Now International, a relief agency based in Oshkosh, Wisconsin, had been providing food, tents and blankets to impoverished Afghans for years. Eight members of their group—a man and seven women—had been arrested by the Taliban in August for showing a film about the life of Jesus Christ and preaching Christianity. They included four Germans, two Australians and two Americans. Under the Taliban's strict interpretation of Islamic law the penalty for proselytizing was death.

Storm said in his Midwest accent, "We have three guys from JSOC arriving tomorrow who will work solely on this with us."

"Fine. Integrate them into your planning. We have to find a way to ensure that the Taliban does not turn the eight hostages over to bin Laden, because that could get ugly."

"I'll have some ideas for you in an hour," Storm answered.

Next I turned to Davis. "You're in charge of high-value targets. I want to find and kill bin Laden, his number two al-Zawahiri, al-Qaeda's military commander Mohammad Atef and Khaled Shiekh Mohammad. Additionally, I want Taliban intel chief Qari Amadullah dead along with his number two and number three. Use Northern Alliance intel resources, our unilateral sources (those CIA penetrations of groups not known by our Afghan partners), SIGNIT, satellites, whatever you can find."

"Yes, sir."

"Hamid, your job on the Shomali Plains is to support George and the military and not get yourself killed by artillery fire on your first tour."

Everybody laughed, except Hamid.

I looked at Amir. "I have something really special for you. You're going to be my personal emissary to ███████████ .

[NOTE TO READER: Gary Schroen, in his book *First In,* describes ███████████ as a Pushtun educated in Egypt, who lived for a number of years in Saudi Arabia. He was funded by the Saudis to support their Wahabbi creed and was Osama bin Laden's first sponsor in Afghanistan. He was also the man who vouched for the journalists who killed Massoud with an explosive device mounted inside a camera. He was now fighting on the side of the Northern Alliance.

On page 117 of his book, Mr. Schroen describes handing ███████ "$100,000 in cash to prepare his troops for the coming fight and assist in any efforts to lure al-Qaida leaders into our reach."]

The studious-looking Arab-American spoke up. "We've given him token financial support. Will that continue?"

"No," I answered. "He gets squat. You're to go meet with him and play him out. See what he'll give up. I don't want him working against us. Convince him as a fellow Muslim that we harbor no ill will toward him. He's a Pushtun and it's likely that Afghanistan will need a Pushtun leader when the Taliban gets kicked out. But I don't want ██████ developing an advantage. Davis, you will accompany Amir on these meetings to make sure the two of you aren't killed in a mysterious accident."

There was more laughter. I was resolved to follow every lead and try to work with everyone. Not being born yesterday, I understood that most leads would probably end up leading nowhere. ████████████
████████████████████████

I cleared my throat. "I have no idea how long this fight will last. Washington wants us to destroy the Taliban forces on the Shomali Plains and then hold the Northern Alliance five miles outside the capital until the United Nations can get in and organize some peaceful transition of power. How these ideas will translate into reality is beyond me at this point. If this does happen, we could have an Afghanistan that is split between the Northern Alliance with our support in the North and a lawless area in the Pushtun areas of the south. If we enter into a protracted conflict like that, we could be vulnerable to all sorts of terrorists attacks. We'll need to develop some kind of secure facility for a long-term deployment."

Our medic, Doc, jumped in. He was a retired Special Forces doctor in his fifties who wrote western novels in his spare time. "In ███████████ a few years ago we constructed a fire base which was a replica of something we had in Vietnam. It included a wall of dirt, a berm, trailers and netting over the top to help reduce the threat of mortars. I don't think it's too early to dust off the plans, do some number crunching and consider what will be needed logistically to make this a reality."

"Thanks, Doc," I said. "Draft a cable to headquarters laying this out. Point out that this facility would be constructed at Bagram Air Base. We need to secure that airfield as a means of introducing more forces into theater. On the subject of transportation, Davis, what happened to the vehicles we paid for?"

"They arrived five minutes ago," Davis shot back.

"Let's go take a look."

All of us filed out to eyeball the vehicles, arriving as Lt. Colonel Haas hoofed his way up the dusty slope.

"Come to check out your new wheels?" I asked him.

Before us stood four, four-door Toyota pickup trucks with extended cabs and two Russian-made jeeps. All of the pickup trucks were riddled with bullet holes. Many of their windows had been shot out.

"Nice of them to include the additional ventilation," Haas said.

The Taliban were known to fight from the back of pickup trucks like these. They had been provided in the thousands by the Saudis. In battle, hundreds of trucks manned by six-man crews would swarm their opponents. While this tactic had worked in the past, it wasn't ideal against an army backed with airpower.

I turned to Haas and said, "You can have one truck and one jeep."

Haas grinned like a kid who'd just been given a pony. "I've been waiting for an Afghan escort to go down and see my men. Screw that. Are these babies gassed?"

"They're full," Davis responded. "I have another hundred gallons stored inside one of the sheds."

Lt. Colonel Haas jumped in one of the Russian-made jeeps and started the engine. The NCO with him grabbed a maroon Toyota pick-up. I cupped my hands and yelled at Haas, "Give it back to us when you leave the country."

With an unlit cigar in his mouth, he shouted: "Whatever," and sped off.

I turned to Davis. "Why am I thinking we're never going to see those vehicles again?"

Davis shook his head. "You just gave away twenty percent of our wheels."

"Buy four more trucks tomorrow," I said.

"How much can I spend?"

"Whatever you have to. Also, buy me the biggest damn truck you can find and keep buying and storing gas."

At 1930 hours Storm and I rode in one of our new Toyotas with Majid pointing the way along an unmarked dirt road approximately five kilometers south. Engineer Aref's* modest concrete and mud house was set back from the main road that cut through the Panshir. The tall, neatly dressed NA ▇▇▇▇ chief looked at me with suspicion as I said: "We need to address the SNI hostage issue first."

"They're being held in the center of Kabul and guarded twenty-four hours a day," Engineer Aref* explained carefully. "We know this because we have a source within the guard force who is reporting to one of our officers in Kabul. We'll alert you if there is any change."

"We have concerns," I continued. "We don't want the eight hostages turned over to al-Qaeda and used as human shields. So I want you to help me identify someone high in the Taliban government who we can pay off to help us secure their release or at least block their transfer to bin Laden."

Engineer Aref* frowned as he thought. "I have the satellite phone numbers of a Taliban Vice Minister who has access to the hostages. He's nervous that we might win. His code name is Gold Falcon. He isn't a source, but we've been negotiating. We might be able to work out an arrangement with him to get the hostages."

"Perfect," I said. "Call him this evening and set up a time when we can discuss terms."

"But they're only women," Engineer Aref* said as though he couldn't understand why we were making such a fuss.

Storm broke in: "Women are even more important. We don't let anybody take our people and if they do, we risk everything to get them back."

Engineer Aref* wanted to change the subject. He asked me when the ███████████ that had been promised would show up in Northern Alliance accounts so they could start buying needed food, ammunition and winter clothing. I said, "I'll check on it right away."

As we left Engineer Aref's* compound, Majid turned to me and said, "A ███████ intel team arrived two days ago and has been waiting to see you."

"Where are they staying?"

"Half a mile down the road from here."

"Let's go."

We bounced north, turned off onto another unmarked dirt road and stopped in front of a handsome two-level house. It was swanky by Panshir standards with chandeliers and plush furniture. I figured it must have been Massoud's.

███

██

████████████████████████████████████

[*NOTE TO READER:* This redacted section describes a meeting with officials of an allied intelligence service.]

Back at the base, our war-planning activities were in full swing. Every laptop was occupied with men typing intel. The click-click-click of the keyboard keys was music to my ears. A three-man team from JSOC (Joint Special Operations Forces) had arrived to help us recover the SNI hostages. ████████████████████████████ If we weren't able to buy or steal the hostages, they were prepared to orchestrate a rescue by force.

*   *   *

In Kabul, the four Germans, two Australians and two Americans from Shelter Now International cowered in the broken mint-colored walls of a Taliban prison. Since their arrest on August 3, the Christian aid workers had been subjected to three weeks of interrogation at a reform school prison before being moved to a high-security intelligence prison in a desolate part of the city. There they learned that they were being charged with spreading "the abolished religion of Christianity." The punishment under Islamic law was death.

Their situation grew more precarious when we started bombing Kabul on the night of October 7. As huge explosions shook the city, one of the two young Americans, Heather Mercer, twenty-four, crawled under a bed, walled herself in with pillows and prayed. The bolder and slightly older of the two, Dayna Curry, who like Heather had graduated from Baylor University in Texas, was drawn to a doorway. "I quietly watched the tracer bullets fly through the air," Dayna explained in the book *Prisoner of Hope*. "A red ball would traverse the sky and a red streak would follow it. The whole sky would light up red. The bombing did not seem terribly close, but the antiaircraft guns were loud. "

Meanwhile, Heather prayed out loud under her bed: "Thank you, Lord, for protecting us. Thank you, Lord, that you are in control."

*   *   *

The sky was a crisp blue and the air bitter cold. First thing the next morning, George, Hamid and our second commo officer bundled in Gortex jackets, hats and gloves and deployed to the front on the Shomali Plains, where they rented a house adjacent to Lt. Colonel Haas and his SF team. To facilitate communications, they cut a hole through the mud walls that separated their two compounds.

Before I left Washington, Hank had told me to share everything with General Franks, but he didn't talk specifically about how to handle the distribution of intelligence to SF teams on the ground. I decided on the spot that Lt. Colonel Haas and his deputy would see everything—intel reporting, ops messages, SIGINT intercepts, the works. Even though they didn't have the proper clearances, I figured, What the hell. Trust and cooperation were of paramount importance to the success of our mission. We might be from separate branches of the government, but we were all trying to achieve the same goals.

In the afternoon Storm, one of the JSOC officers, Majid and I paid another visit to Engineer Aref*. As a propane heater warmed the little living room and we sipped bitter coffee and green tea, Engineer Aref* explained that he had spoken to his Taliban government contact, Gold Falcon, who had expressed interest in cooperating with us.

"Good," I said leaning closer.

"He would like an expression of your interest in the form of a cash deposit," Aref* stated.

I asked: "What sort of expression is he looking for?"

"One hundred thousand dollars to open negotiations."

"Agreed," I answered. "How will you get him the money?"

"He'll send someone to a checkpoint on the eastern side of the front who will accompany a courier through our side. He says he'll deliver the two American women for a million dollars apiece."

The JSOC officer's eyes widened and Storm's jaw dropped.

Storm said, "It's all of them or none of them. The Australians and Germans are our allies."

I backed him up. "My colleague's correct. What I need from Gold Falcon is their exact location and assurance that they will not be harmed or turned over to al-Qaeda."

"We have his assurance of protection," Engineer Aref* said.

I wanted Gold Falcon to know that we weren't playing games. "I want to talk to him right now," I said.

We followed Aref* into a back office where he pulled a three by five card out of his desk and dialed a number on an Inmarsat satellite phone. I listened as Aref* relayed my message in Dari to Gold Falcon exactly the way I asked him to. We'd send him one hundred thousand dollars for his cooperation. He'd tell us where the hostages were being held and guarantee that they not fall into the hands of Osama bin Laden. When Engineer Aref* said that we wanted all the hostages, Gold Falcon told him that he thought it would be difficult.

I interrupted. "Tell Gold Falcon I'm standing here with you and I'm a man of my word. Tell him that if he betrays me or loses the hostages I'll spend every waking moment of my life hunting him down to kill him. Tell him I'm not like any American he has ever met. If he cooperates and is good to his word, I'll protect him and ensure the safety of his family."

Engineer Aref* conveyed the messaged. Gold Falcon asked for one million per hostage to facilitate their escape.

"Tell him to prepare to receive the one hundred thousand dollars and we'll negotiate the full payment for his services at a later date."

That night, alone in my room, I did something I'd never done since I was a kid. I got down on my knees and prayed to God for the safety of the SNI hostages. I asked him to make sure I did nothing to put their lives in jeopardy. I thought of Heather Mercer's brave father, John, who had offered the Taliban to take his daughter's place.

As I prayed for the hostages' terrified families in the U.S., Germany and Australia, I asked for a kind of strength that can't be found in technical equipment or bombs or dollar bills: faith.

* Gary Schroen in his CIA-approved book *First In* refers to several meetings between myself (I'm called Gary 2 in the book) and Engineer Aref. He explains that Engineer Aref occupied Kabul on November 14, 2001, and assumed control of the remnants of the previous intelligence organization, renaming it the National Directorate of Security (NDS), which had a department that worked with the CIA up until 2004.

7

SHOMALI PLAINS

*"We will never be a pawn in someone else's game.
We will always be Afghanistan."*
—Ahmad Shah Massoud

★　　★　　★　　★　　★　　★

Maybe it was because I wasn't as high-ranking as my predecessor Gary Schroen. He was an SIS-3 (the equivalent of a three-
star general) and I was a new GS-15 (the highest senior rank
before entering the SIS corps). Maybe it was because a lot of the
people staffing CTC/███ back at Langley were friends of mine or had
been my students at the Farm. Maybe I was easier to talk to. Maybe it
was because the war was now getting underway.

Whatever the reason, Inmarsat satellite phone traffic from headquarters and CENTCOM to our office in the Panshir Valley increased
five-fold after my arrival. If I blocked out four hours sleep on a particular night, the chances were that I'd be roused at least twice with
phone calls. A lot of them came from the seventh floor. Questions
like: How many people do we have including Agency and military on
the Jawbreaker team? Do you know where they all are? Are all your
people firearm certified?

As tired as I was, I did my best to be patient. I knew that people back at headquarters were under enormous pressure. And I was very grateful to be in the field.

It was my third day in the Panshir—November 5, 2001. First thing in the morning I got a call from Hank and John back at CTC/█. I brought up the ████████ a month we had promised General Fahim to equip and feed his forces outside Mazar-e Sharif and Taloqan and on the Shomali Plains. Hank said that a memo had been drafted and sent to the seventh floor. All we could do now was wait for the signatures of the DDO Jim Pavitt and DCI George Tenet ████████ ████████████████████████████████████.

Hank had given me the authority to spend ████████████ ████████. Still, I informed him of the one-hundred-thousand-dollar payment I had given to the Taliban Vice Minister (code name "Gold Falcon") to help secure the SNI hostages.

Hank said, "Good call."

Back in the '50s and '60s, the Directorate of Operations had operated according to the Lawrence of Arabia school of management. Namely, find a talented officer and send him out in the field to do good work. As a result of unconstitutional activities revealed by the Church committees of Congress in the mid-'70s, the public's trust in the Agency had hit rock bottom. To guard against future embarrassment, the Agency placed layer upon layer of bureaucratic oversight on top of the Directorate of Operations. As a result, the potential for doing mischief had been reduced, but so had the Agency's willingness to take risks.

Herein lay the paradox. Hank had chosen me in part because he knew that I was the kind of officer who was wired to push the envelope. He liked the fact that I took charge and pressed forward aggressively without stopping every five minutes to ask permission. But he didn't want to get blindsided, either. So he asked me to keep him informed.

I told him about George's presence on the front, my plan for dealing with Abdul Rasul Sayyaf and our efforts to locate high-value Taliban and al-Qaeda targets. "I'll let you know every time I make a tactical change of direction," I said.

"Continue to press forward," Hank replied.

* * *

When I dropped in to see Majid before lunch, I found him in a funk.

██

██

██

██

████████████████████████████████████

[*NOTE TO READER:* This redacted section involves a discussion of resources for the Northern Alliance.]

The Northern Alliance had no real strong central authority. It was a loose confederation of Tajiks from the Panshir, Shia Hazaras from central Afghanistan, Uzbeks led by General Dostum in the north, Ismael Khan's people in the far west and Hamid Karzai leading Pushtuns in the south.

If General Fahim controlled the money, he would use it to reward those allies who supported his political agenda. It was no secret that tribal leaders already had their eyes on their roles in a post-Taliban government. We didn't want their political jockeying to interfere with our ability to wage war.

I said, "No." ██

████████████████████

██

██

███

That's when Majid started firing accusations. He said: "It's the fault of the United States that we suffered such a horrible civil war. You and the Pakistanis armed Gulbuddin Hekmatyar. As a result thousands of Afghans died."

"How dare you blame the people of the United States for your past," I shot back. "We helped drive out the Soviets. If it wasn't for the U.S. you'd be speaking Russian now."

His face turned red as he shouted: "Thousands of our people died because the United States did not keep its word and abandoned us the moment the Soviets left."

I said, "I don't have time to fight over who's to blame for your country's history," and stormed out.

Factually, Majid's charges were correct. As Steve Coll described in his Pultizer prize–winning book *Ghost Wars,* we had armed brutal tribal leader Gulbuddin Hekmatyar through Pakistan's intelligence service after Massoud cut a deal with the Soviets in '92. In resisting the Soviets, the Afghans had suffered as many as two million casualties, more than five million displaced citizens and so much political and social disintegration that the viability of their country had been threatened. After the Soviets retreated in '99 we had abandoned Afghanistan to the same brutal sectarian violence that led the Soviets to invade it in the first place.

Yes, our policy over the past two decades had been inconsistent. And, yes, the Afghans had plenty of reasons not to trust us. But countries, including the U.S., have to take responsibility for their own fate.

At first, I was concerned that our dust-up would affect the back-and-forth flow of intelligence. But it didn't. Guys on the Northern Alliance side, like Majid, were hard-bitten realists who didn't get insulted easily. Even if we had screwed them in the past, they knew that they had no chance of ever defeating their Taliban enemies without U.S. help. We continued working together with no hard feelings. The Northern Alliance shared everything they picked up from their human sources and we passed along intel we received from satellites and other sources.

I wasn't alarmed by the lack of intelligence about Osama bin Laden and other al-Qaeda leaders, because I knew they were well-hidden behind enemy lines. But what did surprise me was the volume of intelligence we were getting from the ███████ equipment we'd set up in

early 2000. Intercepted communications between Taliban commanders revealed that they were more determined than ever and confident
of their ability to withstand our air strikes. More than one Taliban
commander pointed out that while U.S. bombers had been hitting
their positions for nearly a month, we'd failed to seize a single city.

*　　*　　*

[*NOTE TO READER:* CIA censors redacted this discussion of fund-
ing and supplying the Northern Alliance.]

Majid greeted me with a solemn face. "Thank you very much for
helping us," he said. Then he took a deep breath. "But, Gary, we have
a serious problem."

"What now?"

"Your man Stan on the Shomali Plains struck one of my men in the
face. My man was humiliated and now wants to shoot Stan."

I knew clean-cut Stan well. He was a former Marine Corps officer
and student of mine at the Farm. I had kept him at the front because
he spoke fluent Russian and, therefore, could communicate with
Northern Alliance General Sharifi. I found it hard to believe that he
would punch someone unless he was severely provoked. I said: "I'll
talk to him."

Majid insisted, "He has to leave the country."

"Who told you about this?"

"Ustad contacted me by radio. He's our ███████ chief at the
front."

I said, "I'll contact Stan immediately and have him back here
pronto."

While Todd relayed the message to Stan at the front, I reviewed the latest intel. The Taliban continued to reinforce their lines with new recruits. As many as five hundred Muslim volunteers per day were streaming across the border from Pakistan. Our sources had located al-Qaeda platoons (made up of forty soldiers) and companies (one hundred and twenty fighters) amassing along the front lines. I radioed the coordinates of their positions to CTC/█ and CENTCOM for priority targeting.

An hour and a half later a nervous-looking Stan arrived with George. They stood in my bedroom covered from head to toe with dust. "Stan, what the hell happened?" I asked him pointblank.

He took a deep breath. "I didn't hit anyone."

"Then why are the Afghans so hot?"

He explained: "The Afghans have instructions to accompany us everywhere. We can't take a shit alone. This morning, one of our planes was getting ready to land, so I needed to get out to the landing field to make sure it was cleared of debris. As I exited our compound, this Afghan jumped in front of me and tried to block my way. I tried to explain that a plane was coming. He didn't understand, so I tried to go around him. He grabbed my arm. When he wouldn't let go, I threw his ass to the ground hard and ran to the airfield, arriving just moments before the plane. It was either him going down hard or our plane making a real rough landing."

George, at Stan's side, added, "Ustad, who is the Afghan █████ chief on the Shomali Plains, is a lazy, shiftless good-for-nothing. Hamid is working directly with his people and we're now getting great stuff. But Ustad resents the fact that Stan keeps making demands on him and his men."

"If you're telling me that you didn't strike the Afghan, I'll go back to Northern Alliance and explain."

"Why?" Stan asked.

"Because they want you out of the country."

"Ungrateful assholes," he snarled.

"I'll straighten it out," I said. "In the meantime, I want you to buy more vehicles. We don't need the Afghans acting as our escorts when we don't need them. We'll never get anything done if they restrict our movements."

Later, in the dining room as we lunched on rice and chicken, I realized that I needed to get down to the front.

Out in the courtyard, I ran into Hamid, who'd driven back with George and Stan. He, too, was covered with thick brown dust. "Get one of the cooks to boil some water for you, improvise a shower, eat some grub," I said. "Then we need you back at the front."

The quick-witted Muslim American smiled from ear to ear. "Doesn't anybody want to tell me what a good job I'm doing?" he asked.

A couple of people stopped what they were doing, but no one said anything.

Hamid continued, "You guys can't do anything without this handsome Muslim man."

Blue-eyed Davis looked up from the equipment he was cleaning and shouted, "Shut up before we kick your ass."

Hamid had everybody's attention now. "Be nice or I will tell all the Afghans that you go both ways, Davis. I am in control here, by the way."

Several of us broke out laughing, including Davis. Hamid was on his first tour of duty and already quite full of himself.

"Can I have permission to slap him silly?" Davis asked me.

"Sure, but don't kill him," I responded.

"See, you all need me!" Hamid shouted with a grin.

He was right. Not only was the Yale University lawyer indispensable when it came to communicating with the Afghans, he was also good for morale. Aside from Todd, our commo officer and the only single guy on the team, who liked to tell us of his adventures at Hooters, we rarely had time to swap stories. We had too much to do.

Early the next morning, I set out for the front in a Toyota truck with Majid. I told him Stan's version of the incident of the day before and explained why he was staying. Majid grumbled, but said only, "Fine."

Driving south, I reacquainted myself with the twists in the road, the huge drop-offs and the dusty villages scattered along the riverbanks. As we passed one small cluster of mud houses, a group of three Afghan women dressed head to toe in light burkas waved and Majid pulled over so they could climb in back. I couldn't tell if they were young or old, beautiful or homely, because even their eyes and mouths were covered with a light blue grille. Twenty kilometers down the road they slapped the top of the cab and Majid pulled over to let them out.

Descending the steep drop to the plains, shaded by huge jagged walls of rock, I saw the brown Shomali Plains gleaming below. In the distance, I made out Bagram Airfield far to our left, dead east. Beyond it, dug into the long sloop, were the Taliban lines. To our right, about a half an hour away, stood General Bismullah Khan's command post perched on a foothill overlooking the battlefield.

We wound our way halfway up and stopped. Gunfire crackled in the distance to our left. Through binoculars I saw Northern Alliance gunners firing machine guns. Walls and mud buildings on our side were receiving fire.

"After dark, with tracers, it would be a lot easier to see what they are shooting at," Majid said almost matter-of-factly. "At night the Taliban forces come in and crowd the front lines close to us so that they can't be bombed."

"Your troops better not get too comfortable with that arrangement," I warned him. "Because one night the Taliban will amass along our lines and overrun us."

We shook hands with Ustad in his office. It was obvious from the way they spoke to each other that Majid was higher in the NA pecking order. As tea was served, Ustad introduced me to a number of lower-ranking Alliance field commanders. They all asked for more U.S. bombing.

I explained that we were focusing on Mazar-e Sharif first, then Taloqan and, finally, Kabul. They expressed gratitude for the Special Forces Triple Nickel team and asked if we could send another. I told them that more teams would move south after we seized the northern cities.

George arrived with Lt. Colonel Haas and Hamid, and we drove further up the promontory to General Bismullah Khan's command post. From this vantage, the view of the western swath of the battle-field was superb. Khan had light hair and a large hooked nose. He wore a traditional *shalwar kameez* tunic and pajama pants, clutched a radio in one hand and kept a pistol strapped to his hip. With Hamid translating, we discussed the need to launch an offensive. Khan said that his forces were ready, but highly outnumbered by the Taliban. They would need close air support to launch an advance.

I told him that I would communicate with CENTCOM to deter-mine a good day to secure a large number of sorties, then let him know. Bismullah Khan nodded.

The sun had started to set as we stepped outside. We watched as in the distance hundreds of Taliban vehicles streamed out of the city of Kabul towards the front lines. With their headlights on, they looked like an endless line of glowing ants. For two hours, the stream of head-lights continued to leave the city and inch toward us. I tried to imag-ine the size of the parking lots they needed to accommodate all the trucks.

As we watched, a quiet tension gripped the air. Thousands of armed men faced us only a few miles away. The sky grew dark and still. Then, suddenly, it lit up with the flames from the tail-burners of a U.S. fighter jet. In the distance we saw flashes that briefly illuminated Tali-ban structures and vehicles and, soon after, felt the rumbles of bombs.

Somewhere down below, Diaz and his SF team were using radios and laser designators to direct attacks against Taliban reserve lines along a mountain range halfway between the Shomali Plains and Kabul. More Stealth fighters swooped in and deep concussions started to overlap one another. I said to my colleagues at my left and right, "The Taliban is catching hell tonight."

Someone replied quietly, "They sure are."

Under my breath, I thanked the engineers at Grumman, Lockheed, Boeing and General Dynamics. And I thanked our pilots. We stood in awed silence witnessing the massive destructive power unleashed by the U.S. armed forces and military industrial complex.

"It's primordial," someone whispered.

"You got that right."

8

MAZAR-E SHARIF

*"I knew when I rode the high-blooded steed, the harder
I pulled its reins the less it would heed."*
—*Afghan poet Rabi'a Balki, 9th century*

*　*　*　*　*　*

t was early in the morning of November 5, 2001. R.J., my buddy
and the leader of ███████ Team Alpha with General Abdul Rashid
Dostum in northern Afghanistan, pulled his large six-foot-two-
inch frame out of the sleeping bag, which lay on the hard cold
ground. Around him the day's first rays of sunlight lit up the vast barren landscape of gorges, desert and mountains.

R.J. along with the rest of team Alpha and U.S. Army Special
Forces Team 595 had spent the last several days on horseback fighting
their way north towards Mazar-e Sharif. It had been an unconventional military campaign to say the least. General Dostum, command-
ing the Uzbek army, was a big bear of a man in his mid-fifties, over six
feet tall, with a barrel chest, bristling mustache and close-cropped
graying hair. Ethnically, he was an Uzbek, but he spoke Dari, Uzbek
and Russian. He was gregarious and unrelenting as he led his band of
horsemen, his head wrapped in a blue turban.

His "army" was made up of fewer than one hundred loyal fighters and as many as two thousand militia who joined his operations for a couple of weeks at a time. They rode horses and looked like something out of a strange Mad Max movie wearing turbans, robes, beards, long checkered scarves, *pakols* and other articles of tribal clothes interspersed with western garb and AK-47s.

Supporting them were R.J.'s eight-man Team Alpha and the twelve soldiers in Special Forces Team 595. Team 595, code name Tiger 02, were Green Berets and arguably the most cross-trained, technologically advanced soldiers in the history of warfare.

Each SF team consisted of two intelligence sergeants, two weapons sergeants, two medical specialists, two demolitions experts, two Air Force combat controllers—a leader and second-in-command.

In this conflict, the most lethal pieces of equipment in Tiger 02's arsenal were the satellite radios carried by the Air Force combat controllers. These allowed them to call in air strikes from the combined air armadas of the Army, Navy, Marines and Air Force from halfway around the world. A close second was the Special Operations Forces Laser Acquisition Marker (known as a SOFLAM), which looked like a giant pair of elongated binoculars mounted on a small tripod with a trigger attached to a coiled length of cable. It shot out a laser beam to mark an enemy target so that a laser-guided bomb from a plane could lock on it and destroy it.

The combat controllers called what they did "scanning for targets." One Air Force combat controller would man an LST-5 satellite radio while his team member scanned enemy positions with a large olive-green scope. Once the scanner located a target, the communicator would call in their position to an AWACS (Airborne Warning and Control System) overhead, which would direct fighter jets and bombers to the stage of operations. Once the planes neared the vicinity, the scanner would light the enemy target with the infrared laser beam of the SOFLAM. From thousands of feet overhead, a jet aircraft would drop a laser-guided bomb whose internal computer would hone in on the SOFLAM's laser signature and essentially "ride the laser" to the target.

Bombers were armed predominantly with another type of munition, the JDAM (Joint Direct Attack Munition), which was a five hundred to two-thousand pound conventional bomb with a GPS guidance system installed. It was programmed to hit within a radius of forty feet. Conventional "unguided" munitions including cluster bombs and string weapons could also be dropped on coordinates using radar and infrared optical systems. Combat controllers on the ground helped orient aircrews by pointing out geographic features such as ridges, roads and ravines.

The combined effect of the "death ray" as General Dostum called the laser designator and U.S air strikes was phenomenal. One Taliban bunker after another containing some combination of Russian-made T-55 tanks, ZSU-23-4 Russian antiaircraft guns, RPG shoulder-held rockets and machine guns was obliterated. The Taliban literally didn't know what had hit them. Seconds after the bombs fell, General Dostum and his cavalry would charge with AK-47s blazing like the hordes of Genghis Khan. For Dostum's primitive, poorly equipped troops, which had been struggling for years to fight a superior enemy, the quick victories were exhilarating.

While the Taliban was forced to give up territory, the size and spirit of General Dostum's army grew. Dostum, who a year earlier had been living in exile in Turkey, was focused on one goal: wresting the Uzbek capital of Mazar-e Sarif back from Taliban control.

R.J. was the perfect man to help the Afghan warlord realize his dream. For one thing, R.J. was a native of New Mexico and had ridden horses most of his life. So he could handle the small Afghan mounts and their hard wooden saddles, while most of his men were sore as hell.

More important, R.J. had developed a solid bond of trust with the headstrong Dostum. Having served in Pakistan during the mid-'80s and later opened the ███████████████████████████ , R.J. knew the culture of northern Afghanistan and spoke the Afghan version of Farsi (known as Dari) well. He made sure that all interaction between Dostum and the SF teams was coordinated through him. What's more, R.J. provided a steady stream of intelligence on Dostum's plans, objectives and moods to CTC/███ , CENTCOM and the White House, which was anxiously awaiting news of progress on the ground.

General Dostum, who had survived two decades of fighting in northern Afghanistan because of his uncanny ability to change sides when necessary, had been able to enlist the cooperation of both General Mohammad Atta (a Tajik and his chief competitor within the Northern Alliance) and General Mohammad Mohaqqeq (a Hazara and commander of the Hizb-e Wahadat forces). Part of R.J.'s job was to keep generals Dostum and Atta from killing each other. He had engaged in more than one shouting match with General Atta's lieutenants when they complained that supplies dropped to General Dostum's troops had not been parceled out in equal quantity to General Atta.

To accommodate both generals, R.J. split his eight-man Alpha Team in half. Since SF Team 595 had already been divided into four separate parts to work with separate Dostum units, Colonel John Mulholland, commander of the 5th Special Forces Group, dispatched a second SF team, ODC 53, to support the impending battle for Mazar-e Sharif. This eight-man team was packed with four Air Force combat controllers armed with SOFLAMs. A third Special Forces team, ODA 534, was airlifted in to join General Atta, camped fifty miles due west.

*　　*　　*

R.J. finished his breakfast of MREs and coffee and wiped the crumbs from his brown, slightly graying beard. Over the last few days, he and ODC 53 commander Lt. Colonel Max Bowers had hammered out a plan for taking the city. It called for simultaneous attacks by General Mohaqqeq's forces through the Darya Balkh River valley in the west and Dostum's forces through the Darya Suf River valley in the east. The two Northern Alliance forces would join where the Balkh and Suf rivers met and proceed north with Mohaqqeq's forces protecting Dostum's western flank.

R.J. peered through his binoculars at the Taliban positions dug deep into the rocky embankment. His commo officer barked, "The MC-130s are on their way."

R.J. turned to General Dostum and Lt. Colonel Bowers and said, "Let's get ready. The show's about to begin."

Each four-engine MC-130 carried a fifteen-thousand-pound BLU-82 bomb. Nicknamed the Daisy Cutter, the BLU-82 was the single largest nonnuclear conventional explosive device in the U.S. inventory and had been originally designed to clear 250-foot-diameter helicopter landing zones in Vietnam. Too heavy to hang on the wing of an aircraft, the BLU-82 had to be pushed out the back of an MC-130 transport at no less than 6,000 feet in altitude. Its 38-inch extender fuse allowed the bomb to detonate just above the ground extending 1,000 pounds of pressure per square inch out over 900 feet.

Keeping track of an enemy that quickly changed positions, while at the same time directing ground fire, artillery and close air support was a difficult task. With the fear of a friendly fire incident foremost in his mind, R.J. carefully monitored the timing and location of the BLU-82 drop. He, General Dostum and senior officers from ODC 53 watched from a distance and listened over a secure radio as the MC-130 called out the extraction of the first BLU-82 from its rear cargo door. They waited with mouths open so the blast wouldn't rupture their eardrums.

The fireball was huge. As the shock wave spread, the Taliban's fortified positions disintegrated and tanks and soldiers were tossed into the air like toys. The bear-chested Uzbek leader and his men let out a long guttural "uhhhhh" followed by gleeful laughter. Two minutes later a second BLU-82 detonated further down Taliban lines and another mushroom cloud rose up high into the sky and hung there for ten minutes. R.J. later described the bombs' effect as "profound."

Before the clouds had a chance to dissolve, Dostum's horsemen let out a yell and charged. Those Taliban soldiers who survived the blast stumbled around in shock with blood dripping from their eyes, ears and noses. They were quickly overrun by charging Uzbeks, who found fewer and fewer bodies as they approached ground zero. Perplexed at first, Dostum and his men soon realized that the enemy had literally been blown to bits.

Almost simultaneously, Mohammad Atta's forces farther west surrounded the village of Akopunk and called for Taliban forces to surrender. They offered to pledge their allegiance to Atta without a fight. But the following morning, when Atta's men tried to occupy the village, the Taliban fought back. Atta's men pulled back while Special Forces Team ODA 534 called in more U.S. air strikes.

Meanwhile, General Dostum's men saddled up and rode north. The next day brought more airstrikes, another Uzbek cavalry charge and more Taliban surrenders. Dostum was elated. He had fewer fighters than his enemy, scant resources and almost no logistics, but with the help of R.J., Team Alpha, U.S. airpower and the SF teams, he was unstoppable and he knew it. The former plumber called Taliban commanders on the radio and bragged to them in Dari: "I have the Americans with me, and they have their death ray. Surrender or die!"

General Dostum directed his men to lay down blankets in the sand so that he, R.J. and the ODC could plan for an assault on the Tangi Gap. Narrow and heavily mined, Tangi Gap was protected by hundreds of Taliban troops, who had dug in around it with artillery, mortars and rockets.

That night, while Dostum's soldiers slept, R.J. filed reports on his laptop to CTC/■ and CENTCOM calling for heavy air support the morning of November 9. Back at Langley, Hank conducted a video conference with CENTCOM in Tampa, Florida, to make sure that everyone from Whiteman Air Force Base in Missouri to the SF team in the Tangi Gap was in sync.

The Predator overhead and Special Forces soldiers on the ground directed one precision bombing run after another on Taliban positions. When the Taliban tried eluding the U.S. planes by moving to other bunkers, the SOFLAMs lit them up again. Then Dostum and his cavalry raised their AK-47s and charged. Within seconds all R.J. and his team could see was a thick cloud of dust. One captain on SF Team 595 described it as "a swarm."

"Dostum's soldiers were coming at them at a gallop, firing their assault weapons and scaring the hell out of the Taliban," he reported. Disheartened Taliban soldiers dropped their weapons and ran. "They would simply ride down any Taliban that attempted to resist them or refused to surrender."

The Taliban defense of Mazar-e Sharif was in full collapse. Dostum and his men galloped the final forty kilometers north. Quickly reaching the outskirts of the city, the Uzbek general negotiated a surrender with the same Taliban forces that had massacred four thousand of his people when they overran the city in 1998.

The next day—November 10—General Dostum and his troops entered triumphantly. The man who had grown up the son of poor peasants stood on the roof of a captured four-by-four and received the adulation of 100,000 liberated Uzbeks. They threw coins at him for good luck and rejoiced.

"It was like a scene out of a World War II movie," said a soldier from SF Team 534. "The streets, the roadsides, even outside the city, were lined with people cheering and clapping their hands."

Then Dostum stopped the vehicle and climbed off. Deluged by the crowd, he walked the last few blocks to the Blue Mosque, which held the remains of Hazrat Ali—cousin and son-in-law of the prophet Mohammad. This breathtaking masterpiece with blue turrets and domes, marble courtyards and magnificent mosaic inlays had been covered with earth in 1220 to withstand the ravaging hordes of Genghis Khan and dug out and refurbished in the 1480s. As Dostum approached its grand entrance, hundreds of white pigeons took flight. Once inside, General Dostum sank to his knees and gave thanks to Allah.

R.J. remained busy. Pleased that our Northern Alliance allies had avoided the house-to-house fighting to clear the city, he now had to debrief prisoners and deal with Taliban forces who were moving east towards the city of Konduz. Exhausted men in Team Alpha and SF teams 595 and 534 informed him that General Dostum had somehow bypassed a *madrash* (Islamic school) packed with eight hundred hardcore Taliban and al-Qaeda troops.

The area had to be surrounded and cleared of civilians before air strikes could be called in. Combat air controllers from SF A-Team 595 used Trimble Navigational Scout GPSs to map the corners of the compound. Then the coordinates were radioed in. After four direct hits on the building, Dostum's troops rushed over whitewashed walls covered with al-Qaeda and Taliban graffiti. When the smoke cleared, Dostum's men counted 450 enemy dead.

*　　*　　*

I followed the fight for Mazar-e Sharif and the battle for the *madrash* on our encrypted satellite radio net. The next morning, I called R.J. to give him his props.

"Team Alpha, this is the Jawbreaker," I said.

"Wildman, how are you?" R.J. asked.

"I'll be great now that your little adventure is over and you won't be hogging all the air power."

"Real men have to stay busy," the big man from New Mexico cracked.

A group of Jawbreaker team members standing around the radio laughed. Davis poked me in the arm. "Are you going to let him talk shit to you like that?" he asked.

"He's earned it," I answered.

Blond, blued-eyed Davis nodded. "Yeah."

"Take care of yourself," I said to R.J., "and congratulations to your men and the SF teams."

"Thanks, I will be moving with Dostum toward Konduz. Alpha out."

"Good luck. Jawbreaker out."

While R.J., Team Alpha and SF Teams 595 and 534 slugged the Taliban up north, my team in the Panshir processed intel at warp speed. Over the past three days our Afghan partners had been inundated with very accurate reports on the location of Taliban facilities in unmarked residences and buildings in Kabul. We quickly transmitted the GPS coordinates to CTC/███ and CENTCOM for targeting and within hours the Taliban facilities were destroyed.

This didn't stop Bismullah Khan from bellyaching about the lack of air assets available to him on the Shomali Plains. I reminded the Northern Alliance general that General Tommy Franks had been crystal clear about the sequence of battle: Mazar-e Sharif first, Taloqan second and, then, the Shomali Plains sometime before Christmas.

At the same time, people in Washington were clamoring for an offensive in the Shomali Plains with or without airpower. But Hank and General Franks stuck to their guns. With Mazar-e Sharif in friendly hands, the Friendship Bridge just north of Mazar-e Sharif could now be opened between Afghanistan and Uzbekistan to facilitate greater logistical support. CENTCOM would then focus its air power on Taloqan.

I spoke to Breen, my young team leader in Taloqan, on a daily basis. He reported that the Northern Alliance commander in the region, Berryelah Khan, was more interested in holding press conferences than managing his area of operation. Early one morning, I listened on my shortwave radio as Berryelah Khan told a group of

Iranian journalists in Persian that the United States didn't know what it was doing. He stated that if he were given control of the air he would win the conflict in a week.

I thought to myself, *This fool couldn't find the gas tank on one of our aircraft and he's going to manage the air war.*

The battlefield around Taloqan was complicated, stretching over more than a hundred miles of rolling hills. Fortunately, Breen had a crack SF A-Team (585) with him commanded by Master Sergeant John Bolduc, who got things moving. Supported by increased airpower, they started to target Taliban targets in Taloqan with regularity. During the evenings, Spectre C-130 gunships swept in. Armed with chain guns, an auto-loading 105mm canon, a 25mm Gatling gun and a Bofors 40mm cannon, the Spectre could cover the battlefield with more rounds per square foot than any combat platform in the world.

Day after day of unrelenting airpower forced the Taliban to relinquish the city and retreat west. Meanwhile, the remnants of al-Qaeda and Taliban forces from Mazar-e Sharif tracked east. Their destination was the city of Konduz, which was fast becoming the last Taliban stronghold in the north. With General Dostum approaching from the west and Berryelah Khan closing in from the east, the battle for Konduz was shaping up to be pivotal.

*　　*　　*

On the afternoon of the tenth Majid sent a messenger requesting a meeting. I climbed the steps to his compound, where he pointed to a map of the North and explained that his sources had told him that Taliban and al-Qaeda troops retreating into Konduz were taking many people hostage to use them as human shields.

Majid said, "Forget about the normal conduct and behavior of combatants. These Taliban forces are desperate and will do anything to escape our attacking forces. This could be very bad."

When an Afghan who has been in combat half his life and has witnessed scores of atrocities tells you something is going to be bad, you listen. I said, "Show me on the map the route that retreating Taliban forces who are not going to Konduz, but are instead fleeing south to the Shomali Plains, will take."

With a pen Majid drew a line directly south from Konduz.

"Now indicate the choke points."

Majid pointed out two separate passes northwest of Kabul.

"Can you get sources out there?" I asked.

"I have people several hours away who can report on any large-scale movement south," Majid answered.

"Good," I said. "We can't let those retreated Taliban soldiers join their comrades on the Shomali Plains where we're already out-manned."

Majid nodded his agreement. He said: "I'll alert my sources. Also, Engineer Aref* would like to see you at eight P.M."

*　　*　　*

Back at our makeshift office, all eight laptops were humming with intel coming in from Taloqan and the Shomali Plains and reports being released to CENTCOM and Langley. I drafted an action-required message to CTC/■■ then called Davis and Storm together.

"Events are unfolding rapidly," I began. "Mazar-e Sharif fell, then Taloqan. In both cases the Taliban waited in dug-in positions until we bombed them. My concern is that a commander worth his salt will learn from experience and now attack Bismullah Khan's force on the Shomali before we get a chance to introduce airpower. We're learning lessons from the battles in the north. Shouldn't we assume that they are, too?"

Davis was the first to answer. "I think they're unlikely to understand the exact nature of their losses and use that understanding to alter their strategy," he said. "If they do attack the Shomali Plains in desperation, they could very well overwhelm Bismullah Khan's forces, and trap and kill our SF team. That would result in a retreat further up into the Panshir, which would leave us bottled up."

Barrel-chested Storm broke in, "I agree. We need to make sure we know where our people are at all times. If something breaks down on the front, we need to be able to account for them."

I said: "Let's go down to the front and talk to George and General Khan tomorrow morning."

That evening Majid, Storm and I found Engineer Aref* in an ebullient mood. "Those BLU-82s you dropped south of Mazar-e Sharif were fantastic!" he exclaimed. "Can you drop one on the Taliban positions of the Shomali Plains?"

"I can arrange that," I answered.

"We received reports that those who survived lost their minds seeing their friends blown into little pieces," Majid said flatly. "They got what they deserved."

"First, we must have more airpower on the Shomali Plains," Aref* stated.

I said, "I'm working on it."

[*NOTE TO READER:* This redacted section concerns a discussion of resources.]

Storm pulled a map of Kabul and the Shomali Plains from his backpack. "It's likely that there will be chaos in Kabul as air strikes increase," he said. "Therefore, we would like to ask Gold Falcon to move the SNI hostages to another facility and arrange for a point where we can do a rescue, or even better, move them to the front lines where we can transfer them to our side with payoffs."

Engineer Aref* studied a map while he considered Storm's proposal. Pointing to a spot along the front lines, not far from Bagram Airbase, he said: "We pay a Taliban commander at that position who has been cooperating with us for over a year. He allows our people to pass into Kabul and, then, out."

Big paramilitary officer Storm carefully marked the spot, then followed the road to Kabul asking Aref* and Majid about the location of Taliban checkpoints and how they could be avoided.

"Do you have a man who could cross the lines and guide Gold Falcon and the hostages out if this can be worked out?" I asked.

Engineer Aref* thought a minute, then answered, "Yes. We can use the same man who passed the hundred thousand dollars to Gold Falcon. He's one of my most important operatives. His father was Tajik and his mother a Pushtun. He speaks both languages and moves around Kabul with ease."

"Next time you speak to Gold Falcon on the satellite phone," I said, "tell him I want him to talk to senior Taliban officials about the need to move the hostages to a separate facility. I also want to make sure that he has control of the guards."

Engineer Aref* nodded. "I spoke with him this morning and he told me that two of the guards are his men. He also said that some of the bombing has been close to where the hostages are being held. A few of the hostages are having a hard time."

"Tell him I will pay four million dollars for all eight if he can surrender them to us," I said. "But it has to be all eight." I had no fixed guidelines from Langley on the amount I could spend securing the hostages. I would clear the four million with Hank the next time we spoke.

Aref* wrote something down, then looked up. "I'm scheduled to call Gold Falcon tomorrow morning at eight A.M. I'll pass on the message."

Storm had more questions about the route across the border, then asked if he could conduct a visual reconnaissance the next day.

I thought to myself, *Grabbing one or two of the hostages is tough enough, but all eight is close to impossible.* Any forced rescue would be fraught with peril, not only for the hostages, but for members of the rescue team as well.

On a daily basis we collected additional intelligence on the whereabouts of the SNI hostages, their conditions and possible ways to extract them safely. In the office, I posted a board with their photographs, personal details and the latest intel we had collected. Someone had written in a felt-tip pen above their names: "The Delta Force of Evangelists." More than once I asked myself, What the hell were they thinking when they decided to come to Taliban-controlled Afghanistan? Young men would have to risk their lives to get them out.

*   *   *

Back at the compound I was reading through a stack of recent intel when Davis hurried in looking like he'd been buried in dirt. Hamid filled the space behind him looking just as grungy.

"How come you two dirt hogs aren't down on the front?" I asked.

"They're shooting one another down there," Hamid said with a laugh.

Davis, the hard-boiled ex-Marine, turned to the Muslim-American and barked, "Shut the hell up!"

Hamid laughed even harder and, pointing both hands at his chest, boasted, "Yale Law School, baby. Top ten percent of my class."

Davis fired a serious look my way and said: "We need to talk."

The two men followed me into my room where we sat facing each other in old wooden chairs. "Hamid here has hit on something," Davis started. He explained how earlier in the afternoon he had met a Pushtun warlord who ██████████████████████ had recently traveled south to Jalalabad with Ayman al-Zawahiri (bin Laden's number two man), who was visiting his sick wife in a hospital.

"I think we can kill him either outside the hospital, or even in the room with his wife," Davis said.

I sat up. "Let's try to nail him on the street. We don't need to harm his wife so long as she doesn't fly multiengine commercial aircraft."

"Fine with me," Davis responded.

"Anything else?"

Davis wasn't finished. "I met with the ██████████ commander who was so ferocious against the Soviets and asked me to convey his continued appreciation to the United States. He wants to work with us."

I asked, "How many men does he have near the front?"

"Several hundred here and a few thousand up in Bamiyan province. He's not a major force, but can help us."

"Good," I said. "Keep the contact active. We might need him as things fall apart. General Fahim and the Tajiks have their own agenda and it might be useful to have other commanders we can call on with forces close to the capital."

I turned to Hamid, who seemed to be enjoying himself. "How are things going with Bismullah Khan on the Shomali front?"

"The relationship's a bit strained," he answered. "He wants assurances of air support before he orders his troops to attack."

"I'll go back down with you in the morning to talk to him. Good job, guys. Now get some sleep. I want to leave no later than 0700 hours."

It was 11 P.M. One of Majid's men rushed in to tell me that his boss wanted to see me right away. I threw on a Gortex jacket and scooted over to his building, where I found Majid looking worried.

"What up?" I asked.

"Gary, I just got a call from one of my men in the Northwest," Majid started. "There's more than a thousand heavily armed Taliban fleeing south in several large convoys. Tomorrow, they'll reach the passes that we talked about. The roads are terrible, so they're not making good time. Even if they drive all night they won't clear the passes by eleven tomorrow morning."

"Give me the coordinates," I said, "and I'll deal with them."

Together, we walked to the map and plotted the coordinates. There were two separate passes that were long and narrow and perfect for an aerial ambush.

Back at the office I asked Todd to get CTC/█████ on a secure line. Hank's executive officer answered.

I said, "I've something important which needs to be handled ASAP."

"I'm standing by," he answered calmly.

I told him about the Taliban convoys fleeing south and gave him the coordinates of the passes that they would cross within the next ten to sixteen hours. I said, "I need you to call CENTCOM so they can start looking at the satellite coverage. This has to take priority. Whatever else they have tomorrow, they need to refocus on this and nail those guys."

He agreed. "Hank is standing right here and is preparing to do a video conference with Tampa in the next hour," he said. "This will go to the top of the list."

"Thanks. The SF teams have direct communication with aircraft, but I don't. So I won't be able to follow it."

"Not a problem. Airpower is being shifted south so there will be air assets available for this tomorrow."

I asked, "How are things going in Konduz?"

That's when Hank got on the phone. "Gary," he said, "we've had some victories but this is far from over. Dostum and R.J. are enroute to Konduz now. We could have a bloodbath there and at the moment we have little reporting on disposition of forces. Anything you can add will help."

"I'll talk to Aref* and Majid and see what else they can tell us."

"Gary," Hank continued, "I know you're catching a lot of heat from Fahim and Aref* about the lack of sorties on the Shomali Plains. Assure them that the air war is going according to plan. In addition to bombing Mazar-e Sharif and Taloqan, General Franks is eliminating every kind of infrastructure the Taliban has in the South. When the collapse comes we want it to be total."

"I'm seeing Bismullah Khan in the morning and I'm bringing my crying towel."

"Tell all your men that both Cofer and I are very proud of them. Keep pressing the enemy. CTC/███ out."

"Jawbreaker out."

Davis, Todd and I stayed up until 0130 hours finishing the day's intel reports. Then I ordered them to get some sleep.

* * *

At 0700 hours we breakfasted on coffee, flat bread and yogurt, then hit the dusty road in our shot-up Toyota extended-cab pickup. It was another sunny, bitterly cold day. Davis drove with Hamid up front. Majid and I sat in back with rifles and our packs, which held things we would need in case of an emergency escape—maps, water, food, a beacon to call for a search and rescue helicopter and a blood chit. The chit was a short necklace with a small tin medallion that held a message in Dari saying that anyone who helps the person wearing this necklace return to U.S. hands will be rewarded twenty-five thousand dollars. It was vital for those Americans who did not speak Farsi or Dari. If I was injured and recovered by friendly Afghans, I planned to tell them I was worth four times as much.

We stopped halfway down the Panshir Valley to have a drink and stretch our legs. A group of children with dirty faces from a nearby village collected around us. I handed out crackers and chocolate from our MREs. The kids smiled and shouted their few words of English: "United States! My friend! Rock 'n' roll!"

In the distance, the sky spread in shades of pale and deeper blue. I watched the white vapor trails of three B-52 bombers inch slowly from north to south. They were at least 40,000 feet high and, from their trajectory, headed towards Kabul.

It was quiet on the Shomali Plains where we hooked up with George and Lt. Colonel Chris Haas for the short drive to Bismullah Khan's headquarters. General Khan had lighter hair and skin than most Afghans and light brown eyes.

With Hamid translating, I asked him to give me the exact day and time he planned to attack so I could coordinate with CENTCOM to make sure he had airpower.

He answered matter-of-factly: "I will launch the attack in two days at dawn."

I cleared my throat. "General," I started in with a serious voice. "Before my arrival here discussions were held between the U.S. side and the Northern Alliance regarding the disposition of Kabul. In those discussions it was mutually agreed that we would assist you in destroying the Taliban forces on the Shomali Plains and you would stop five miles out of the city so that the United Nations could enter and negotiate a final agreement to avoid further violence and the destruction of the city. Are you aware of those discussions and prepared to abide by them?"

"Yes," he answered without hesitation. "I'm aware of those discussions and won't enter Kabul with my forces."

"General, " I continued, "it also appears that Taliban forces escaping Mazar-e Sharif are moving south through mountain passes and will try to link up with Taliban forces on the Shomali Plains approximately fifty to seventy miles west of your western flank. Is it possible for you to move a battalion west through mountain passes to help interrupt that escape route?"

"No," he answered, shaking his head. "The Taliban have positioned a lot of artillery on my western flank. I can't move without taking significant losses. Can you deal with the retreating columns from the air?"

"We'll try, General."

*   *   *

By early afternoon Davis, Majid and I were back in the shot-up Toyota driving north. Davis was stretching out his legs in the back when I turned to Majid behind the wheel. "I want to talk to you about your ██████ friends," I said.

Majid looked at me uncomfortably, as if to say: Please don't bring this up.

"Make no mistake, the American people after September eleventh aren't going to take any more shit from Islamic fundamentalists who think it's okay to attack us." ████████████████████

████████████████████████████████

████

"You will cause a lot of problems, Gary."

"If you're uncomfortable delivering the message, let's stop and see Engineer Aref*."

Majid sighed deeply. "That won't be necessary. I have received the message and it will be delivered," he said.

It was my firm belief that if we were going to finish the Afghan war quickly and with minimal losses, we had to convince the Iranian government that we meant business. For way too long, Iran had been given a pass when it came to the taking of American lives. For years, foreign policy pundits had talked about trying to advance the interests of the so-called moderates in Tehran, which was fine. What they failed to say, however, is that the Iranian constitution established a theocracy that views terrorism as a viable instrument of foreign policy.

* * *

I passed through a little den on the way to our office. Seated in the dark on a sofa were the three men from the Joint Special Operations Command hostage rescue team watching a movie on a laptop.

I had never seen a movie played on a computer before. "What are you guys watching?" I asked.

"*Enemy at the Gates*," answered one of the JSOC team members.

As I bent down to take a closer look, actor Ed Harris stood out in the open wearing a German uniform. Suddenly, he took a bullet in the head. Wham!

I thought to myself: *Enemy at the Gates*, how appropriate.

Inside our office, I told Marlowe, the ex–Navy Seal who was now with CIA Science and Technology, that I wanted him to drive down to the front lines in the morning and scout Bagram Airbase. I had been told that the front lines ran right across the runway, so I needed an assessment of the serviceability of the runway and surrounding buildings.

"Sure thing."

Red-bearded Storm was writing at another laptop. "Storm, we need to talk," I said, interrupting. "Tell the JSOC guys that they need to be in on this, too."

We walked to the den where the movie was winding down. The camera panned a huge room filled with wounded Russian soldiers following the battle of Stalingrad.

I explained that first thing in the morning we would hear from our source who was in touch with Gold Falcon, and learn if it was possible to move the hostages to the front line position. The JSOC team and Storm had already surveyed the area. But since we were launching an all-out offensive in less than forty-eight hours, which couldn't be delayed to facilitate a hostage rescue, they needed to come up with a Plan B.

"Will do," Storm said.

Before going to my room, I called CENTCOM on a secure satellite phone and spoke to our Agency representative. He said that General Franks and Hank had hoped that the Northern Alliance would send forces to help cut the Taliban escape route from the North, but they were now prepared to take care of it themselves. U.S. Air Force fighter jets and an AC-130 Spectre gunship were on their way.

I lay down at 2 A.M. and thought of my family and friends halfway around the world. *They'll be pleased with the progress we're making*, I thought to myself. *Events are accelerating, pushed by determination and a shared sense of purpose. But who knows what tomorrow will bring?*

* Gary Schroen in his CIA-approved book *First In* refers to several meetings between myself (I'm called Gary 2 in the book) and Engineer Aref. He explains that Engineer Aref occupied Kabul on November 14, 2001, and assumed control of the remnants of the previous intelligence organization, renaming it the National Directorate of Security (NDS), which had a department that worked with the CIA up until 2004.

9

AMIR

"This I will say for the Afghan—he is a treacherous, evil brute when he wants to be, but while your friend he is a first-rate fellow. The point is you must judge to the second when he is going to cease to be friendly. There is seldom any warning."
—*George MacDonald Fraser,* Flashman

*   *   *   *   *   *

Arab-American Amir and blond-haired, blue-eyed Davis, with his hair neatly parted and combed, wound their way slowly down the steep ravine road to the Shomali Plains for their first meeting with warlord ███████████████. Since members of Gary Schroen's team had passed ████████████, he was our ally for the time-being, which was of questionable merit since he had the reputation of changing sides when it suited him and playing one side against the other. We also knew he was close to Osama bin Laden and could possibly be of help.

████████████████████████████████████

████████████████████████████████████

████████████████████████████████████

████████████████████████████████████

███████████████

Despite his political ambitions, the elderly warlord had never been able to establish a substantial base of support within Afghanistan, in part because his strict Wahhanism clashed with the Hanafi system of beliefs accepted by most Afghans (including the Taliban). Both he and Ahmad Shah Massoud had been members of the Burhanuddin Rabbani government, which was pushed out of Kabul by the Taliban in 1996.

I knew that ███████████ understood the dynamics of Afghan politics better than I ever would and had ambitions to be part of a post-Taliban government. I also knew that he maintained contacts with the Taliban and al-Qaeda and had talked Massoud into receiving the team of Arab journalists who had assassinated him.

*　　*　　*

As Davis drove, Amir gazed down into the rocky ravine at the rusting tanks and armored personnel carriers—refuse from the three Soviet attempts to take the Panshir by force. Children carrying bundles of wood and burka-clad women hauling buckets of water walked along the edge of the road trying to avoid the dirt shoulder that could be mined.

As a high school student in the United States, Amir had dreamed of joining the anti-Soviet mujahideen in Afghanistan and "fighting the good fight." His interest in Afghanistan continued during his years in the U.S. Navy as civil war raged and the Taliban seized power. As a Muslim he was deeply offended by the way the Taliban misinterpreted his religion and treated its citizens. His anger grew when al-Qaeda established training camps in Afghanistan and declared jihad (Holy War) against the West.

Despite the objections of his pregnant wife, Amir joined the Jawbreaker team to rid the world of the criminals who had used Islam to kill innocent people in Kenya, Tanzania, Yemen and New York City. He was on his first assignment. This had become his "good fight."

Davis slowed to a stop at a checkpoint manned by Afghan teenagers armed with AK-47s and RPGs. For the first time in his life,

Amir had an automatic weapon pointed at his face. Gathering himself, he explained who they were and the nature of their mission. The two Americans were waved through and continued their spine-twisting journey south.

Two hours after they started out, they arrived at the elderly warlord's compound—a large, low-slung mud hut—where they were welcomed by twenty heavily armed men, some wearing camouflage, others in traditional Afghan clothes. Davis and Amir were escorted to a sitting room and served glasses of sweet tea. After fifteen minutes ███████ walked in looking like Charlton Heston playing the part of Moses in the *Ten Commandments*. Towering over six feet tall, he dressed the part of a prophet with a long white beard and impeccable white robes.

The Kharruti warlord poured on the charm, addressing the two Americans first in English and, then, reminiscing about Cairo with Amir in eloquent Arabic. He struck Amir as clever and treacherous, so he dubbed him *tha'lab*, which in Arabic means "the fox."

When Amir asked ██████ about the whereabouts of Osama bin Laden and other members of his terrorist group, the warlord's mood changed. He would have to check his sources, he said gravely, before he could give the Americans a response.

The following day, the three men sat on carpets as the warlord's men served a meal of hot bread, tea, cheese and honey. When Amir once again brought up the subject of bin Laden's location, ██████ said that bin Laden and "the Arabs" had left Afghanistan shortly after September 11. Both Davis and Amir knew this wasn't true.

Next, Davis held up photos of men who we knew were members of al-Qaeda and allied radical groups and had been living in Afghanistan. ██████ denied ever meeting them and said he had no idea where they were. All the information we had indicated otherwise.

Despite the fact that ██████ had not given the two Americans a single shred of useful information, he still had the gall to ask for money. He needed American dollars, he said, to arm and supply his troops ██ .

It was a typical Afghan warlord performance: Trust no one, play both sides against each other to your own advantage, only reveal information that directly benefits your own quest for power.

* * *

CENTCOM was far more reliable, dispatching aircraft in large numbers to destroy the columns of Taliban troops fleeing south from Mazar-e Sharif we had identified the day before. Throughout the morning of the 6th I received multiple calls from CTC/███ , which was in contact with the JFACC (Joint Forces Air Component Command) in Saudi Arabia. They sent back word that AC-130 Spectre gunships had left a long swath of Taliban dead.

In the late afternoon I received a surprise call from Mary, my former boss at the recruitment center, on my satellite phone. In her distinctive Oklahoma accent she said: "Hello, Gary. Are you behaving yourself out there?"

"I'm sure trying," I answered. "To what do I owe the honor of this call?"

"I'm in San Francisco at the moment, sitting in the office of the FBI's Special Agent in Charge. Believe it or not, they have an Afghan contact here who says his brother is on the front lines as a commander with the Taliban opposing you but would like to cut a deal."

Small world, I thought, *and one that seems to be growing exponentially smaller by the second.* "How's this guy in San Francisco communicating with his brother?" I asked.

"He says his brother, the Taliban commander, has been calling him with a satellite phone."

"Do you have a phone number for the brother in the Taliban?" I asked.

Mary was ready. "Just so happens that I do."

As she read the number I marveled at how globally connected even a Taliban commander in a backwater like Afghanistan could be with the right piece of technology.

"Mary, give me your number and have the FBI keep their Afghan contact on a short leash in case I have problems contacting his brother, the commander."

"Will do."

Mary was thorough and provided the commander's full name, date of birth and some biographical background. I headed next door to share the information with Majid.

"Sure, we know him," Majid said. "He used to be one of our commanders and defected to the Taliban when he thought they were going to win."

"I'm going to call him," I said, impatient to close the deal.

Majid held up his hands. "Let's wait for Engineer Aref*."

An hour later we were sitting before the well-dressed Northern Alliance Chief of ████, Engineer Aref*. When I leaned forward to hand him the Taliban commanders' number, he waved me away. "I have it already," he said. "When Mohammad switched sides, he took one of my Inmarsat phones."

Aref* dialed the number and spoke in Dari. Then listening intently, he turned to me and said into the phone, "I'll talk to the Americans and call you back in thirty minutes."

I followed him into a small parlor, decorated with sofas covered in clean white sheets. "Mohammad says he has almost a thousand men under his command," Aref* reported. Then he walked over to a map and pointed to a position northeast of Kabul. "He's defending this position on the Shomali Plains and says he wants a half a million dollars to surrender all his forces, which he says he can arrange within a week."

"Does he really have that many men?" I wanted to know.

"If not a thousand, then close to it," Majid responded. Engineer Aref* agreed.

██

████████████████████████████████. "Tell him if he doesn't surrender under those conditions, I'll call in B-52 strikes and kill him and all his men by mid afternoon since I now know his position."

Aref*, ever suspicious, then raised the issue of another Taliban commander in the north who was ready to surrender and wanted to know if we would still honor the CTC/██ offer of ██ per soldier. I told him that if Hank had promised that, I would make good.

"Please contact Hank to confirm this," Aref* asked.

"Let's finish with our friend on the Shomali Plains first."

Engineer Aref* looked at me skeptically, then dialed again. The Taliban commander, named Mohammad, was waiting. As Aref* conveyed my offer, I heard him use the Persian verb *"nabud karda,"* which means to annihilate by force. Aref's* facial expression indicated that there was a problem. He put his hand over the phone.

"Mohammad has twenty al-Qaeda fighters with him and wants to know what to do with the Arabs," Engineer Aref* said.

"Tell him to kill them all, because if he doesn't they will kill him when he tries to switch sides. Then he and his men should cross the lines with their weapons slung down and hands up," I replied.

Aref* smiled as he conveyed the message. It was a deal.

The next order of business was the SNI hostages. Engineer Aref* had spoken to Gold Falcon who was willing to trade all eight SNI hostages for four million dollars. Gold Falcon said that he was hoping to gain enough control over the hostages so that he could arrange their escape within five days. Three of his most trusted aides would cross the battlefield with the hostages and receive the money in exchange.

"The four million is ready," I said. "I'll get Storm to work out the details with Majid. Storm will be traveling with three military specialists to conduct the exchange."

*   *   *

Back at our compound, I called CTC/▇▇ and filled Hank in on my call from Mary, my conversation with the Taliban commander and

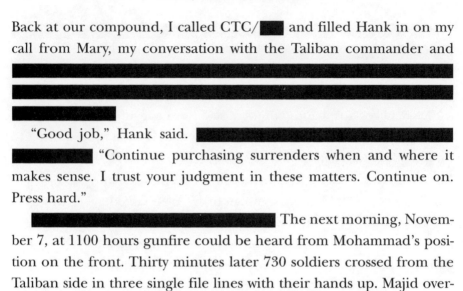

"Good job," Hank said. ▇▇▇▇▇▇▇▇▇▇▇▇▇▇▇▇▇▇▇

▇▇▇▇▇▇▇▇▇ "Continue purchasing surrenders when and where it makes sense. I trust your judgment in these matters. Continue on. Press hard."

▇▇▇▇▇▇▇▇▇▇▇▇▇▇▇▇▇▇▇ The next morning, November 7, at 1100 hours gunfire could be heard from Mohammad's position on the front. Thirty minutes later 730 soldiers crossed from the Taliban side in three single file lines with their hands up. Majid oversaw the quick bloodless transition, which lasted less than fifteen minutes. The Taliban soldiers simply marched into the Panshir and joined our side. They explained that the gunfire we heard was the sound of them killing the al-Qaeda fighters attached to their unit.

This defection punched a gaping hole in Taliban lines that I hoped would make General Bismullah Khan's offensive easier. George reported that NA troops were prepared to launch at dawn the next day (the eighth).

At midnight, as we were winding down, one of Majid's ▇▇▇▇ officers appeared in our compound with Amir. Hafiz was a serious, cooperative and professional young man of about five-foot-eight with a pockmarked face.

"What's up?" I asked. Both Amir and Hafiz looked exhausted from twenty-hour days.

"Chief, I think we have something interesting," a very serious Amir said.

"What's that?"

The Arab-American explained that Hafiz had just received a satellite phone call from a source ▇▇▇▇▇▇ who said that Taliban military ▇▇▇▇▇▇▇ was currently in Kabul conducting a meeting with senior officials. Hafiz said he knew the location and could pick it out with complete accuracy on a city map.

"Get the best map you can find," I ordered. "And wake up A.C. and Reno, the JSOC Air Combat Controller, and get them in here."

Todd, who was sleeping in the other room, sat up and called CTC/███ to ask if they had an armed Predator near Kabul. ██████████████████████████ After checking with the Global Response Center (GRC), an executive officer came back on the line to confirm that there was a Predator in the Kabul area that was armed and ready. I asked for GRC's direct number so that I could speak to the Air Force pilots who were flying the Predator from a virtual cockpit ██████████████.

With my tech guy A.C., Reno the Air Combat Controller, Amir and Hafiz crowding around me, I spoke on a secure line: "We have fresh intel on a priority target: Mullah Akhund in Kabul. ████████████ Hafiz, who is standing with me, knows the neighborhood." I turned to A.C. and asked, "What do we have in the way of imagery?"

"I have full imagery of Kabul on a disk that we can load onto a laptop," black-bearded A.C. replied.

"Wonderful. Set the laptop close to the phone and do your stuff." A.C., the youngest member of my team, was a whiz with anything technical. I knew that I could count on him.

I looked at Hafiz, whose eyes were bugging out of his head. "Hafiz, if we show you good pictures of the entire city will you be able to show us the house?"

Hafiz, who understood English better than he could speak it, answered: "Yes, I show you, Agha Gary. Yes."

"Reno," I said. "Work with Hafiz to locate the neighborhood, and then the house. Then I want you to talk directly to the pilot who is handling the Predator. ████████████████████████████."

A.C. loaded the satellite photo software that he had specifically requested before deployment. Then, he moved aside so Reno could sit at the laptop flanked by Hafiz and Amir. A satellite photo of the entire city came up on the screen and Hafiz pointed to the general location of the house near a stadium. Using the mouse, Reno zoomed in closer and closer until they were within a few blocks. Then Hafiz ran to his office to contact his source ███████████████ .

He returned beaming with confidence and pointed to a residence in a densely populated neighborhood adjacent to a small hotel. Reno spoke directly to the pilot at ██████████ . Since Reno was a combat controller whose specialty was working with pilots, he had the Predator on target in less than twenty minutes.

███
███
███
███

███████████████████ "Good work, men," I said, shaking hands with Reno, Amir, A.C. and Ali. "Rest up for tomorrow."

My mind was still racing as I closed up the office, so I took a walk around the compound to check on the guards. Two pairs of them strolled by with AK-47s slung over their shoulders and we exchanged a few words in Farsi in the cold, quiet, crystal-clear night.

Four years earlier I had hiked for ten days into the Everest region of Nepal with my son and a small group of friends. Tonight I was reminded of the same high clear sky framed by jagged mountains.

███
███
███
███
███
███
██████████████████████
███
███
███

As I walked back, I thought about my wife and children. Remembering that it was the middle of the day on the East Coast of North and South America, I climbed the steps to my office and dialed the satellite phone. I couldn't get through to my wife in ████████. So I called my daughter in Charlottesville, Virginia.

"Good afternoon, Alexis," I said. "This is your father. How come you're not in class?"

She laughed at my jesting and asked how I was doing.

I missed my family a lot. It was the price I had to pay for serving my country. I loved them both.

* Gary Schroen in his CIA-approved book *First In* refers to several meetings between myself (I'm called Gary 2 in the book) and Engineer Aref. He explains that Engineer Aref occupied Kabul on November 14, 2001, and assumed control of the remnants of the previous intelligence organization, renaming it the National Directorate of Security (NDS), which had a department that worked with the CIA up until 2004.

10

THE FALL OF KABUL

"We will encourage our friends to head south across the
Shomali Plains, but not into the city of Kabul itself."
—President George W. Bush, November 7, 2001

*   *   *   *   *   *

Early in the morning of November 8, 2001, George and Lt. Colonel Haas scanned the sky over the Shomali Plains. Directly in front of them more than ten thousand Taliban soldiers lay waiting—dug into fortified bunkers and trenches with fifty-plus tanks, armored personnel carriers and trucks mounted with ZSU antiaircraft guns.

"Where the hell are they?" Hamid asked, looking overhead for vapor trails.

"There should be one group of B-52s arriving north from the States, and another group coming from Diego Garcia in the South," George drawled in his Texan accent.

"General Khan and his men are in position," Hamid reported.

George was a man of few words. "Tell 'em to wait."

The plan called for a two-pronged attack. One group of Northern Alliance fighters would advance across the desert floor east along the new highway from Bagram Airfield. A second force would attack from

164

the west along the old highway carved into a wall of cliffs. Since the terrain favored the Taliban defenders, airpower was critical.

Everyone was in place. General Bismullah Khan and several thousand Northern Alliance fighters wearing newly American-bought, Chinese-made uniforms clutched their AK-47s. Chief Warrant Officer Diaz and his Triple Nickel SF team with radios and SOFLAMS were prepared to direct the close air support. Hamid was on hand to provide important translation so that George, Haas and the Agency and SF teams could communicate with General Bismullah Khan and his subcommanders General Sharifi and General Babajan.

As the sun rose higher, they all asked together, "Where are the fucking planes?"

George called several times to our compound in the Panshir and repeated the same question. I was flummoxed. CTC/█ had been badgering me for weeks to get General Khan to advance on the dug-in Taliban positions guarding access to Kabul. Only a few days earlier, George, Lt. Colonel Haas and I had gotten a commitment from Khan to launch a Northern Alliance offensive with the promise of massive U.S. air support. The date had arrived and the airplanes were nowhere in sight.

At 1 P.M. two lone F-16s appeared in the skies over the Shomali Plains, fired Maverick missiles at Taliban positions and left. General Bismullah Khan was about to explode. "Where are the big bombers?" he shouted in Dari. "What are the Americans doing?" Lt. Colonel Haas and George had carefully reviewed every aspect of the operation with him. Engineer Aref* had assured him that the Americans would cover the NA advance with air support. But the planes had not come.

I reached our liaison officer in CENTCOM. He said JFACC in Saudi Arabia had directed the majority of planes north around Konduz to deal with an emerging problem. A few remaining planes were targeting Kandahar in the South.

"Why the hell didn't anyone tell me?" I demanded. "What the hell is going on there?"

"Gary," he answered. "I'm as surprised as you are."

That wasn't good enough. I said, "My guys on the front have had their relationships with the Afghan commanders strained to the limit because of this. The loss of credibility is huge!"

Our liason at CENTCOM was sympathetic. "I understand completely," he said. "Explain to them that the threats up north are real. We've taken some cities, but there's a lot of chaos. We could take serious losses up there if we don't act now."

I asked, "What can you do to help me out?"

"I can give you a list of numbers of available aircraft per day, types of aircraft and times of anticipated arrival in your area of operation," he said. "You can pass that to Bismullah Khan so he has a tangible means of measuring our ability to deliver. That's the best I can do from here."

"Thanks. That will help."

"I'm glad."

"It's not like the Northern Alliance is going to turn against us," I added. "I just don't need additional complications when I'm already anticipating a problem when we get to Kabul. Washington wants us to stop outside the city and wait for the U.N. They're the guys who did such a stand-up job protecting civilians in Rwanda, remember?"

"I remember," the Agency liason said.

"I'll write up something and talk to you tomorrow. Jawbreaker, out."

Even though I was still hot, reason took over. I didn't think this was a conspiracy to lengthen the conflict. Nor did I think it was the result of some one-star general's egomania. We were engaged in a complicated operation in a faraway land where needs outnumbered resources. Still, it was my duty to draft a cable outlining the consequences of the screwup that had just transpired.

███

███

███

[*NOTE TO READER:* This redacted section deals with several meetings with Northern Alliance military officials to coordinate the upcoming offensive and apologize for the failure to deliver airpower at a time it had been promised.]

Outside George turned to me and muttered, "I think that went okay."

I told him that A.C. and Marlowe, the two Directorate of Science and Technology officers, would need help setting up some gear on the frontlines.

I stopped at the linked Jawbreaker and Triple Nickel compounds before making the gut-wrenching drive up to the Panshir. Waiting for me at our compound was a helicopter with a full crew and a mechanic. It was big, with lots of lift, and could perform well at high altitude. The biggest problem was fuel. When the crew wasn't flying they spent most of their time filtering what little fuel we could get our hands on. Over the past several years bad fuel and engine failure had been the leading cause of helicopter crashes in Afghanistan.

*   *   *

Up north, the Taliban was in a state of collapse. After Mazar-e Sharif, the cities of Shiberghan, Meymaneh and Murghab farther west toppled one after the other. To take advantage of the rapidly changing political landscape, Hank and John at CTC/█ worked with Special Forces 5th Group Commander Colonel John Mulholland to insert two additional SF teams—one with the Hazara led by Dr. Karim Khalili in central Afghanistan and one to join Ismael Khan near Herat in the far west.

Meanwhile, Storm focused on the details of the SNI hostage rescue. He had worked out where and when he would link up with Gold Falcon's men to exchange the money, the route the hostages would take out of Kabul and the location on the front lines where they would cross. And he coordinated everything with Lt. Colonel Haas's guys who would provide security, while he and the JSOC team handled the exchange.

I made sure that they covered all contingencies, but otherwise stayed clear. Too many times in my career, I'd seen senior officers insert themselves into an operation at the last minute and foul it up. All Storm and the JSOC team needed now was for Gold Falcon to deliver the hostages in exchange for four million dollars. In the event that the hostage exchange couldn't take place on the Shomali Plains, Gold Falcon had agreed to move them to a prison directly east of Kabul.

███

███

███

███

████████████████████ All of us, in concert with CTC/███ and CENTCOM, agreed to a new date to launch the coordinated air assault and ground offensive—November 14.

*   *   *

The morning of November 12 I woke to a full sun and a growing sense of inevitability. Over the past two days, the highly anticipated air assault over the Shomali Plains had finally begun. The day before U.S. aircraft had conducted twenty-five strikes, annihilating more than two thousand enemy soldiers, twenty-nine tanks and six command bunkers.

I was in daily contact with our liason at CENTCOM and General Tommy Franks's J-2 General Kimmons, who assured me that they were carefully synching their targeting to our intel reports. In two more days a BLU-82 would be dropped to commence the coordinated air and ground offensive.

As I exited my bedroom toward the office, a workaholic first-tour officer named Yale strode towards me in a hurry.

"Chief, Majid's sources in the city are reporting that a full evacua-

rear gate
area

This is the scene that greeted me as I arrived at the bombed-out U.S. Embassy in Dar es Salaam, Tanzania, on August 10, 1998. My fellow investigators and I captured many of the conspirators, but the bombing was a grisly wake-up call regarding al-Qaeda's intentions towards the U.S. *(Courtesy of the author)*

Osama bin Laden and his second-in-command Ayman al-Zawahiri in Afghanistan in 2001. Al-Zawahiri was the mastermind behind the bombings of the U.S. Embassies in Kenya and Tanzania, and a primary target of the massive airstrike we called in over Tora Bora in December. *(Reuters/Hamid Mir)*

An unmanned Predator drone armed with a Hellfire missile. *(Agence France Presse/US Air Force)*

Northern Alliance military chief General Mohammed Fahim reviews his troops on the Shomali Plains, November 5, 2001. I was present when CENTCOM commander Gen. Tommy Franks conducted a heated negotiation with Fahim over resources the latter had requested. Balancing Fahim's political ambitions with our needs was a constant challenge. *(Reuters/Yannis Behrakis)*

Me sitting in a helicopter in the Panshir waiting to leave for Bagram Airbase, November 12, 2001. The Northern Alliance choppers in particular were poorly maintained and often crashed. *(Courtesy of the author)*

Here's a look at the control tower of Bagram Airbase as we approached by helicopter. The base would be my outpost as we tried to get a handle on which parts of Kabul were safely under Northern Alliance control. *(Courtesy of the author)*

The charismatic Northern Alliance leader Ahmad Shah Massoud in his Panshir Valley headquarters in June 2001, three months before he was assassinated by al-Qaeda terrorists posing as reporters. He was killed two days before the September ll attack. *(Agence France Presse/Getty/Joel Robine)*

Triumphant Northern Alliance soldiers ride into liberated Kabul carrying a poster of assassinated leader Ahmad Shah Massoud, November 13, 2001. *(Getty/Tyler Hicks)*

Lt. Colonel Chris Haas *(left)* and myself on the steps of the U.S. Embassy, Kabul, November 14, 2001. We were among the first Americans to enter the Embassy in fourteen years, and we felt as if we'd entered a time warp as we spotted rotary telephones and official photographs of President Reagan on the walls. *(Courtesy of the author)*

A riot broke out on November 19, 2001, as Afghan men stormed the Bakhar movie theater in central Kabul, desperate to see the first public film shown since the fall of the Taliban. *(Reuters/Yannis Behrakis)*

One of the many Taliban/al-Qaeda bases on the Shomali Plains. We stopped to inspect several of these abandoned bases as we drove from liberated Kabul back to our main base at Bagram. *(Courtesy of the author)*

Northern Alliance Foreign Minister Dr. Abdullah Abdullah *(left)* and U.S. Special Representative James Dobbins *(right)* meet in Tashkent, Uzbekistan, on November 18, 2001, to discuss the future of Afghanistan. I had to do some careful negotiation with Abdullah and Fahim to organize this meeting, and I gave my own briefing to Dobbins just before his meeting with Abdullah. *(Agence France Presse/Anvar Ilyasov)*

Northern Alliance forces battle rioting Taliban and al-Qaeda prisoners for control of Qala-i Jangi fortress, November 27, 2001. Tragically, CIA tour officer and former Marine Mike Spann was killed in the riots, becoming the first U.S. casualty in Afghanistan. *(Getty/Oleg Nikishin)*

Bodies of dead al-Qaeda and Taliban soldiers following the riot at Qala-i Jangi. *(Getty/Oleg Nikishin)*

Northern Alliance General Rashid Dostum, who styled himself as a modern-day Cossack traveling on horseback, greets reporters as he arrives at Qala-i Jangi on November 28, 2001. Dostum ordered his troops to pump ice-cold water into the basement where the rioting prisoners were hiding, finally forcing the remaining holdouts to surrender. *(Getty/Oleg Nikishin)*

A U.S. airstrike on al-Qaeda troops in Tora Bora. This photograph, taken by a member of my Juliet Forward team, gives a sense of the awesome firepower we rained down on the region. *(Courtesy of the author)*

Qaeda prisoners captured during the fighting in Tora Bora, December 17, 2001. *(Getty/Chris Hondros)*

Hamid Karzai *(left)* greeting Interior Minster Yunis Qanunu *(right)* and General Mohammed Fahim *(center)* as he arrives as Bagram Airbase, December 12, 2001. When Karzai landed, he was mobbed by excited Northern Alliance troops. Fortunately, I was able to quickly get him into a car before he was trampled. *(Reuters/Reuters Television)*

CENTCOM commander General Tommy Franks on a visit to Kabul in May of 2002. *(Reuters/Vasily Fedosenko)*

tion of Kabul by Taliban forces began last night," Yale said. "Bismullah Khan is moving against Taliban positions on the Shomali Plains. The Taliban are retreating."

I took a deep breath and said, "Get everyone into the office . . . now!"

Continuing to the NA intel building, I listened to Majid confirm that the Taliban in Kabul were in a complete panic because of the defections of Taliban commanders and the severity of U.S. airstrikes during the last forty-eight hours. I jogged back to the office. In ten minutes the whole team had assembled under the flat-roofed building that had served as our headquarters for the last week and a half. They stood amidst chairs, tables, laptops and communications equipment.

I said, "Kabul is reported to be in a state of confusion. The Taliban are withdrawing. We need to move quickly in order to receive maximum benefit from our enemy's retreat."

Everyone agreed. I started issuing orders: "Davis, contact George down on the front. Tell him to stick close to Bismullah Khan and do whatever he believes is appropriate as circumstances develop. Tell him I'm going to close up shop in the Panshir and reestablish the body of the Jawbreaker team at Bagram Airbase. I have to drop commo in the process, but will reestablish contact with him later in the afternoon.

"Davis and Storm, I want you to take the helicopter and do a fly-over of Bagram. Coordinate with Chris Haas and his SF team before going in to make sure that the area is secure enough to enter without getting shot down. Everyone else, start packing up. Weapons, commo gear and basic provisions, everything. Haul it down to the helicopter pad. Providing there's no serious groundfire, the copter will make a second trip with personnel and gear."

I turned to Amir. "Take the huge five-ton truck and load everything else onto it. I want you and a team of Afghans to drive everything that we can't get onto the helicopter down to Bagram. Remember guys, only your packs, weapons, ammo and commo gear on the bird. Amir takes the rest."

Todd, our commo officer, asked if I wanted him to inform head-quarters about the collapse.

"Yes. Write a simple cable that says that a retreat and collapse of the Taliban is taking place. But don't tell them about our move. I'll inform them myself when we get to Bagram. I'm sure Hank and Cofer will have no problem, but I don't want anyone on the seventh floor getting in our way."

Each man nodded his approval. Then Storm spoke up: "I'm going to ask Majid if he has anything on Gold Falcon and the SNI hostages."

"Good."

Concern was written deep into Storm's face. How would we contact Gold Falcon in all the confusion? What would he do with the hostages? Would we find them in an abandoned building with their throats slit?

We had to quickly seize the initiative and hope for the best.

$$* \quad * \quad *$$

It took us three hours to break down the gear and load some of it in the helicopter, then lift the rest on the truck. Amir drove off with several Afghan guards.

Storm and Davis reported that their recon flight over Bagram had been uneventful. East of the airfield they spotted a large *wadi* (dried-out riverbed) that had served as a Taliban bunker before the Triple Nickel SF team called in a GPS-navigated air strike. Now Taliban bodies lay strewn alongside a destroyed concrete bridge.

Majid, Davis, Storm, Todd, Yale, Sean the medic, the three JSOC officers and I climbed in the copter and lifted off. We slowly headed north a hundred yards, then banked in a full circle and bore south. As the big ███████ gained speed and altitude, I followed Amir's truck winding its way through the Panshir. Then it moved out of sight.

At 1,500 feet we passed between rugged mountaintops. The valley below was spectacular, dotted with highly defensible steppes. Patches of lush green ran along the river like ribbons of hope.

We climbed higher, over the eastern tip of the valley and then into more mountains. A faint yellowish brown haze hung in the sky.

For the first time in weeks, I remembered the disposable camera I'd been carrying in my pack. The ten of us took turns looking out the porthole windows and snapping pictures. After ten minutes we cleared the mountains and saw the Shomali Plains spread before us in full tableau. Kabul rose thirty miles ahead at two o'clock. Bagram lay to our left at ten.

The land below was brown and devoid of vegetation. Patches of mud huts surrounded by mud walls were the only sign of life. A few houses were still intact, but most had been destroyed by artillery fire.

What a brutally hard life, I thought to myself. The harsh landscape was bad enough, but the fact that its inhabitants also had to suffer through a decade or more of warfare seemed more than cruel.

The pilot, a man in his fifties with long gray hair and mustache, circled the base first, passing aprons filled with dozens of burned-out Soviet-made aircraft and hangars that had been blown apart. Borrowing a phrase from Teddy Roosevelt's wife, Edith, Bagram looked like "hell after the fire went out."

The ugly yellow control tower and a small building behind it were the only two structures that looked intact. We swung over the *wadi* and the destroyed bridge littered with corpses, then hovered over the middle of the runway and gently touched down.

As soon as we did, two Afghans approached. One was a rotund man in a drab olive uniform; the other, a skinny fellow in civilian clothing. I exited the chopper alone and shook the hand of the uniformed man who introduced himself in Dari as General Babajan, one of Bismullah Khan's commanders. He explained that he had just taken command of the airbase. That's when I noticed that the slimmer man was operating a small video camera.

Hours later the enterprising young man with the camera sold the footage he was shooting to several foreign news outlets. Pictures of me exiting the helicopter and shaking hands with General Babajan accompanied the lead story that night on ABC, CBS, NBC and CNN. My mother watching in Florida immediately recognized her bearded son, called my sister in New York and demanded to know what I was doing getting off a helicopter just outside of Kabul. My sister tried denying it was me at first. But after she saw the footage replayed again, gave up and admitted, "Yeah, Mom, that's Gary. He sure gets around."

*   *   *

George's men pressed forward with General Bismullah Khan's force in a convoy of vehicles traveling south on two parallel roads. One hugged the western boundary of the Shomali Plains, the other ran along the east in a classic envelopment maneuver. Occasionally they encountered a pocket of Taliban soldiers that tried to swarm around them. If the resistance was strong, Chief Warrant Officer Diaz's SF team would dial up an AWACS and call in close air support.

Each time a U.S. bomb or missile destroyed a Taliban tank or truck, Northern Alliance soldiers raised a cheer. They had to be careful to stay on the paved road because the land beside it was littered with antipersonnel and tank mines. The problem was steering around craters left by B-52 two-thousand-pound bombs that were big enough to swallow a car.

The land Bismullah Khan's army passed through had been completely decimated by the Taliban. Orchards, trees, fences, houses and vineyards were smashed and burned to the ground to punish the inhabitants of the Shomali for their resistance. Years before, wells had been poisoned and water pipes and dams blown up by the Taliban to deprive the plain of vital water. What had once been the breadbasket of Kabul was now more like a rock-strewn desert.

The bodies of fallen Taliban soldiers had been covered with stones or buried in accordance with Muslim practice. But foreigners and al-Qaeda bodies were left to rot in the sun.

As they pushed south, Northern Alliance commanders allowed hundreds of Afghan Taliban soldiers to switch sides. Some were friends or relatives of NA subcommanders; other had been allies in the past. This was the sixth time since 1996 that sovereignty of the plains had shifted between the Taliban and Northern Alliance.

General Khan had promised to my face that he would stop his forces five miles out of Kabul. But the political crown of Afghanistan was too tempting to resist. "The American bombing had been very effective," Khan explained later. "So we started to attack in the morning, and by two P.M. reached the gates of Kabul."

Members of the Triple Nickel SF team who traveled with Khan's forces were well aware of the agreement, but unable to enforce it. "I went to General Sharifi and he said, 'Sure. We'll stop, but some of the local commanders have family down there,'" one Triple Nickel soldier explained to *Frontline*.

Whether they were pushed by pure momentum, political ambition or their claim that bandits were looting the city, Bismullah Khan's troops continued into the city. Stan, Parker and members of Triple Nickel entered with them, not stopping to communicate with George or myself. Although there was some scattered violence, most of it was the result of Kabul residents beating Taliban stragglers to death.

*   *   *

As I helped unload the helicopter at Bagram, I realized that I had men all over the place. Davis, Storm, Todd, Yale, Sean the medic and the three JSOC officers were with me. George was somewhere on the battlefield. Stan and Parker rode at the front of Khan's army. Marlowe and A.C. were stationed on the opposite end of the Shomali Plains with a Northern Alliance security detachment. I needed to get our commo up fast.

███████ (The General) accompanied me on an inspection of the building behind the control tower. The first floor was more or less intact, but filled with a foot and a half of soil and soot. Since all second-floor windows had been blown out, there were only two rooms that were not piled high with flying dust. The rest had to be shoveled out by hand.

I trotted back to the helicopter and shouted at Todd: "Top floor to your left. That's where we put the commo. It's a damn mess, but at least it has a roof."

███████ (The General's) men produced shovels and we got to work. In order to establish commo, we needed a power source. Back in the Panshir we ran a good-sized generator, which we hadn't brought with us. George had a second one with him somewhere on the front. Now Todd set up a generator the size of a lawnmower engine.

Todd said, "The dust and dirt are superfine and are going to mess up our equipment within a day or two."

The temporary solution was sheets of plastic duct-taped across the windows. The next time I saw ███████ (the General) I told him that I needed a contractor as soon as possible to install new doors and windows, clean and paint the place and get the water running.

With our communications up, the first call I made was to CTC/ ███ in Washington. Local time there was 0730 hours when Hank's deputy, John, answered.

I said, "John, this is Gary. We've had a collapse on the Shomali Plains and the Taliban are fleeing."

"I know," he said. "It's all over the major media."

"I've moved Jawbreaker out of the Panshir. We've established ourselves with Northern Alliance ███████ at Bagram."

He sounded surprised. "You're at Bagram now?"

"That's correct. We need to be closer to the action."

"Gary, are you aware that two of your men, Stan and Parker, have entered the capital with Bismullah Khan despite the fact that the

White House specifically wanted Bismullah Khan to stop five miles outside the city to avoid widespread killing?" he asked.

"How do you know?"

"They called us from a satellite phone."

I said, "I'm a little spread out at the moment. But I'll take an armed group into the city immediately to link up with them and report back to you on the situation."

"Good luck."

John gave me the location of the guesthouse where Stan and Parker were staying. Then Hank got on the line. "The DDO is panicked about your guys going into the capital, but the DCI doesn't seem that concerned," Hank said. "You did the right thing to move forward."

"Thanks."

"Go into Kabul and give me an immediate assessment of the situation. Theorizing in Washington about possible violence helps no one. I need to know if there is house-to-house fighting, random killings or if large Taliban contingents are still holding parts of the city."

"I'll call you from the satellite phone when I get there."

"Be alert."

Once again, I realized how lucky I was to be reporting to men like Hank and John who understood that events were moving rapidly and I was dealing with them as best as I could. I could just as easily have received a world-class ass-chewing for not having better control of my men.

As I called my guys together, Lt. Colonel Haas drove up in a jeep looking pissed. "That damn Bismullah Khan violated his promise to stop five miles out of the city!"

"I know."

I told him about my conversation with CTC/▮▮ and invited him to join me for the ride to Kabul. Eight of us loaded up in two Toyota four-door pickups. Majid drove one vehicle with Lt. Colonel Haas, an SF Sergeant named Andy and myself. Two Northern Alliance soldiers climbed in the first truck with Yale and Storm. It was 4 P.M. when we started south and the sun was just starting to set.

Turning to Majid, I said, "I want to link up with my men, but let's go to Taliban Intelligence Headquarters first."

"Good idea."

We exited Bagram through a side gate onto a dirt road covered with a foot or two of fine dust. Majid knew the way, making turns at unmarked intersections and avoiding roads that lead to obscure villages. At dusk a figure jumped out at us from behind a thicket of trees. Screaming "EAAAST!" in a shrill, frightened voice, he pointed his AK-47 at our heads. Both drivers slammed on the brakes.

Majid rolled down his window and yelled at the terrified young man in Dari. Looking through the gun's sight, the trembling young soldier inched his way slowly from my side of the truck to Majid's. The whole time the NA ███████ officer kept up a steady stream of commands. A long, tense minute passed before the soldier realized who Majid was and lowered his weapon. The rest of us loosened some tightly clenched muscles and sighed with relief.

Ten minutes later we entered a partially paved, dark and empty road. Majid hit the pedal, accelerating to a steady fifty miles per hour. We zoomed past blown-out vehicles and the occasional corpse.

That's when I noticed headlights from a large truck approaching from behind. "Who the hell's following us?" I asked, looking over my shoulder. Majid let it pass, then immediately picked up speed and started flashing the lights. When the truck ahead took a left fork, we followed at sixty-five miles an hour, tossing violently every time we hit a pothole. Majid started leaning on the horn.

"What're you doing?" I wanted to know.

Majid shouted excitedly: "That's our truck! That's Amir! The road we have entered is mined ahead!"

Despite the cold temperature, I started to sweat big bullets as we flew down the dark road, horn blaring. The next two minutes lasted too long. Finally, the truck slowed and pulled to the side of the road.

Majid jumped out and in a stern voice told the driver that the road was mined two miles ahead.

"It's a good thing you saw us," said a shaken Amir.

"No shit."

Turning back and taking another road, we started to cut diagonally to the far west side of the Shomali Plains. That's where we met a paved road that sloped gradually south. The SF sergeant sitting next to me, Andy, started to tell me about Peter Lynch's book *Learn to Earn,* which he claimed was a great introduction to the history of capitalism. A stocky fellow with a red beard, Andy explained that modern man had a choice of being an "adventure man" or a "finance man." He had chosen the former, he said.

"Me, too."

We were entering a middle-class neighborhood on the northwest outskirts of Kabul; the streets were completely vacant. The eerie quiet continued as we drove deeper into the city of two million, which was larger and more spread out than I had imagined. After fifteen minutes, we reached a large traffic circle with four uniformed men. When they leveled their weapons, we screeched to a stop and Majid lowered his window to identify himself. After a few words in Dari, the men waved us forward. They were part of Bismullah Khan's force.

What had once been a city of prosperous citizens, universities and well-stocked shops, including the first Marks & Spencer in Central Asia, was now a war-ravaged shell. In the early '90s, Massoud, who controlled large parts of Kabul fought a standing battle with rockets and artillery against Abdul Rashid Dostum and Abdul Rasul Sayyaf, who occupied separate prominitories outside the city. The Red Cross estimated that between '92 and '96 more than fifty thousand people had lost their lives during warlord infighting. That's before the Taliban took control and singled out educated Kabulis for their most severe repression. Ten of thousands of them had fled into exile, leaving the city's infrastructure of roads, telephones, water sanitation and electricity in shambles.

I looked at maps and satellite photos to try to get oriented. We passed through three more traffic circles manned by Northern Alliance sentries, but still hadn't seen a single civilian on the streets. Finally we approached a large gated compound manned by ten armed guards with rifles and big smiles who let us in.

Passing down a long, well-manicured drive, around a curve, we arrived at a large concrete structure. I saw several hundred armed Afghans out front. As soon as they saw us, they started to cheer.

Suddenly I felt like I was reliving a scene out of one of the war movies I had watched on TV as a kid. *Why me?* I asked myself. *How is it that someone from a background like mine has ended up here?*

In the midst of the celebration, Majid turned to me and said, "Gary, welcome to Taliban Intelligence headquarters. This is the building Dr. Najibullah used for years, first as Chief of Intelligence and later as President. Most recently it has been Taliban Intel Chief Qari Amadullah's headquarters."

I had read about Dr. Najibullah. He was the Soviet puppet and psychopath who enjoyed torturing his political opponents. A brazen man to say the least, he sought United Nations protection when the Taliban descended on Kabul in '96. The last two remaining members of the U.N. staff had been unable to prevail against the Taliban who seized Najibullah and his brother, beat and tortured them, then hung them from a lamppost in Ariana Square.

We pushed our way through the crowd with Majid leading the way. Soldiers patted us on the back and shouted cries of exultation. At the door two armed men let the eight of us in and held back the rest of the crowd.

We followed Majid three floors up a stone staircase with wood-paneled walls filigreed with Islamic designs, through double doors, into the office of Taliban's Chief of Intelligence Qari Amadullah. Qari had not hung around to welcome us.

It was a massive room with a large wooden desk, expensive stuffed furniture and a table that sat at least twenty. Majid spoke into a hand-held radio, then, turned to me and said: "Engineer Aref* will be here in twenty minutes."

To amuse ourselves, we took turns sitting at Qari's desk with our feet up and big grins on our faces. Majid noted that most people who entered this office hadn't left smiling. It was a sobering thought.

Arriving with three armed men, Engineer Aref* crossed the room and shook my hand, saying in Persian, "This is a fine day." He seemed nervous and was probably expecting a tongue lashing as we sat down at the big table, Americans on one side, Afghans on the other.

With Majid interpreting, I began, "On behalf of the United States Government I'd like to congratulate the Northern Alliance on its victory over the Taliban on the Shomali Plains. However, I'd like to remind you you'd made a commitment to remain outside the city limits to allow for a United Nations peacekeeping force to arrive and establish control."

Aref* sat cringing. I couldn't tell him that I was personally thrilled that we'd seized the city and could now get down to the business of going after al-Qaeda safehouses and training facilities.

"We had reports of violence and looting and did not want a breakdown in civil order," Engineer Aref* explained. "Please pass on to Washington that we will do everything possible to retain order and that there will be no reprisals from our forces upon former Taliban or Taliban supporters."

We were all well aware that the Sunni Tajiks had massacred thousands of Shia Hazaras on the streets of Kabul ten years ago. Now that the Tajiks and Hazaras were fighting a common enemy, there was at least tacit cooperation between the two groups. I was under no illusion that this would be a permanent state of affairs.

I said, "I've been asked to report back to Washington on the security situation. You must do everything possible to ensure that your forces don't abuse any segment of the population. If so, you'll have terrible difficulty with us."

"We came here to liberate this city, not to conquer it," Aref* responded.

Storm broke in: "What have you heard about the SNI hostages?"

"Our people checked the building next to the Ministry of Justice where they were being held," Engineer Aref* answered. "The hostages aren't there and there's no evidence of violence against them."

"What about the prison west of the city?"

"They're not there, either. Our contact, Gold Falcon, is not answering his satellite phone. I'll continue trying."

There were deep sighs and groans from our side of the table. Storm raked his hand through his reddish gray hair.

Engineer Aref* tried to make us feel better. "Gold Falcon knows how important they are to you," he said. "You've acted in good faith in providing him an advance. He surely must believe that you'll provide the balance of the money you promised. I don't think that they're dead, because they're of greater value alive."

I understood the logic of his words and the fact that Afghans had a history of bartering hostages. During the first Afghan War, Lady Sale had bravely bargained for her life and the lives of British women who were captured by Afghans. Her husband, British Colonel Fighting Bob Sale, organized a group of men to rescue his wife, only to find her leading a column of British ladies on horseback. Money was paid nonetheless.

I also understood the concept of revenge. General Tommy Franks and CENTCOM had been bombing the living hell out of the Taliban and al-Qaeda practically nonstop. Our enemies had very limited ways to strike back. It wouldn't take much for a guard who had lost family members in the bombing to put a gun up to the heads of the SNI hostages and shoot them in cold blood.

We returned to the subject of security. Engineer Aref* assured us that after initially entering the city with a large force, General Bismullah Khan was in the process of repositioning his armor and artillery outside the city to maintain a softer hand.

We shook hands. Then Majid led us to the house where Stan, Parker and several members of the Triple Nickel SF team had bivouacked for the night. It turned out to be a government guesthouse that formally housed visiting VIPs. Northern Alliance guards directed me to the second floor, where I found Stan and Parker lounging in the bedroom with assault rifles by their sides.

"Good evening, gentlemen," I said.

They sat up surprised.

"A call would've been nice," I added.

They looked at me with sheepish grins.

"You know of course the plan was to stop five miles outside the city. You two will either be fired or get medals."

Stan, the Russian-speaking former Marine, responded immediately: "We'd prefer the medals."

*　　*　　*

At approximately the same time in another part of Kabul, the eight SNI hostages—Kati Jelinek, Silke Duerrkopf, Diana Thomas, Ursula Fischer, Peter Bunch, Georg Taubman, Dayna Curry and Heather Mercer—were pushed into the back of a truck by Taliban soldiers and driven south. They sat crammed and terrified amid rocket launchers and ammunition, watched by armed Taliban guards. As bombs exploded around them, they sang, prayed and read aloud from the Bible. Just outside of the city limits, their truck, which had joined a caravan of fleeing Taliban tanks and vehicles, stopped by the side of the road. Dayna Curry turned to the turbaned guard next to her and asked in Dari: "Where are we going?"

The guard answered, "Wardak." Wardak was a Taliban village on the road to Kandahar.

Then Danya overheard the driver say: "*Kabul gereft. Kabul gereft.*" (Kabul has been taken.)

A two o'clock in the morning, the truck stopped again on a hill next to several metal shipping containers. The leader of their group, Georg Taubman of Germany, was asked by a group of Taliban officials if he could get a large sum of money from his government to buy their release. Georg explained that none of the hostages' governments knew of their whereabouts. A heavyset Taliban intelligence official promised to bring a satellite phone in the morning so Georg could call.

In the freezing cold, the eight hostages, dressed in light clothes and slip-on sandals, were led at gunpoint into a twelve-foot-deep shipping container where they huddled together for warmth. One of the American hostages, Heather Mercer, refused to go inside. She was afraid that the Taliban would lock them in and either leave them to freeze to death or blow up the shipping container. When the angry guards threatened to shoot her on the spot, she went inside.

It was too bitterly cold to sleep, so she huddled against a wall of the metal container and prayed. "God, what miracle are you going to perform to get us out of this?" she asked.

* Gary Schroen in his CIA-approved book *First In* refers to several meetings between myself (I'm called Gary 2 in the book) and Engineer Aref. He explains that Engineer Aref occupied Kabul on November 14, 2001, and assumed control of the remnants of the previous intelligence organization, renaming it the National Directorate of Security (NDS), which had a department that worked with the CIA up until 2004.

11

KABUL

*"We do not need foreign troops in Afghanistan.
It has been shown that we have the power to tackle
terrorism ourselves."*
—Northern Alliance General Bismullah Khan, November 19, 2001

*　*　*　*　*　*

At 6 A.M. the next morning (November 13) a cold mist hung in the air as two cooks attached to the Kabul guesthouse whipped up scrambled eggs, flat bread and tea. The guesthouse was large and undamaged, so I asked Majid if we could use it long-term.

He said, "That can be arranged."

Ordering Stan and Parker to stay put, the rest of us headed back to Bagram Airbase, passing people leaving their houses for the first time in post-Taliban-controlled Kabul. The years of harsh repression were over. This was truly the first day in the rest of their lives.

A few cars and a thicket of bicycles appeared on the road as the sun started to burn through the gray mist. We passed the boarded-up U.S. Embassy that had been closed for more than a decade. Certain parts of the city lay in ruins.

Working our way along the western perimeter of the Shomali Plains this time, we stopped to quickly inspect military camps that had formally housed Taliban and al-Qaeda soldiers. They were mostly

183

flat-roofed mud structures with room for four to five hundred. We saw Taliban armored personnel carriers cut in half by U.S. bombs and others that had been thrown upside down by near hits.

The valley was huge—at least one hundred square miles—and dangerous. According to one estimate there were eleven million unaccounted-for land mines buried throughout the country, many of them concentrated around Kabul. I figured that it would take twenty or more years to disarm them all. In the meantime, hundreds or even thousands of Afghans would be maimed and killed.

A group of journalists tried to film us as we drove through Bagram's gate with our tinted windows rolled up. George, in my absence, had started putting things in order. A.C. and Marlowe closed up their technical outpost on the western flank. Hamid and others traveling with Bismullah Khan had returned.

We tried to conduct a meeting, but were soon overcome with dust stirred up by the workers ███████ (the General) had hired to clear the buildings. ████████████████████████████████████ ███████████████████████████████ It struck me as highway robbery, but I knew I wasn't likely to find another contractor by looking in the Yellow Pages. Besides, I wasn't planning on sticking around long. Tons of ordinance had been exploded around the airbase in recent years, so the dust we were breathing had to be badly contaminated.

George pulled me aside as we were unloading a truck. "I hope we're not planning to get too comfortable here," he said. "We need to get to those al-Qaeda safehouses in Kabul and see what we can find."

"I agree. But Hank needs a day to calm down the folks back in D.C. first. By tomorrow, I hope to have approval to move the entire Jawbreaker team into Kabul. If not, I'll move half of you guys in, unofficially."

George drawled, "That works for me. I'll talk to Majid and do a map recon of potential sites in the city. I'll also make sure we get the runway cleared of debris so we can start landing fixed-wing aircraft."

George anticipated that humanitarian support, logistical gear, weapons and uniforms would soon be arriving hot and heavy from the U.S. I thought, *What a pleasure to work with such a skilled and thoughtful deputy.*

Afghans and Americans worked together to get the place in order. While hauling gear to the second floor, Andy, the SF Sergeant who had accompanied me into Kabul the night before, unstrapped his shoulder harness and 9mm Beretta pistol and set it on a crate. When he returned minutes later, the Beretta was gone.

We did a search, which turned up nothing. Then Lt. Colonel Chris Haas pulled me aside to tell me that Andy was meticulous about his gear and certainly didn't misplace the pistol.

"Gary, if you can," Chris said, " I really do need that weapon back."

"I'll take care of it," I said with certainty. Then asked: "Has anyone seen Hamid?"

Soon I heard my men calling, "Oh, son of ▮▮▮▮ , your services are required."

Hamid poked his head in and smiled. "How may I be of help?"

I sat him down with Lt. Colonel Haas and explained our dilemma: "We believe that one of the Afghan guards has stolen Andy's Beretta."

Hamid took a deep breath. Over the past week and a half he had gotten to know the guards and learned to appreciate the hardships they went through to put food in the mouths of their families.

In a serious tone Hamid said, "That Beretta's worth a half a year's full salary to these men. Looking at all of us, with all our gear, they think we're all millionaires. You can't tempt them like that."

"Hamid," Lt. Colonel Haas answered just as gravely, "Colonel Mulholland's going to land here tomorrow afternoon and I'm going to have to report this incident. Mulholland could relieve the guy and send him packing. It would be a shame to have that happen because an Afghan picked his pocket, so to speak."

"Give me some time with them," Hamid said. "I'll talk to them as a group."

"If you need to, offer a five-hundred-dollar reward with no questions asked to the man who hands it over," I added.

"Thanks, Chief," Hamid said. "That'll help."

Hamid called a meeting of all twenty Afghan guards and very diplomatically explained the situation. He left them to sort it out among themselves. While he was doing that, Majid told me that his sources in Jalalabad, the largest city in Nangahar province to the east of us and the stronghold of al-Qaeda, were reporting chaos in the city and large numbers of al-Qaeda company-sized units moving about the province.

As the afternoon wore on, ██████████ arrived with cooks and staff, and Hamid met with the guards again. This time he prayed with them. Afterwards several of the more senior Afghans spoke of the importance of trust and how this was a matter of honor. Suspicion fell on two of the most recent recruits—both men of about twenty—who loudly professed their innocence.

After the meeting Hamid brought the two young men to me. Trying not to sound judgmental, I told them that I could understand if they had made a mistake. I said that I blamed no one. I only wanted to save the career of a soldier who had come to fight with them. They still maintained their innocence.

*   *   *

That same morning, the eight SNI hostages were taken from the shipping container by a heavyset Taliban ██████ officer, placed in the back of a van and driven south toward the Taliban stronghold of Kandahar. The four Germans, two Australians and two Americans bolstered one another's spirits with prayers and songs as the van wound through several hamlets and entered the hillside village of Ghazni. As U.S. bombs exploded around them, the hostages were escorted into a dilapidated building that looked like a bombed-out military facility. The Taliban ██████ official told them they were entering a prison. Later, as they sat within the crumbling cement walls in a circle and prayed, they heard loud shooting outside. Looking past the shards of glass that remained in the window, Dayna Curry saw their Taliban guards running toward the center of town.

As the hostages continued to pray, everything turned silent. Then they heard someone pounding on the front door of the prison, followed by hurried footsteps reverberating up the stairs. They huddled together in terror. Suddenly, the door flung open and a scruffy man with wild hair, rounds of ammunition strapped around his chest and guns in both hands stared at them panting. "Hello," he blurted out in English. Then in Farsi, "*Aazaad! Aazaad!*" (You're free! You're free!) "*Taliban raft.*" (The Taliban have left.)

*   *   *

It was a cold, windy night. We worked until midnight with the plastic that Todd had fixed to the windows flapping in the breeze, then slept in sleeping bags on pads lined along the concrete floor. Those who had to use the latrine we had dug thirty meters away made sure to walk carefully along a designated path so they didn't step on a land mine and get blown to bits.

The next morning, Andy's Beretta had still not been found. Special Forces 5th Group commander Colonel Mulholland was scheduled to arrive at noon. Hamid, at my instruction, upped the reward to $1,000 and said that whoever recovered the weapon would be assigned as the personal driver and bodyguard to Agha Gary, the Chief, for the duration of his stay in Afghanistan.

At 11:30 A.M. I was in commo reading intel traffic when I heard a commotion below. Looking out the window, I saw men fighting in an area where some of the vehicles were parked. Majid was in the middle of it beating one of his men.

Running downstairs, I helped my men pull the Afghans apart. One of the Afghans held the Beretta in the air and screamed in Dari: "I have it! I have it!" The man who'd been beaten wore full combat gear and appeared to be in his mid-twenties.

Gasping for breath, Majid explained: " I asked two of my men to get in this jeep and escort me to a meeting. As one of the soldiers bent down to get in, the other soldier spotted a metal object sticking out of the back of the first soldier's belt. The second soldier pulled the man's shirt up and removed the weapon. That's when we started to beat the thief."

The alleged thief was pinned now against the wall by Davis, an SF soldier and Hamid. The Afghan who had seized the pistol proudly handed it to Lt. Colonel Haas.

Majid walked over to me, and pointing at the alleged thief, said harshly, "I want him! I want him now!"

"Hold on a minute," I answered. "First, let me see the man who found the weapon and the two soldiers who were falsely accused."

Majid barked orders and within thirty seconds the men stood in front of me, no more than six feet away from where the thief was still pinned to the wall. I handed the man who found the weapon five hundred dollars, and the two men falsely accused two fifty each. "Is that fair?" I asked in Farsi.

"*Baleh*," was their answer. Yes.

Then the thief who was shaking and covered with sweat spoke up. "You said I could be your driver," he pleaded in Dari.

"I said whoever turned in the weapon could be my driver," I answered in Farsi. "You had plenty of chances to surrender it and did not."

"He'll go to jail," Majid said ominously.

I was trying to buy time so tempers would cool. But Majid was in a hurry to mete out punishment. "He's ours, Gary," he said. "He shamed us in front of you. We have little property, almost no resources and even less money. What we do have is our honor as soldiers. He has none."

"Take him," I said.

Hamid looked crestfallen. He had gotten to know the Afghans and felt sorry for the young man. "They might kill him," he warned.

"We're not the Red Cross," I answered. As much as I appreciated

Hamid's concern, I knew we needed to move on. "We have a city to get into," I told him. "We have al-Qaeda safehouses to search and bin Laden to find."

*　*　*

At 2 P.M. I called Hank at CTC/■■ and said, "We need to set up in Kabul, not here."

"Proceed," he ordered. "And I'll work it out on this end."

He also informed me that General Gary Harrell, who led the famous *Black Hawk Down* rescue in Somalia, would be arriving in a few days to take over the humanitarian support mission.

By noon the next day we were on our way south in two huge trucks and a dozen four-wheel-drive vehicles. No sooner had we arrived at the guesthouse, than I was confronted by two Afghans in their mid-forties with beards worn Taliban-style to their waists. They identified themselves as "government managers" and said that they had been running the facility for the past five years.

With Majid's assistant, Hafiz, and Hamid by my side, I said to Hamid in English, "Call the senior Afghan guard."

When the guard arrived, I told Hamid, "Tell these men two things. One, I am firing them as of this moment. Two, if they ever return to this guesthouse, I'll have them shot."

Hamid's eyes opened so wide I thought they were going to fall out. "But, Chief," he said.

I explained, "We can't afford to have anyone affiliated with the Taliban bringing in explosives or poisoning our food. ■■■■■■■ alone will handle the cooks and housekeeping staff. Tell the chief guard that I want these men escorted to retrieve their personal items, then instructed never, repeat never, to return again. You understand?"

"Yes." Hamid nodded and translated my instructions into Dari. When he got to the part about shooting the pair, the lead Northern Alliance guard leveled his weapon at their heads.

I said to the guard in Farsi, "Let them leave today in peace." Then turning to Hafiz, added, "You're the manager of this facility. Work closely with the chief of the guards."

"*Baleh Agha.*" (Yes, sir.)

Then Davis and I toured the facility. The guesthouse itself contained at least thirty rooms. I designated the back of the second floor for our work area. Two outer buildings would house the Afghan guards.

The whole compound was surrounded by a seven-foot wall and gated entrance, but the dining room side of the building was close to the street. Against the rear wall fifty meters back stood a three-story abandoned building that could serve as a great place to attack us with rockets.

Davis had a recommendation: "We might want to have some steel connex shipping containers stacked across the back lot which would absorb incoming RPG rounds."

"Talk to Majid and see what you can do."

Until headquarters dispatched a security team to reinforce our position, I would use the guards creatively to patrol our perimeter. The important thing was to press forward aggressively and not let security slow us down.

By 2100 hours Todd had the commo up, so I called Hank on the STU-111 secure phone.

"We've launched a team of ▌▌▌▌ officers your way," he announced. "They'll be followed by Billy Waugh and Hoss."

Revealing my ignorance, I asked: "▌▌▌▌ officers, what's that?"

▌▌▌▌▌▌▌▌▌. They should arrive at Bagram tomorrow. Use Billy Waugh and Hoss however you like."

Billy Waugh was a legend in Washington. Now seventy-two years old he had spent his career in Special Forces and was currently in CIA ▌▌▌▌ paramilitary. At fifteen he'd tried to sign up with the Marine Corps to fight in World War II, lying his way past the recruiter only to be found out when he reported to Camp Pendleton. Two years later he joined the Army, fought in the Korean War and completed six tours of combat in Vietnam. After thirty years service, he retired and came to work for us. ███████████████████

███████████████████ Billy Waugh's book *Hunting the Jackal* features surveillance photos he took of Carlos the Jackal that led to the Jackal's arrest in Khartoum, Sudan.

Hoss was a Navy Seal Lt. Commander detailed to CTC who had traveled with me to Dar es Salaam as part of the EDT.

Hank had more. "Gary, we have a Special Forces Colonel Alexander detailed to Special Activities Division who has been working on a special project for us together with a full SF team. I'm sending all of them at you as well. We're going to need to train indigenous terrorist pursuit teams and these are the guys to do it."

I liked keeping Jawbreaker at a manageable size. The last thing I wanted was idle bodies getting themselves into trouble. I said, "Hank, I'm not sure I need another SF team."

"Trust me, Gary," he countered. "Your mission is going to expand at a rate that you have yet to comprehend. I have complete faith you'll find gainful employment for everyone."

I knew better than to argue with my biggest supporter, an incredible leader and a man who thought three-dimensionally. "Okay, send them my way."

"Gary, don't let up."

"We're just getting started," I told him. "Jawbreaker, out."

I looked up from the phone to see Davis and Hamid standing in front of me with AK-47s slung across their shoulders.

"We're going out to do two ops meetings," Davis said. ████████
██
██ "The second meeting is with the ███████████ commander we've been talking to."

"Be careful," I warned them. "There are lots of NA checkpoints around the city and not many people on the streets. Do you want another vehicle with armed security?"

"They'll just raise our profile," Davis responded. "If we get stopped or harassed, Hamid will talk us through."

Hamid smiled. "Yeah, right."

"Proceed and take a radio," I said.

I invited George and Stan to join me in the room I had taken at the front of the building to talk about al-Qaeda safehouses and training facilities. The room was small but luxurious by wartime standards with a single bed, sofa and two chairs.

Stan reported that Majid had provided him with a list of five al-Qaeda locations in the city and promised more by morning. As George started to speak, the electricity went out. Soon a houseboy arrived with a kerosene lantern.

George suggested that Stan lead the initial search of the al-Qaeda facilities for intelligence and evidence of labs for producing toxins. In the lantern-lit room, we worked out the sequence of searches, which I told them would be taken over by the ▮▮▮▮▮ team when they arrived.

After dismissing Stan and George, I continued one-on-one with Lt. Colonel Chris Haas. He said, "I think it's important to move my intel and admin components into the city with you so we can continue to be connected."

"I completely agree. I'll have my commo officer make all our message traffic available to you so we don't cross wires. But since you guys are not fully cleared and polygraphed, Washington will never approve. So don't say anything."

"If it's okay I'll have my eight-man team and Triple Nickel all living with you here."

I remembered Colonel Alexander's Special Activities Division SF team that was also arriving and said, "If there comes a day when we need more space, I'll rent you your own facility somewhere in town."

"Only if you can pay," Haas countered. "Getting money out of the Army for this sort of thing would be a lot more complicated than your just handing me the cash."

*   *   *

That afternoon the eight SNI hostages were told by a group of scruffy armed men that it was safe for them to leave the Ghazni prison. They followed the fighters, ducking gunfire and praying to Jesus. Entering the town bazaar they were greeted by celebrating men, women and children shouting, "The Taliban left! We're free!"

As the townspeople rejoiced and wished them well, Tennesse-born-and-bred Dayna Curry thanked God for letting her be part of this new day for the people of Afghanistan. She later learned from an English-speaking businessman that they had entered Ghazni at roughly the same time that two hundred al-Qaeda fighters retreated south.

That night the former hostages rested comfortably in the house of an ex-Taliban official as their leader Georg searched for a satellite phone so he could contact their embassies in Islamabad, Pakistan.

*   *   *

Three large tables of Jawbreaker and SF team members sat together for breakfast the next morning and cracked bad jokes. As the sun shone in the windows and we chowed on fried eggs, steak strips, flat bread, yogurt, honey, coffee and tea. Then Stan and a group of SF soldiers grabbed their gear and left with a contingent of Afghan guards.

I went upstairs to the work area where I overheard part of Team Delta in Bamian province communicating with headquarters over our radio net. I recognized the voice of a young SAD paramilitary officer named Klesko who was on his first deployment. It seems that Team Delta had split in two. The team leader had positioned himself with Hazara commander Dr. Karim Khalili inside the city of Bamian, while Klesko, a Farsi-speaking case officer, and three military detailees remained south of Khalili's position waiting to be resupplied. They were now in urgent need of additional radios, vehicles and MREs.

As I listened, headquarters explained that they would have to wait for the next available resupply flight, which could take more than a week. I checked a large map of Afghanistan on the wall and saw that they were 250 miles west of Kabul.

"Team Delta, Jawbreaker has all the items that you need," I said on the radio. "There's a road network that will make overland travel into Kabul possible, but be on the lookout for Taliban and al-Qaeda units fleeing south."

"Roger that, team Jawbreaker. We'll get permission from our team leader and meet you in Kabul for resupply."

As the transmission ended, Lt. Colonel Haas entered the work area. "We just cut the front door open to the U.S. Embassy and checked it for booby traps," he said. "It looks secure. I was wondering if you'd like to do a walk-through with me."

The Embassy was five minutes away. The large, unattractive concrete-and-stone building sat inside a large compound surrounded by high walls. Even though the windows and doors were boarded up, it looked largely intact. Before 9/11/01, the Taliban had hoped to negotiate a political rapprochement with the U.S.

A close friend of mine had served as a military officer in Kabul during the early 1980s when the Soviets controlled the city. He told me that back then a young Russian soldier jumped the fence of the U.S. Embassy and sought refuge inside. The Soviets responded by surrounding the building with tanks and cutting off telephones, power and water. After a several-week standoff, the Russian soldier surrendered himself to the Soviet Army.

Davis, Lt. Colonel Haas and I climbed concrete steps past the United States seal, which had remained untouched for fourteen years. Entering the lobby was like entering a time warp. Our flashlights illuminated President Ronald Reagan's official photo beside Vice President George H. W. Bush. On a reception desk off the main lobby I spotted the first rotary-style telephone I'd seen in years.

Upstairs we saw evidence of vandalism, but most of the furniture was intact. We moved carefully in case the SF soldiers who initially searched the building had missed a booby trap.

On the floor of the Ambassador's office lay broken framed photos of President Jimmy Carter and former Secretary of State Cyrus Vance at an outdoor ceremony that looked like a funeral. Both men wore black suits. Another picture showed a casket lying in state guarded by servicemen in dress blues.

I realized that I was looking at the funeral of U.S. Ambassador Adolph Dubbs, who had died in Kabul in 1979 after being kidnapped by terrorists and shot in a hotel room during a botched rescue attempt.

For some reason, I said out loud, "Top hats and tails."

"Excuse me, sir. What did you say?" asked one of the SF soldiers with Lt. Colonel Chris Haas.

I remembered hearing Senator Phil George of Texas utter that phrase, "top hats and tails," to imply that U.S. diplomats spent all their times at cocktail parties living the high life. It always struck me as a disgraceful thing to say. The truth is that Foreign Service officers serve bravely all over the world, sometimes at tremendous risk to themselves and their families.

I turned to the soldier and said, "I'm sorry. I was just thinking out loud." Then, I picked up the photo and tucked it under my arm.

Inside the Defense Attaché's office on a side table sat a huge collection of maps. One of the soldiers said, "These could be useful, sir. Is it all right if we take a few?"

"Gentleman," I answered, "take whatever you need. There isn't a single citizen of our country who would begrudge you guys anything to help you do your missions."

Lt. Colonel Chris Haas smiled at me and said: "Good point."

The soldier wrapped his arms around the stack of two hundred maps and took the whole lot.

We worked our way downstairs and into an area that held the ██████████████ . In fourteen years, no one had tried to use a torch to cut through. On the front steps we paused to take some photos, then climbed back into the trucks. It was a sobering visit that reminded me of our own precarious position in a country where political fortunes changed fast.

*   *   *

Back at the guesthouse, I asked Storm from SAD and Amir to meet with me in my room. "Given the fact that the city collapsed so precipitously, the Northern Alliance must have taken a number of prisoners," I began. "I need you to talk to Majid and have his people escort you to the prisons where I have a feeling you'll find Arabs and other foreigners affiliated with al-Qaeda. Somewhere among them is information about the next planned attack against our country. Storm, you handle security and target selection. Amir, you do the talking. It's critical that we begin now."

"The information is out there," Storm responded. "We'll find it."

Amir nodded and added: "Let's go find Majid."

[*NOTE TO READER:* This redacted section deals with the arrival of individuals tasked with inspecting al-Qaeda sites.]

Later that evening, after the electricity went out, George, Davis, Storm and I sat around two kerosene lamps to review two separate reports that Majid had received saying that Osama bin Laden had been seen fleeing the Kabul area toward Nangahar province and the city of Jalalabad in the East.

I said, "Strap your seat belts on. It's time to get back on the offensive."

All three men were chomping at the bit. "Gentleman," I continued, "we need to create two forward deployments, one into Jalalabad to the east and one into Lowgar province directly south. These are areas where al-Qaeda has trained and operated for the past decade. It's time to pay them a visit with boots on the ground. George, you're going to lead the team that is going into very unfriendly Jalal-abad."

The tall Texan sat up. "Now I know you'd rather stay here in Kabul and handle admin details like a good deputy," I continued, "but since you did such a good job getting the Afghans to stop five miles outside the capital, I'm going to throw you back into the fray."

We all laughed.

"It's a punishment I gladly accept," George responded.

"Davis, since you're constantly bitching at Hamid, I've decided to select you to lead the team into Lowgar province. This is the Pushtun heartland where we're hated and known as infidels. I know you'll enjoy it. By the way, Hamid is going with you along with Storm from SAD to keep an eye on you both."

Davis, the blond-haired former Marine, smiled.

"I remember that Diane back at headquarters told me about a war-lord from the small Pashai tribe who is affiliated with the Northern Alliance by the name of Babrak," I continued. "He held a valley at the northern tip of Nangahar province for the five years under Taliban rule. They couldn't force him out. I'm meeting with Engineer Aref* tonight and I'm going to ask him if he can track Babrak down to work with George."

"Sounds like our kind of guy," George drawled.

"Davis, your situation is going to be a bit more complicated because the Northern Alliance doesn't want to go south. So you need to ask our ▮▮▮▮▮▮ commander contact if he will lend us, or ▮▮▮▮▮▮ us, a force of two hundred that can penetrate south and initiate contacts with southern tribal leaders."

"The ▮▮▮▮▮▮ are not from the South," Davis shot back.

"I know that," I countered. ▮▮▮▮▮▮▮▮▮▮▮▮▮▮▮▮

▮▮▮▮▮▮▮▮▮▮▮▮▮▮▮▮▮▮▮▮▮▮▮▮▮▮▮▮▮▮▮▮▮▮

▮▮▮▮▮▮▮▮▮▮▮▮▮▮▮▮▮▮

I turned to Storm. ▮▮▮▮▮▮▮▮▮▮▮▮▮▮▮▮

[*NOTE TO READER:* The redacted sections above cover discussions of resources and strategy.]

"I'll take care of it," Storm said.

* * *

As I spoke, the eight SNI hostages stood waiting on an old abandoned airstrip outside Ghazni. Georg, their leader, was communicating with U.S. officials in Islamabad, when the battery on the satellite phone he had borrowed died. In the pitch-black night, the two Americans, four Germans and two Australians heard two enormous helicopters approach, circle the field and leave. The copters did this twice. The next sound they heard were dogs barking and the voice of a local militia commander who told them to leave. He shouted: "This is too dangerous! You'll all be killed!" The town of Ghanzi, he explained, was expecting a Taliban counterattack that night.

The helicopters approached and retreated one more time. That's when Georg told his fellow SNI members that it was probably safer for them to return to the city. But the two Americans—Heather Mercer and Dayna Curry—were determined to stay. Heather found some matches and set fire to her scarf. Dayna added hers and others. The local militia commander and some of his soldiers helped, adding planks of wood and blankets. Minutes later the helicopters circled closer to the ground than before and left again.

Twenty minutes passed before several huge shapes emerged from the shadows looking like Martians and covered with gear. A man asked: "Do you speak English?"

Dayna Curry shouted: "Don't shoot! Don't shoot!"

The eight SNI hostages were quickly helped aboard a MH-47 Chinook helicopter, which took off east towards Pakistan. Tacked on the ceiling was an American flag. "It was a beautiful flag," Heather Mercer wrote later.

Over the roar of the engine, one of the Delta Force soldiers said: "I want you to know that my family and I have been praying for you since the first day you were taken captive."

*   *   *

It was past midnight when I sat down with Engineer Aref and Majid, who had taken a room at the guesthouse. They both seemed relaxed. From their standpoint, they had accomplished more than they ever dreamed of by taking Kabul. They had no desire to engage the Pushtuns in the South. They looked at me with a bemused expression, as if to say: What does this crazy American want from us now?

First, I asked for a group of soldiers to escort the ███████ team into Gardez, which they agreed to provide. Then, I asked for their help in identifying a commander we could work with in the East. They both thought that Babrak was a good choice and agreed to contact him.

The following morning, the members of Team Delta who had been deployed in Bamian arrived in a blue van that looked like it had once belonged to the Partridge family. With them was a young Hazara leader who spoke English, which he claimed improved during the last four years he had spent in a Taliban prison. Outside of the city, Team Delta had stopped so that the young Hazara could ask directions since he hadn't been in the city since he was a boy. First, the young Hazara was verbally assaulted by four Tajik Northern Alliance soldiers, then physically attacked. When the Americans stepped in with guns ready, the Tajiks backed off. They explained to the angry American that they had simply been beating a slanty-eyed Shia Hazara. Clearly this was a country where tribal hatreds ran deep.

I reported the incident to Majid, who tracked down the culprits and offered to have the offending soldiers beaten while the young Hazara watched. He asked only that the offending soldiers be told that Hazaras are human, too, and that they have families and children and a desire to improve their country. I was impressed.

With that out of the way, the members of Team Delta from Bamian province sat down to brief me. They said that Special Forces Team ODA 553 had entered Bamian on October 31. After linking up with Dr. Khalili's forces on November 10, they hammered the Taliban with air strikes. Within two days the battle was over and the Taliban withdrew. "The Army SF team did outstanding work," one of them said.

"But there's something else," SAD officer Klesko continued. "We've had terrible disagreements with our team leader. His view is that we're only here to collect intelligence. We believe we're here to kill the enemy. Who's right?"

"Both of you."

"We almost came to blows with him," Klesko explained. "We've been following you on the radio and love the fact that you and your men are taking it to the Taliban and al-Qaeda."

"I thought 11 September taught us all a lesson, but I guess some people still don't get it," I said. I could see right away that these were highly trained, smart men with double type-A personalities.

"With your approval we'd like to stay here a week or so to plan some operations and execute them," Klesko added. "Specifically, we have a contact who's communicating with Taliban ██████████ . We want to arrange a meeting with him. He can either agree to help us capture bin Laden or be taken into custody."

I smiled and said, "I like the fact that you guys are thinking big. I'd love to have a face-to-face discussion with ████████ if you guys can arrange it. Davis on my team is handling the high-value targets. He's a stud and will help you. Just keep him up to speed."

They looked pleased.

No sooner did I leave my room to go downstairs to read the incoming message traffic, when one of the guards told me in Dari that two British men were at the gate asking for Agha Gary.

I walked out with him hoping that they weren't members of the press. ██
██

████████████████████████████████

████████████████████████████████

███████████████████

Returning to the work area, I read a message from Islamabad ████████ reporting that the eight SNI hostages had been successfully rescued and were now reuniting with their families in Pakistan. The Special Operations Forces rescue team had flown in three MH-47 Chinook helicopters off U.S. ships in the Arabian Sea in a mission that had taken eighteen hours to complete. I shattered the relative quiet of the work area with a loud, heartfelt: "Thank God!!!"

12

TEAM JULIET

"War is too serious a thing to be left to the military."
—*Charles-Maurice de Tallyrand-Périgord*

★   ★   ★   ★   ★   ★

Our base of operations in the Kabul guesthouse was electric with activity as events broke fast all over southern and eastern Afghanistan. The bubble of Taliban control over the capital had burst and I was determined to take advantage of the resulting Taliban and al-Qaeda retreat.

On the fourteenth of November four Blackhawk helicopters dropped another ████████ Agency team, Echo, and Special Forces ODA 574 outside of the village of Tarin Kowt to hook up with Pushtun leader Hamid Karzai. Tarin Kowt was twenty-five miles east of the ancestral home of Taliban's one-eyed religious leader Mullah Omar and seventy miles north of the Taliban's religious capital, Kandahar. The Taliban vowed to hunt down Karzai and kill him because they viewed the fellow Pushtun as a potential threat to their political legitimacy in the Pushtun-dominated south.

At midday on the sixteenth, two hours before they were scheduled to land, I learned that one hundred–plus British forces were arriving at Bagram to encamp in a half-destroyed hangar several hundred meters north of our previous position. They were met by Brigadier General Gary Harrell, who arrived a day earlier to manage the huge humanitarian relief effort that was needed to house and feed thousands of Afghan refugees.

General Harrell shot up to Kabul a day after his arrival for a one-on-one. A huge, clean-shaven man in his forties, he was said to bench press four hundred pounds. He was determined to get supplies to the population before the outbreak of winter. The Northern Alliance was thrilled to see him. But they didn't feel the same about the British who had a long history of involvement in Afghanistan and had arrived unannounced. I sent a message to General Fahim through Majid and Engineer Aref: "The British are our closest ally and they're here to help."

That's when the STU-111 phone rang. It was someone by the name of Phillip who said, "I'm going secure."

Phillip, who was calling from somewhere in Europe, was from the ▮▮▮▮▮▮▮▮▮▮ and a specialist in South Asia. He said, "I've just been assigned to Jim Dobbins staff, who has just been named as Special Representative for Afghanistan."

"This is the first time I'm hearing about this," I answered.

"Dobbins is going to be the point man for the U.S. Government in directing the process which will hopefully create an interim governing authority and eventually a government in Kabul," Phillip said.

I knew Jim Dobbins's reputation. He was a no-nonsense diplomat who'd been called in to resolve the crises in Kosovo and Haiti. I remembered hearing that he'd clashed swords with Senator Jesse Helms of the Foreign Relations Committee over Haiti, and Helms had sworn to block Dobbins's approval should he ever be nominated ambassador.

Phillip said, "Dobbins would like you to bring the Northern Alliance Foreign Minister Dr. Abdullah Abdullah up to Uzbekistan for talks."

"Gee, Phil, I happen to be a little busy at the moment," I quipped.

"I know," he countered. "But this is extremely important. We've got to get moving now to help them set up the next government."

I said, "I'll raise it with Fahim when I see him tonight."

"Thanks, Gary," Phillip replied. "And call me when you're done. We need to get Abdullah Abdullah out soon. Dobbins needs to move quickly."

"I'll do my best. Jawbreaker, out."

I humped down the corridor to Majid's room where he was writing something at a desk. I told him about Dobbins and the need to talk to Abdullah Abdullah about traveling to Uzbekistan with General Fahim.

"I'll try to arrange it," he said.

Downstairs I grabbed up a cup of tea. Exiting the dining room I ran into Lt. Colonel Chris Haas. "What about the security escort that the ███████ team needs to travel south to Gardez?" I asked.

"I checked with Colonel Mulholland and the answer is 'negative,'" Colonel Haas answered shaking his head. "Too many bad guys running around the area. He says it's not even close to being secure enough."

I felt myself tense up, then remembered that it wasn't Lt. Colonel Haas's call. Colonel John Mulholland was now the senior Special Forces officer in-country. I said, "We'll put Gardez at the bottom of the list of sites and check back with you in a couple days."

*   *   *

Our efforts to interview al-Qaeda prisoners had been frustrating as hell. Night after night, Storm, Amir, and others were told by our Northern Alliance counterparts that they could interview Arab prisoners only to have those meetings canceled at the last minute. Finally on the fourth night Amir and Storm were instructed to go to a badly lit school building in a bombed-out section of Kabul. After having automatic weapons stuck in their faces and questioned by guards, they were granted permission to enter. The building was ice cold with few lights, few intact windows and water dripping from the ceiling. Amir couldn't determine if the source of the water was melting snow, rain or a broken pipe.

The first prisoner brought to them was a short, pudgy Saudi in his early twenties. He told Amir in Arabic that he was from the South of Saudi Arabia near the Yemeni border and thought that Amir was an official who'd come to take him home. It was clear that the young man had only the most primitive education. As they spoke, guards with long wooden and metal poles entered periodically to check on the prisoner. Amir asked him if he'd been abused.

"No," he said, "but there is another Arab here who needs medical care."

When Amir asked what the young man was doing in Afghanistan, he said, "I was working for a charitable foundation helping poor Afghans when the war broke out. I was trapped."

Both Storm and Amir doubted that this was true.

The next prisoner they interviewed was another uneducated Saudi in his early twenties who had been badly wounded by a U.S. bomb a week before. He lifted the blanket covering his shoulder to reveal a wound the size of a baseball that was so deep Amir could see the bones of the young man's shoulder blade. Both Storm and Amir were amazed he was still conscious. The young Saudi also claimed that he had come to Afghanistan to do charitable work for an unnamed foundation.*

*   *   *

[*NOTE TO READER:* The redacted section above refers to the intelligence-gathering activities of my team.]

*The previous section is based on interviews conducted by Ralph Pezzullo.

As soon as ▮▮▮▮▮▮▮▮ (we) reported that al-Qaeda fighters had fled Kabul east toward Jalalabad and south into Lowgar province, CENTCOM started pounding those sectors. On the sixteenth we got word through the Northern Alliance that al-Qaeda's military commander, Mohammed Atef, had died in an air strike outside Gardez. Atef, the number-three man in al-Qaeda after bin Laden and Ayman al-Zawahiri, had planned the attacks on our embassies in Nairobi and Tanzania in '98. A former Egyptian police officer, Atef had traveled to Somalia in 1992 and 1993 to train clans opposing U.S. forces. He assumed military command of al-Qaeda in May 1996 after the death of Abu Ubaidah Al-Banshiri during a ferry accident on Lake Victoria.

Davis, who was handling high-value targets, had one of his Afghan sources inside the Taliban confirm Mohammed Atef's death. Davis also informed me that al-Zawahiri's wife had been moved from the hospital that we were watching. Zawahiri and other al-Qaeda leaders had stopped driving in Toyota truck convoys since many of them had been the targets of Predator attacks. They were now said to be moving alone in taxis, which made identifying them with a Predator almost impossible.

*   *   *

Stan and his team were back from their initial inspection of al-Qaeda safehouses and wanted to talk. We met alone in my room, where they told me ▮▮▮▮▮▮▮▮▮▮▮▮▮▮▮▮▮▮▮▮▮▮▮▮▮▮ they found a false-documents facility and ▮▮▮▮▮▮▮▮▮▮▮▮▮▮▮▮▮▮▮▮ ▮▮▮▮▮▮▮▮▮▮▮▮▮▮▮▮▮▮▮▮▮▮▮▮▮▮▮▮ ▮▮▮▮▮▮▮▮▮▮▮▮▮

Also recovered were an array of U.S. military manuals, which described infantry tactics, patrolling and survival skills. Other manuals written in Arabic outlined the step-by-step construction of booby traps and improvised explosive devices. Nelson—an African-American officer with the bodybuilder's physique who had just arrived—said, "Chief, what we found is that al-Qaeda appears to have run a university system of terrorism. In one building nonnative speakers would be given a course in Arabic. In another, recruits were given basic instruction in algebra and chemistry. At another facility, they learned more advanced chemistry, including formulas for making basic poisons. They were also taught basic natural science, physics and an advanced course in improvised explosive devices. Using this system over several years al-Qaeda could have trained thousands of terrorists."

I said, "Gentlemen, good work. Turn over what you have to Marlowe and A.C. who will send it back to headquarters for analysis. And get back to checking al-Qaeda sites."

"Yes, sir!"

*　　*　　*

Storm and Amir returned from the schoolhouse prison to report on their interviews with Arab and Pakistani prisoners, ███████████

███
███
███
████████████████████████████

"What kind of bullshit answer is that?" I said strongly. "I'm supposed to believe that these morons arrived here in the middle of a U.S. bombing campaign to do business? Come on!"

Amir adjusted his round wire-frame glasses and wiped his head. "I didn't say I believed them," he explained.

"Good." I called the whole team together and said, "We're in Afghanistan, not a U.S. court of law. There will be no presumption of innocence until proven guilty here. If we encounter Arabs, Chechens, Chinese Wiegars, Muslims from Burma or non-Afghans, they're not businessmen or aid workers. They're the enemy until proven otherwise, and the burden of proof is on them."

Amir spoke up. "Some of the people in prison are in need of medical attention or they might die. I would like your permission to bring our medic to help them."

I took a deep breath as I pondered his request to divert the unit's medic. "We're a small team," I said. "We have to do everything quick as we hunt bin Laden and al-Qaeda. Go ahead and provide medical aid to these pieces of crap that came here to fight America. But remember, we're not Amnesty International."

"The Arab prisoners are all scared to death now that they're under the control of the Afghans," Amir added. "If they have something important to trade for their lives, they will."

Storm spoke up: "███████████████████████████████████
████████████. Having our medic treat them will help. Give us a few days and we'll get results."

"Do it," I said. "I don't have a lick of sympathy for the Arab and Pakistani prisoners captured by the Northern Alliance. I would bet money that ninety-nine percent of them would have gladly tortured and killed us if the shoe were on the other foot."

It was closing in on 1900 hours, so I hurried down the hall to Majid's room.

"Time to see General Fahim and Dr. Abdullah Abdullah," I announced.

Without saying a word he stood up and grabbed his coat. Downstairs in the parking lot two vehicles staffed with armed guards waited. The streets of Kabul were dark and empty. Northern Alliance armed guards monitoring major intersections and checking documents waved us through.

Engineer Aref had taken over Taliban intel chief Qari Amadullah's headquarters, which I had visited my first night in Kabul. For Aref, it was a homecoming of sorts. This had been his headquarters in the early '90s before the Taliban drove the Tajiks out of Kabul.

We entered the same large office where General Fahim, Aref and Dr. Abdullah Abdullah were already seated. They rose and shook my hand, then an Afghan man in his fifties served tea.

"If you have no objection," I started, "I will do this in English and

Majid can translate for General Fahim." I knew that Aref and the Foreign Minister spoke fluent English.

General Fahim nodded his approval. I told them of President Bush's appointment of Special Representative James Dobbins, who would work with them and other Afghan opposition groups to form a government.

Dr. Abdullah Abdullah said, "We're aware of his selection."

"Excellent. Special Representative Dobbins would like to meet with you, Mr. Foreign Minister, immediately in Uzbekistan."

"This is a very difficult and complicated time for us," Abdullah Abdullah responded. "It's not the best time." Fahim and Aref said nothing.

I leaned forward and looked Abdullah in the eye. "Mr. Foreign Minister, you must go. With the death of Massoud you're now the sole Afghan political figure known to the outside world. I'll be honest. The political leadership in Washington is comfortable with you, because they know you understand that this is a critical moment in your country's history. If you refuse to meet with Special Representative Dobbins, you're turning down a request made by my president."

General Fahim spoke gruffly and avoided eye contact: "Our helicopters are busy. It could take a few days to work out transportation."

"I'll arrange the transportation," I said.

I sensed another political issue running through their heads. Maybe Fahim wanted to send someone other than Abdullah Abdullah. It could be that they wanted to maximize their position within the Afghan opposition before meeting with Dobbins.

Without responding to my invitation, Abdullah Abdullah asked: "Why have British forces arrived without our permission?"

I took a deep breath. "Mr. Foreign Minister," I answered, "the British are our allies and have come to provide security at Bagram and to assist with the humanitarian relief effort."

His arms cut through the air sharply as he spoke. "How can they provide security when they haven't been asked to come?" he asked. "This is a violation of our sovereignty. If we are not to be a sovereign nation I should resign. We would prefer that they leave."

The threat to resign struck me as overly dramatic. "Please," I said, trying my best to be diplomatic, "the British are an important part of our coalition. It was clearly a mistake on their part not to communicate through proper channels, but their participation as coalition members is critical to our success."

The Foreign Minister wasn't backing down. "You have communicated every detail of your deployments and operations with our people. Why have they not done the same?" he asked.

"Sir, I can't answer that question. I can only ask that you accept their early arrival as an honest error made with the best of intentions. They are here to help you and the Afghan people."

That's when Engineer Aref entered the discussion for the first time. He said, "Gary, we're concerned about the situation in Konduz. As many as fifteen thousand Taliban and foreign fighters have flooded the city from Mazar-e Sharif and Taloqan, breaking into houses and taking people hostage. General Dostum has surrounded the city with his men, but even though we're allied with Dostum, we can't control him. If the negotiations between Dostum and those holding the city fail, there could be a tragedy of enormous proportions up there."

I said, "We're aware of this and have a team with Dostum outside of Konduz. From our perspective, we would ask that General Fahim maintain regular communications with General Dostum and keep us advised of any possible problems or factors on the ground that you believe are significant."

"I'm speaking regularly with Dostum," Fahim said.

I sensed that the critical moment had come, so I turned to him and said: "General Fahim, when this meeting is over I have to call Special Representative Dobbins and give him your reply. Will Dr. Abdullah Abdullah travel to meet Special Representative Dobbins or not?"

General Fahim didn't hesitate. "He'll be prepared to travel with you in two days." Abdullah Abdullah sat motionless and betrayed no emotion.

"Thank you," I said. "I'm sure that President Bush will be pleased."

███

███

███

██████████

[*NOTE TO READER:* This redacted section concerns a discussion of strategy in the South.]

*   *   *

That same night, Storm and Amir returned with the Special Forces medic to the schoolhouse prison. As the medic treated the wounded Saudi, Amir continued to interrogate other Arab prisoners. For the most part, they fit the same profile: poor, uneducated, seemingly clueless young men—the kind you might find in the States joining a street gang for some sense of identity.

They parroted the same stock answers: They had come to Afghanistan recently for the purpose of doing business or working for a charitable organization and had been trapped by the outbreak of fighting. They didn't believe Amir and others when they told them that Muslims and Muslim Americans had died in the World Trade Center attacks.*

*   *   *

At approximately 1100 hours the next morning Colonel Alexander stepped off an unmarked aircraft at Bagram. He was a Special Forces Colonel detailed to the Agency who'd been working out of CIA Special Activites Division for the past two years. He'd also been part of multiple plans to capture bin Laden during 1999 and 2000, all of which had been canceled at the last minute.

*This section is based on interviews conducted by Ralph Pezzullo.

He drove straight away to the guesthouse and requested to see me. I stood facing a tall, black-haired man of ███████████ heritage who said, "I've been instructed to create Afghan counterterrorist pursuit teams that will be used to hunt al-Qaeda units as they flee south."

I'd seen the cable traffic and knew that he had an SF team detailed to him to help conduct the training.

"We're going to need bodies who are willing to be trained," he continued, "and a facility in Kabul to use as our base."

"Let me be frank with you, Colonel," I said. "By the time we assemble Afghan teams, get a building and put the infrastructure together, most of your targets will have vanished. There's nothing wrong with the concept of Afghan pursuit teams, but we're going to have to be our own pursuit team if we want to kill a sizable number of al-Qaeda before they flee the country."

"What are you thinking?" he asked.

"It's not what I'm thinking," I answered. "It's what I've done. I've found a ██████████ commander affiliated with the Northern Alliance who's agreed to accept one of my teams. I'm preparing to deploy George and a group of men into Jalalabad to pursue al-Qaeda fighters and leaders who have fled into the East. Once I have done that I'll deploy a team dead south into Lowgar. If we don't take care of this final part ourselves, it won't get done."

"What does headquarters think of your plan?" the Colonel asked.

"They don't know about it yet. After I've put the pieces together, I'll inform Hank."

A cloud came over Colonel Alexander's face.

"Don't worry," I said. "If my plan is aggressive and bold, Hank will approve it. He expects me to create opportunities not wait for orders."

Colonel Alexander said, "My men will arrive in Uzbekistan tomorrow."

"The day after tomorrow I'm traveling up with the Foreign Minister Dr. Abdullah Abdullah to meet with Special Representative Dobbins. You'll fly up with me, accompany me to the meetings and then we'll meet with your men."

"Good."

I said: "I'll try to get you a shot at bin Laden."

"If you can do that, I'll be one grateful guy."

* * *

The following morning, Colonel Alexander and I drove down to Bagram to huddle with General Gary Harrell. The former Commander of Delta Force wanted to talk about coordinating the humanitarian support. He argued strongly for a joint military-Agency team to plan the operations out of Bagram. I suggested instead that he operate belly to belly with me in Kabul, since I was the one generating the intelligence and already in the middle of planning all sorts of operations.

But Harrell had been a big-time player in Special Operations and clearly wanted to expand his humanitarian role into something more. He said that he'd already discussed his idea of setting up a team at Bagram with CTC.

Next, Colonel Alexander and I met with 5th Group Special Forces Commander Colonel John Mulholland. I came right to the point. "John," I said, "I have intel that bin Laden and his men have fled to Jalalabad and plan to give pursuit. I've arranged with the Northern Alliance to insert a team into Jalalabad with a Pashai commander named Babrak. The team is leaving in the next few days and I'd like one of your SF teams paired with mine to provide extra security because Nangahar province is in a state of flux."

"Do you have detailed intel on the security situation in Jalalabad?" Colonel Mullholland asked.

"It's bad. Nobody's really in control and large groups of armed Taliban and al-Qaeda fighters are still creating havoc."

"Do you have a fixed location where you're going to set up?"

"No, I don't. But Babrak is sending some of his people to lead my men in and commence operations. They'll inform me once they get there."

Colonel Mulholland shook his head. "Look, Gary," he started, "I'd like to help, but you want me to send my men in with a commander you haven't yet met or worked with. The situation is chaotic and you have no idea where they're going to set up."

"That's exactly right."

"When do I get briefed on the positive aspects of your plan?" Mulholland asked with a grin.

"This is what I know," I told him, leaning forward and looking him in the eye. "Bin Laden and a large contingent of Arabs have gone east. Another group of al-Qaeda went south. I'm deploying teams to pursue them. I'd prefer that you were with me, but I'm not prepared to wait for security to improve. I'm going now."

"Fine," SF Colonel Mulholland said. "Send your team in. If in a week they're still alive and operating, I'll send a team to work with them. The same thing goes for the team you send south. Are you talking about Lowgar province?"

"Exactly. I'm putting a team south of Gardez."

"Gary," Mulholland explained, "I'm just not prepared to send my men into a place where we don't know the commander, lack significant intelligence and what we do know indicates a high probability that a small force could run into an extremely large force and be overwhelmed."

Colonel Mulholland was no shrinking violet. He was a tough, experienced leader, who was mission-focused and deeply concerned about the welfare of his men. I, too, was concerned about my men. But I knew that if I didn't deploy my teams immediately, critical opportunities would be missed.

*　*　*

The very next day, November 18, Babrak's nineteen-year-old nephew arrived at the guesthouse in Kabul with ten men to lead my team into Jalalabad. They were outfitted in fatigues and armed to the teeth.

We had just received a report that a group of journalists in a convoy of six vehicles had been stopped by a force of Taliban soldiers, marched into the hills and executed. Initial reports indicated that those killed included an Australian cameraman, an Italian correspondent, a Spanish correspondent and an Afghan photographer. Their driver survived by getting on his knees and reciting the Islamic creed. Hours later a bus filled with Afghans was stopped and all the men who had shaved their beards (in violation of Taliban law) had their ears and noses hacked off.

While Babrak's nephew and his young cohorts rested, George and his team loaded their vehicles. George was taking Parker, Yale, A.C., the three JSOC officers and an SF medic.

Team Juliet, as we called it, departed in eight heavily armed vehicles by late afternoon. The road was barely passable in places full of torturous bends, some of which had been practically washed out. Massive boulders clung tenuously to the cliffs above them, threatening to to break loose at any second. The long, arduous drive took seven hours.

While they were on the road I sweated like hell. *Damn, we're taking a big risk*. A band of roving Taliban or al-Qaeda could easily overrun them.

The minutes dragged by until midnight when Majid reported Team Juliet's safe arrival in Jalalabad and I heaved a big sigh of relief.

*   *   *

That same morning, Pushtun leader Hamid Karzai, Team Echo, and Special Forces ODA 574 found themselves trapped in the small provisional capital of Tarin Kowt, seventy miles north of the Taliban stronghold of Kandahar. Intelligence from Karzai supporters said that five hundred Taliban fighters were bearing down on them in eighty trucks, vowing to kill every man, woman and child in the town.

"I won't say it was panic," SF Captain Jason Amerine later told *Frontline*, "but on our side we had eleven Special Forces soldiers and a bunch of highly motivated but untrained guerrillas numbering between thirty and sixty."

Captain Amerine ordered the Team's Air Force combat controller, Sergeant Yoshi Yoshita, to get on the horn and tell JFACC that they were going to need AC-130 Spectre gunships and as much air support as they could get. Then, Captain Amerine and Master Sergeant J.D. David moved a handful of Afghan fighters, Sergeant Yoshita and two other SF operators several miles south into a mountain pass that overlooked the highway. When they arrived at 0700 hours, the Taliban were only three miles away.

Sergeant Yoshita wasted no time radioing in the enemy's coordinates to Navy F/A-18 fighter pilots approaching the area, then started pointing his SOFLAM so they could lock in. The first bomb missed, but the second one hit the lead Taliban Toyota dead-on, flipping it over twice and tossing it into the desert. "They were just pouring in the birds," SF Staff Sergeant Wes McGirr said of JFACC, "because we were in the hottest situation going at the time. We were in immediate contact and in immediate danger, so they started throwing in the birds, and they just raked them up."

The close air support was so effective that four hours into the battle only three Taliban trucks had made it through the pass, rocking and jolting through the wreckage and deeply rutted terrain. The three Toyotas holding a dozen Taliban fighters were quickly finished off by Karzai's men and the other SF soldiers on Captain Amerine's team.

Air strikes continued streaming in throughout the day, first bombing the front of the convoy, then the rear so they couldn't retreat. One bombing run after another systematically turned the middle into an inferno of carnage and hot, twisted metal.

The battle was over in seven hours, leaving more than forty Taliban vehicles completely destroyed and more than three hundred Taliban soldiers dead. It proved to be a devastating blow to the Taliban in the South.

In a society dominated by warlords, Karzai's victory gave him immediate credibility. "That's when it became apparent that he was the guy who was going to lead Afghanistan in the future," Special Forces Lt. Colonel David Fox said later. "He took on a completely different amount of significance."

Every member of Special Forces Team ODA 574 was later awarded a Bronze Star medal for heroism. Several also received Purple Hearts for their wounds.

*   *   *

On a cold, frosty November 19th morning Colonel Alexander and I boarded a large unmarked white turboprop transport aircraft with Dr. Abdullah Abdullah for the trip to Tashkent. My right-hand man Davis would be acting as team leader in my absence, since George was in Jalalabad without full communications.

Waiting for me in Uzbekistan was my tall, stocky African-American support officer named Donovan, ███████████████████████ ███████████████████████████████. He was the guy who kept my teams supplied with money, weapons, commo equipment and everything we needed. Anytime I sent him a message, he responded the same day.

After telling Dr. Abdullah Abdullah that he was scheduled to meet with Special Representative Dobbins at 1400 hours, and ushering him to a waiting vehicle, Donovan showed Colonel Alexander and me to his car. "Get in," he said. "You're staying at the Intercontinental, but first you're going to see Dobbins and an entourage at the Ambassador's residence. It's showtime, my friend."

It was a clear, sunny day in Tashkent and unseasonably pleasant for late November.

I shut my eyes as we drove down wide Soviet-built boulevards past mosques, Soviet-style apartment blocks and a huge statue of Tamerlaine, the great Tartar warrior of the 14th century.

"What's an average salary for a worker in Tashkent?" I asked.

"Uzbekistan has fallen on real hard times since the breakup of the Soviet Union," Donovan answered. "One hundred dollars a month is considered a good salary."

We pulled up to a large house with distinctive Uzbek Islamic features, surrounded by uniformed Uzbek police. "This is it," Donovan said with a smile. "Have fun!"

I was wearing a dark green/black Gortex jacket, turtleneck shirt and tactical black pants with boots and hadn't shaved in weeks. Colonel Alexander wore a black leather jacket, dark jeans and a pullover shirt. We were met in the entrance by Phillip, ███████████, who had first called me. "Good job in getting Abdullah Abdullah out so quick," he said, shaking my hand.

"You're welcome."

"Dobbins, the U.S. Ambassador to Uzbekistan and about twenty Department of State staff and military officers want you to brief them on the operation thus far. They also want your assessment of the Northern Alliance."

"Not a problem," I answered. "I'm not shy about talking."

"That's what I've heard."

We entered the dining room, where Phillip made the introductions. Dobbins was a tall man in his midfifties, balding and wearing a suit. In a very serious tone, he asked me to take a seat at the dining room table and begin.

He said, "I'm considering conducting talks at Bagram."

"Sir, that won't be possible," I responded. "Bagram looks like hell after the fire went out."

Not getting the joke, Dobbins asked, "Was there a fire at Bagram?"

"Yes, the fires of hell," I answered. "There's only one building remaining with a roof. The rest of the place has been totally destroyed. It's not a good place for a conference."

Everyone broke out laughing except for Dobbins, who stared at me hard. I said, "Sir, let me provide a quick narration of events beginning with our entry into the Panshir."

"Go ahead," answered Dobbins.

For the next hour I briefed Dobbins on everything starting with the ███████████████████████, previous Jawbreaker deployments, ██.

"Do you trust Fahim, Engineer Aref and Abdullah Abdullah?" Dobbins asked.

"Only in the execution of specific missions. I think we can count on them to act strongly to defend their own narrow interests," I answered. " We have detected serious rifts and competition between the Tajiks, Hazaras and Uzbeks. Afghanistan truly is a zero sum game. Anytime anyone advances all others consider this to be at their expense."

"What's the security situation like in the Kabul at the moment?" Dobbins asked.

"Stable. There have been no counterattacks or terrorist bombings by Taliban or al-Qaeda stay-behinds so far. But I can't assure you that they won't start tomorrow. The Northern Alliance lacks the resources and ability to identify possible Taliban or al-Qaeda teams in the city. They have their hands full just maintaining order. If you want to visit Kabul at the moment, you and your staff can stay with my team. We'll ensure your security."

"Thank you," Dobbins said. "But, first, I'm going to bring all the key Afghan political players together somewhere in Europe. What can I expect from Abdullah Abdullah today?"

"He threatened to resign two nights ago over the unannounced arrival of British forces," I answered. "I'm sure Tony Blair would appreciate it if you could straighten that issue out."

Dobbins smiled for the first time.

"Abdullah Abdullah is carrying a message from General Fahim," I continued. "But I don't know what that will be."

"What about the south and east of Afghanistan?" Special Representative Dobbins asked.

"The Northern Alliance has no desire to enter either the South or East. Honestly, they're waiting for us to solve that problem."

"What's going to happen there?" he asked.

"It's too early to tell," I answered. "We're just beginning to link up with indigenous forces in those sectors. I've got a team in Jalalabad now led by my deputy. It's risky and we're likely to lose officers. Instead of dealing with major Pushtun commanders, most of whom are Taliban, we have to deal with minor ones and help build their forces."

Dobbins stood and shook my hand. As we left, Phillip informed me that I wouldn't be included in the meeting between Dobbins and Abdullah Abdullah that evening.

"Don't worry, I'm not offended," I said.

Donovan was waiting for me outside. "You ready to go to your hotel?" he asked.

"A hot shower would be nice. We only have one setting on the shower in the guesthouse and it's cold."

First thing I did after checking into the hotel was calculate the time difference between Tashkent and the ████████████ of South America. I figured it was late afternoon in ████████████, so I called my wife.

"Hello, Rebecca, it's Gary," I said.

"Hey! How are you? Or should I ask where are you?"

"I'm in Uzbekistan for the night."

"How are you?"

"I'm fine."

She said, "I told everyone you were in Washington, then while watching CNN, they saw you in Afghanistan. It's kind of embarrassing."

"Sorry about that. How are the kids?"

"They're fine. Alexis is traveling here for Christmas. If you can get back by then it would be great."

"I have no idea on timing. I'm taking this one day at a time."

"I know. I'm not putting pressure. But please be careful. Please!"

After years in the Agency, I had developed the ability to compartmentalize things. I missed my family terribly, but could push the loneliness aside and concentrate solely on the mission. Laserlike focus is what made me good at what I did.

Rebecca remained calm as we continued, as though she was talking to her husband at work down at the mill in some small town in America. It was great hearing her voice. Even though I loved her and missed her, I was exactly where I wanted to be.

13

BILAL

"We sleep safe in our beds because rough men stand ready in the night to visit violence on those who would do us harm."
—George Orwell

*   *   *   *   *   *

The phone rang as I lay on the bed of the Tashkent hotel. It was Phillip, who said that Special Representative Dobbins had decided to travel back to Afghanistan with me and hold a press briefing with Abdullah Abdullah at Bagram airbase.

"He also wants to know if he can then use your plane to fly right back to Tashkent, because he has to go to Europe for meetings."

"No problem," I responded.

He thanked me again and said that everyone was impressed with all my team had accomplished. Also, the meeting with Abdullah Abdullah went better than expected.

"I'm glad to hear it."

"Get some rest."

I put on my hat, gloves and Gortex jacket and walked into the cold, night air to clear my head. Snow was just starting to fall on the wide streets as streetcars clattered by, punctuated by the occasional crack of

222

electricity. Cold Soviet architecture and colossal government buildings on large tracts of land dominated the city.

As people passed on the sidewalk they could tell from my clothing that I was a foreigner. A woman in her thirties walked by with two young boys. One of the boys stopped to stare back at me, and his mother dragged him away by the arm.

I had studied Russian at the University of New Mexico and developed a passion for Russian literature. The works of Pushkin, Gogol, Turgenev, Dostoyevsky, Chekhov, Bulgakov, and Solzhenitsyn fascinated me and taught me a deep respect for the Russian people. Having grown up during the Cold War, I'd expected that we'd be fighting the Soviets forever.

I had to remind myself that the Russian government of Vladimir Putin, the Uzbek government of Karamanov and the Tajik government were all on our side. Even though ten years had passed since the fall of the Soviet Union, the fact that we were now friends and had so many interests in common seemed odd.

Back at the hotel, I watched news of the war in Afghanistan. Talking heads on CNN reported that the Taliban were regrouping in the South to launch a counteroffensive against the Northern Alliance. The "experts" on CNN agreed that the U.S. effort to form an interim government was headed for disaster.

*   *   *

After a good night's sleep Colonel Alexander drove me to the U.S. Embassy, which occupied an old Soviet library that had once housed books extolling the virtues of communism. On the second floor, in a small conference room, I greeted the dozen members of his SF team. One face was familiar, a former JSOC officer who had once tossed a flash grenade into a shoot house where I was standing as an observer during a hostage rescue exercise. Fortunately, I'd been wearing ear protectors and goggles at the time.

I briefed them about our mission in Afghanistan, then Colonel Alexander spoke. "I know that many of you have trained and sacrificed for years only to be denied the opportunity to use your skills to their fullest extent. Gary here will get you in the fight."

* * *

At noon, when I stepped back onto the large white unmarked turbo-prop transport, Jim Dobbins and Dr. Abdullah Abdullah were already aboard with an eight-man contingent from Diplomatic Security. Special Representative Dobbins shook my hand firmly and thanked me again.

"Whatever you need, sir," I responded. I was anxious to get back.

During the flight, Special Represenative Dobbins spoke privately with the Northern Alliance Foreign Minister who said he understood the need for a Pushtun to lead the new Afghan government. Pushtuns were the largest ethnic group in the country comprising roughly forty-two percent of the population. Twenty-seven percent of Afghans were Tajiks, nine percent were Uzbeks and another nine percent Hazaras. The rest were a combination of Aimak, Turmen, Baloch and others.

Dr. Abdullah suggested Hamid Karzai as someone who might head a new interim government. This was the third time the State Department representative had heard Karzai's name. The first time was when Karzai entered southern Afghanistan in late October. Karzai had been mentioned again by the head of Pakistani Intelligence during Dobbins's recent visit to Islamabad.

"What about ex-President Burhanuddin Rabbani who is currently occupying the presidential palace?" Dobbins asked. President Rabbani was the political head of the Northern Alliance and, in theory, Dr. Abdullah's boss.

Dr. Abdullah Abdullah's answer took the U.S. diplomat by surprise. "I suggest that you tell him he has to leave," the foreign minister said.

As the plane approached Bagram, I asked the pilot to circle so that Special Representative Dobbins could see the full extent of the destruction. Then as Dobbins and Dr. Abdullah went to the front gate to address the press, I left with several of our Afghan guards who were waiting to bring me back to Kabul.

* * *

George, with Team Juliet in Jalalabad, reported that his first face-to-face meeting with Babrak had been friendly, but hampered by difficulties in communication. Babrak, a man in his early forties who spoke his native Pashai and Pushtun had brought along a young aide who spoke only rudimentary English. This turned out to be immensely frustrating for the big Texan. As George outlined the U.S. plan to pursue bin Laden, it became obvious to him that the full meaning of his words was not getting through. Despite the torturously slow translation, Babrak did communicate his willingness to help the Americans who'd fought to free his people.

George learned that while Babrak's men seemed to have control of the city of Jalalabad itself, armed groups of one hundred to two hundred Taliban and al-Qaeda soldiers continued still roamed the province.

The leader of Team Juliet needed a Pushtun speaker to serve as his translator. Amir and Hamid spoke only Arabic and Dari. I immediately thought of Adam Khan, who was back at Langley translating marriage certificates, old newspaper articles and notes written on menus recovered by Agency and SF teams from al-Qaeda facilities. I'd tried and failed to get Adam to accompany me when I first deployed, but would fight for him one more time.

* * *

Bilal, the former Marine who'd dropped by my office during the ▓▓▓▓▓▓▓ case two years ago, waited in the lobby of the Tashkent hotel. On the morning of 9/11, he'd been riding in a taxi on the way to the Detroit airport to catch a flight to an Agency assignment in the Middle East when his brother called to tell him about the World Trade

Center attack. All commercial air traffic was suspended by the time he reached the terminal, so he rented a car and drove nonstop to D.C.

Bilal had missed Jawbreaker's deployment because he was on assignment to another Middle Eastern country. While he was away, he heard about the harassment of Arab-Americans from friends and relatives back in Dearborn, Michigan. Back home, Arab-American businesses shut their doors. The price of gasoline rose immediately to six dollars a gallon. And rumors ran rampant. Among them: President Bush was going to lock away all Arab-Americans in concentration camps. And, the attack on the World Trade Center had been a Zionist plot.

Bilal was anxious to get into Afghanistan and join Jawbreaker, but stayed clear of the other American military types milling around the lobby. He felt differently about Donovan, a fellow Agency officer, and approached him. "You just missed, Gary," Donovan said.

"Again?"

"Don't worry," Donovan replied. "We'll get you in on the flight tomorrow. The war isn't over, yet."

On the morning of November 22, Bilal waited on the tarmac of Tashkent's international airport with Donovan and Colonel Alexander's Special Forces detachment. Bilal introduced himself to the tall, dark-haired ex-JSOC officer whom I'd recognized the day before.

"Are you going in to work with Gary?" Bilal asked him.

The tall man nodded, then asked: "You, too?"

* * *

The five men who'd joined us from ████████ Team Delta (originally deployed to Bamian province) crowded in my room, leaving their Afghan translator waiting in the hall.

[*NOTE TO READER:* The redacted section above, which runs for several pages, involves a discussion of Team's Delta's plan to meet with a top Taliban intel official.]

*   *   *

It was late afternoon before Bilal landed at Bagram and found transport into Kabul. Dropping his gear in the lobby, the thickly built ex-Marine climbed the stairs and entered the base where ten laptops were running and men were trading jokes.

Someone cracked: "We're here to hunt and kill Arabs" just as the Arab-American Bilal walked in the room.

In a big voice Bilal bellowed, "There's at least one Arab who will kick your collective asses if you screw with him."

Every man in the room froze. They'd never met Bilal before.

I smiled and said, "Gentlemen, say hello to Big B. Former Master Sergeant Bilal Hassan of the United States Marine Corps."

Bilal strode through the room like he owned it and gave me a hug. "Hello, Chief," he said. "You think I'd let you go to war without me?"

"I'm real happy to see you," I replied. "We've got a hell of a lot to do."

The charismatic ex-Marine then worked his way around the room shaking hands with everyone. He had a deep confidence about him that won people over immediately. When he got to Amir, he addressed him in Arabic. The two men had never met.

"Get Bilal a weapon, a room, some chow, and let's meet in my room in an hour," I said to Amir.

Storm from Special Activities said, "We don't have any more 9mm Glocks, just AK-47s."

Under normal circumstances, Agency officers carried only ▮▮▮▮▮ approved arms. I had scrapped that rule. Instead, Storm was buying AK-47s on the local market and issuing them to new arrivals. Any officer who hadn't fired an AK-47 before was given a quick training session and a chance to fire his new weapon behind the guesthouse.

I handed Bilal my handgun. "Here, take my Glock. Where you're going, you're going to need this more than I am."

"Thanks, Chief," he said with a big, ready smile. "Sounds like my kind of mission."

*　　*　　*

Also arriving at the guesthouse were Colonel Alexander and his SF team, who started packing into two rooms. Accompanying them were two ▮▮▮▮▮▮▮ officers who'd been sent by headquarters to examine the passports and ▮▮▮▮▮▮▮▮▮ we had seized from al-Qaeda facilities. I hadn't been informed ahead of time, which wasn't unusual. People were arriving and departing at a steadily increasing pace.

I held up a faxed photo of an unshaved, exhausted-looking face as Bilal, Amir, Davis and Storm entered my room.

"Who the hell's that?" Davis asked.

"It's purportedly one of the sons of the Blind Sheik Abdel Rahman, who is in jail in New York State for conspiracy in the first WTC bombing." The Blind Sheik had helped launch Ramzi Yusuf, who set off a truck bomb in the World Trade Center garage back in 1993.

"CTC/███ was informed by a journalist that this man in the photo, the sheik's son, is being held captive in prison in Kabul." The face in the photo screamed with desperation. I asked, "Have you seen this guy, Amir?"

"No," he answered. "But in addition to the two Northern Alliance prisons we've checked out, a number of Afghan entrepreneurs have captured Arabs and are holding them in metal shipping containers with an eye towards trading or selling them in the future."

Davis broke in: "They never miss a chance to make a buck."

"Make a copy of this photo and put it in the hands of Majid's boys," I instructed. "If the Blind Sheik's son is being held here in prison, I want to know where. I'll buy him from the Afghans just to send him off to a prison in the U.S."

Red-bearded Storm spoke up: "Some of the prisoners that the Doc treated are improving. And there's a newly arrived ████████ case officer named Ronald who's been focusing on one of the Pakistanis."

"Ronald isn't a native speaker," Amir added, "but he has a real strong command of the Arabic."

"If ████████ are working on a particular prisoner, move on to other prisoners," I said. "We're sharing everything with each other so we'll get whatever intel they extract soon enough."

I turned to Bilal and Amir. "I've got a strong feeling that the Northern Alliance is holding more prisoners up in the Panshir. I say this because when we commenced this operation, the Northern Alliance was capturing Taliban and al-Qaeda on the front lines. ████████

██

██

██

Eleven September was only their first shot at us. I know in my heart that bin Laden has planned at least one more major attack on us either inside the U.S. or outside the U.S. while we're vulnerable. I need you guys to find a lead."

"Don't worry, Chief," Bilal responded. "We'll dig deep."

There was a knock on the door and one of my officers stuck his mustached face in to tell me that Phillip, Special Rep Dobbin's assistant, was on the line and the ██████████ were waiting downstairs.

I finished with Bilal, Amir and the others by saying, "You guys work out the details of how you're going to proceed."

The ████████ team leader, his ████ deputy and two men in their thirties stood in the lobby. I said, "Give me a minute, I'll be right back." Then I hurried to the phone through a hallway where SF soldiers had at least three card games going.

Phillip was calling from Bonn, Germany. He asked me to go see Dr. Abdullah Abdullah as soon as possible and tell him that Dobbins wanted him to travel to Bonn for a conference next week.

"Sure, Phillip. I'll take care of it."

The ██████ and I sat at a large table in the dining room, where the team leader, ██████, introduced Ronald, who'd been bonding with the Pakistani prisoner and trying to get him to talk.

██████ said: "If there's any way we can expand our cooperation or help you, please let me know."

"I understand you, too, are working the prisoners," I said. "I would ask that you inform me immediately of any interesting developments or leads."

"Absolutely," ██████ answered. "We're all at risk of future attack."

As soon as the ██████████ departed I told Majid that I needed to meet with Dr. Abdullah Abdullah. Back at our work space, I was confronted with a room full of men working communications gear and banging laptops.

I patted ever-dependable Davis on the shoulder and said, "Get two AK-47s and come with me."

We loaded into the back of a waiting jeep with an Afghan driver and armed guard in the passenger seat. "The house of Dr. Abdullah Abdullah. Quick!" I ordered in Farsi.

Dr. Abdullah Abdullah had taken up residence in a modest house ten minutes away. The decor reminded me of the bland Drexel furniture normally provided to Department of State employees.

Abdullah Abdullah greeted us, and a young man brought tea. I explained that Special Representative Dobbins had asked me to personally invite him to a political conference in Bonn.

"Who else is being invited?" he asked.

I said I didn't know specifically, but based on what Special Representative Dobbins had said to me in Tashkent, I assumed that other Afghan political groups both inside and outside of the country would be represented. Abdullah Abdullah seemed to be especially interested in how the U.S. viewed the potential role of the Afghan King Mohammad Zaher Shah currently living in exile in Rome. I said that he would have to address that question to Special Representative Dobbins.

He said, "Tell Ambassador Dobbins that we'll send a lead representative and a delegation, but I might not be in attendance."

"Why's that, Mr. Foreign Minister?" I asked.

"Internal dynamics," was his answer.

Davis and I shook hands with him and exited. The meeting had lasted no more than fifteen minutes. We headed back to the guesthouse and a mountain of intelligence reports that had to be read and released before I could hit the sack at 2 A.M.

*　　*　　*

Sometime around 8 P.M. I fielded a phone call from CTC/█ informing me that General Franks was likely to arrive at Bagram in the next few days. No sooner had I hung up the phone than a large explosion went off outside our work area. The windows blew in and oxygen was literally sucked out of the room. I watched in slow motion as Storm from Special Activities bent down and starting slamming magazines into AK-47s stacked against the wall. The rest of us stood frozen in shock and only started to come out of it when Storm slapped loaded weapons into our hands.

Together, we ran downstairs to face our attackers. But this time it wasn't a car bomb or an RPG round fired by an al-Qaeda terrorist. It was a tank shell that exploded when two kids tossed it into a fire they had built in a vacant lot ten meters from our perimeter wall. One of the boys was badly injured. We rushed in to help.

As a crowd hustled the injured boy into a taxi for a trip to the hospital, I thought to myself: *In the States we tell our children not to play with matches. In the new Afghanistan we're going to have to run public service messages instructing children not to play with crew-served weapons.*

It was a strange war.

14

GENERAL TOMMY FRANKS

"Associate yourself with men of good quality if you esteem your reputation; for 'tis better to be alone than in bad company."
—*George Washington*, Rules of Civility

*   *   *   *   *   *

The night sky over Bagram was pitch black with a sliver of moon obscured by clouds. Mountains formed a forbidding perimeter in the distance. U.S. Army Lt. Colonel Mark Sutter and I climbed out of a brand new blue Ford pickup that had been flown in for him and his three-man JSOC team. The cold wind bit into us, so we pulled on hats and gloves.

Since the first Joint Special Operations Command (Delta Force) advance team—that had been initially deployed to support rescue of the SNI hostages—had been folded into my team and sent south into Jalalabad, CENTCOM decided to dispatch another JSOC advance team to work beside me. The rest of them, minus their leader Lt. Colonel Sutter, were now comfortably resting in our guesthouse in Kabul and would prepare the ground for a large JSOC contingent to follow.

Events were moving at breakneck speed, so I was anxious to wrap up this meeting and get back to Kabul, where my men were tracking the movement of Osama bin Laden and his forces south and east.

During our rugged drive north, Lt. Colonel Sutter told me that

233

once upon a time he'd been a Division I university soccer player. He was now in his late thirties and hard as nails. I looked down at my watch, then up at the mustard-colored empty-looking Bagram control tower that stood in front of us. Beyond I could barely make out the ruins of buildings and hangars shredded by war.

"It's 2100 hours," I said, scanning the sky for some sign of General Tommy Franks' C-17.

"He should be touching down any minute," the Lt. Colonel replied.

I kept thinking back to General Tommy Franks' pledge to General Fahim three and a half weeks earlier on a similar tarmac in Dushanbe: First Mazar-e Sharif, then we open a land bridge to Taloqan, then we defeat the Taliban on the Shomali Plains and I visit you before Christmas.

It looked like the general would be arriving several weeks early. Without warning, I heard a tremendous roar of engines as the big plane touched down and taxied north to the south. As it passed I saw lights for the first time emanating from the rear of the aircraft. Speeding down the runway past several security vehicles, the plane braked into a turn, headed back toward us and stopped facing north.

With the engines still running, the back hatch opened and a dozen U.S. soldiers with helmets, weapons and night vision goggles spilled out. One of them crossed the fifty meters of apron to shake the Lt. Colonel's hand, then escort him back to the C-17.

Two minutes later, General Tommy Franks, commander of CENT-COM stepped out and two dozen soldiers formed a perimeter around him. When the circle reached me, it opened up and General Franks, with Colonel Mark beside him, firmly took my hand.

I said, "Welcome to Bagram, General Franks," as his security detail stretched to form a circle twenty feet in diameter.

"Good evening, Gary," the General replied. "How are you?"

"I'm fine, sir. I believe Colonel Mulholland will have General

Fahim here to meet you in thirty minutes. I thought you might want to chat with me before we go in."

"Yes, I do," General Franks answered in a low, no-nonsense drawl. "Tell me: What is Fahim doing now that he has control of the capital?"

"He's spending most of his time organizing and positioning himself to influence the creation of the next Afghan government. Former president Burhanuddin Rabbani had moved into the old presidential palace, but it doesn't appear that he has the full support of the Northern Alliance."

"I see."

"I recently flew up with Dr. Abdullah Abdullah to meet with Special Representative Dobbins in Uzbekistan. The Northern Alliance has agreed to participate in the upcoming Bonn talks, but Abdullah Abdullah will not be leading the delegation. My sources tell me they're sending Younis Qanooni, who is, at the moment, the acting Chief of Security for the city. Qanooni was a former Interior Minister."

"Interesting choice," General Franks said. "Tell me about the Northern Alliance entry into Kabul."

"I'd been reporting that they would stop five miles outside of the city after defeating the Taliban on the Shomali Plains. None of us anticipated the sudden Taliban withdrawal and evacuation. It resulted in a power vacuum and some looting. The Northern Alliance saw an opportunity and moved in."

"Where's bin Laden?" the general asked.

"I've received multiple reports that have him traveling south into Nangahar province."

"Good."

"How is the local population reacting to Northern Alliance control of Kabul?"

"They seem to have accepted it. I haven't seen or heard of a single incident since their arrival."

"Okay," the general nodded. "Is there anything I can do to help you in your dealings with Fahim?"

"Yes, sir. There is," I answered. "I've just deployed an eight-man team into Jalalabad in Nangahar province made up of several of my Special Activities officers, three JSOC who have been loaned to me and one of Mulhullond's SF medics. ████████████████████ ██ ████████████████████████████████."

Out of the corner of my eye I noticed that the security perimeter had opened up to allow Special Forces Colonel John Mulholland to enter. General Franks called out, "Good evening, John."

I sensed a strong bond between them. Colonel Mulholland said, "It is good to see you, sir, and you too, Gary. We have a bit of time, so why don't we walk over and you can meet some of the men before we go in to see Fahim."

General Franks turned back to me and asked, "Is there anything else you would like me to raise with Fahim?"

"Not at the moment, sir."

General Franks said, "Then, let's take a walk." The security circle moved with us past the first building my team had inhabited, which was now surrounded by barbed wire, along a dirt road fifty meters into a structure with a half-destroyed roof that had been closed with tarps. The dozen or so U.S. Special Forces soldiers inside snapped to attention. They were hardly the picture of military spit and polish with beards and a combination of military and local garb.

General Franks said, "At ease."

The big Texan moved through the room, shaking hands and spending a few minutes with each soldier. After thirty-five years in the Army, Franks might have developed into a ruthless strategist and tactician, but it was clear that he still cared about his men.

Following a short conference with Colonel Mulholland, the three of us together with an Iranian-born U.S. soldier Mulholland brought to serve as Frank's translator walked five minutes to General Fahim's office. The short, fat Northern Alliance commander met us in a parlor wearing fatigues with no insignia. He welcomed General Franks with a big smile.

Franks said: "Didn't I tell you we'd be here together before December twenty-fifth?"

"You did indeed," Fahim responded.

It was clear right away that General Fahim was anxious to amend the awful impression he had made during his first meeting in Dushanbe. His confidence had been boosted by victories in Mazar-e Sharif, Taloqan and Kabul.

General Franks congratulated Fahim on those victories, never alluding to the fact that they would not have been possible without the massive air strikes and SF teams provided by CENTCOM. The normally dour-looking Fahim grinned broadly throughout.

General Franks then walked Fahim through what CENTCOM was planning in terms of personnel deployments to support humanitarian relief. He also expressed the United States' desire to expand operations in the South and East. Turning to me, he asked Fahim to commit his support to the Agency team in Jalalabad.

Instantaneously the smile disappeared from General Fahim's face. He clearly preferred praise from the commander of CENTCOM over dealing with this CIA officer who was constantly prodding him to do more.

Franks then asked Fahim for his assessment of combat operations in various parts of the country, including those led by Dr. Karim Khalili in Bamian, Mohammad Atta in Mazar-e Sharif and Ismael Khan in Herat. Fahim quickly briefed him on the state of the Taliban's collapse and the prospects of their regrouping in the South.

Following another round of meetings with Colonel Mulholland

and some chow with the SF soldiers, General Franks flew out. Meanwhile, Lt. Colonel Sutter and I bounced our way back to Kabul.

*　*　*

It had been another full day. Hoss, the former Navy Seal, and Billy Waugh had arrived that same morning. Billy, at seventy-two years of age, immediately started pressing me on when he could be deployed forward. "I don't want to miss anything," he kept saying. When I explained that I needed him in Kabul for a week to ten days he groused that he didn't come to Afghanistan to "fiddle-fuck" around a headquarters.

I said, "I'll give you ample opportunity to ███████████████, if you give me a week."

I ordered Hoss to prepare to accompany Bilal and Amir to the Northern Alliance prison in the Panshir.

In the midst of everything else, I received a call from Islamabad ████████ recommending that I contact a Pushtun warlord named Nuruddin who might be able to help us in Jalalabad. Nuruddin was not ███████████, but had informed Islamabad ██████████ of his intention to return from exile in Dijon, France, to his native Nangahar province and fight the Taliban. A former mujahideen commander during the anti-Soviet jihad, Nuruddin claimed he could raise a force of more than a thousand men.

I thanked Islamabad for their suggestion, then instructed George to talk to Babrak about bringing Nuruddin and his men into the army we were creating in the South and East. Babrak considered Nuruddin a rival for political influence and told George he didn't like the idea of cooperating with him. In what later turned out to be the biggest mistake I made in the deployment, I ordered George to establish contact with Nuruddin. We needed sizeable forces in the South not only to attack the Taliban and al-Qaeda, but also to reestablish order. George did as he was told.

*　　*　　*

The next morning, bright and early, I received yet another report from Majid placing bin Laden south, in Nangahar province. Two days before the fall of Kabul (on November 12), the London *Sunday Times* reported that the al-Qaeda leader was seen entering Jalalabad in a convoy of white Toyota trucks surrounded by commandos in green fatigues carrying shiny new Kalashnikovs rigged with grenade launchers. At midafternoon as U.S. bombs fell on the city, bin Laden had a meal with local tribal leaders consisting of kebabs and rice. Then he spoke at the Saudi-funded Institute for Islamic Studies, where he tried to rally local supporters. Dressed in loose gray clothing and his signature camouflage jacket, bin Laden said, "God is with us, and we will win the war. Your Arab brothers will lead the way with weapons and technology. What we need most is your support. My God grant me the opportunity to see you again."

The following morning, as U.S. bombing stepped up, bin Laden was spotted by Jalalabad residents standing outside a mosque, holding hands with the local Taliban governor. Cradling a Kalakov machine-gun, he then barked orders to his sixty armed guards and left in a convoy of four-wheel-drive vehicles.

This same convoy of approximately two hundred Toyotas and Land Cruisers was seen two days later passing through the village of Agam two hours south. "There were many nationalities in the convoy," one villager told *Sunday Times* reporter Anthony Loyd. "Some were black-skinned, some white. Most were Arabs. They were well-armed and good Muslims carrying the Koran in one hand and their Kalashnikov in the other."

Billy Waugh plotted the location of this latest sighting on a map with the last four reports we had received from Northern Alliance spies. They showed a steady movement south and east towards the Pakistani border. All five reports noted that the al-Qaeda leader was moving with a large group of armed Arabs.

His flight towards the southeastern mountains made sense. Osama bin Laden had fought his first battle against the Soviets in 1987, at Jaji, an Afghan village in Nangahar, just a few miles west of the Pakistani border. We knew that he had a training camp at the base of the Tora Bora mountains and maintained a complex of as many as two hundred highly defensible caves at higher elevations that had been developed during the anti-Soviet jihad. Because they offered easy access by foot to Parachinir, a region of Pakistan that juts into Afghanistan like a parrot's beak, the snow-covered mountains were a great place to hide and, possibly, escape. Bin Laden probably calculated that the U.S. would run into problems if we tried to pursue his al-Qaeda fighters into neighboring Pakistan where he enjoyed strong popular support.

Billy fixed the map on the wall and continued to plot each new bin Laden sighting. As expected, his progress continued east towards Tora Bora. All this was reported immediately to George, who was fifty miles north of Jalalabad.

[*NOTE TO READERS*: The redacted section above deals with a meeting between my deputy, George, Babrak and other warlords we were assembling into a force which became known as the Eastern Alliance.]

* * *

Up north, the tense standoff around Kunduz continued. More than five thousand Taliban and two thousand foreign fighters, many of whom had retreated from Mazar-e Sharif and Taloqan, remained hunkered down in the city prepared to make their last stand. They were holding a large portion of the city's population hostage. Surrounding them were Northern Alliance generals Mohammad Daoud and Dostum on the west and Beryallah Khan on the east. From overhead they were being pounded daily by U.S. airstrikes.

Among the Taliban and foreign forces that fled by foot to Kunduz was a tall, lanky American citizen named John Walker Lindh. The twenty-one-year-old Lindh had left his family in Marin County, California, four years earlier to travel to Yemen and Pakistan for the purpose of immersing himself in the study of Arabic and his newfound faith, Islam. In letters home he soon began parroting a hatred of the United States that flowed through mosques and conservative religious schools across the Middle East. In May 2001 he crossed the Pakistani border into Afghanistan to fight alongside the Taliban. Throughout June and July he attended bin Laden's al Farooq training camp outside of Kandahar, where he met the al-Qaeda leader before being airlifted north to fight the Northern Alliance. "My heart became attached to the Taliban," he explained later. "I wanted to help them in one way or another." It didn't seem to bother him that the Taliban forbade women to work outside their homes or receive an education and routinely violated people's human rights.

Like other Taliban and al-Qaeda fighters trapped in Kunduz, John Walker Lindh had spent the last ten days scrounging for food and water and trying to protect himself from the bitter cold and ferocious U.S. air strikes. On the night of November 23rd Northern Alliance sources claimed that two Pakistani planes landed in Kunduz under the cover of darkness to extract key Pakistani advisors to the Taliban and several high-ranking Taliban officials. I had no way to confirm this, but wasn't surprised. Pakistan's Inter Service Intelligence Directorate (ISID) had helped create the Taliban and had been a close ally of their government for years. I assumed from the beginning of the conflict that ISID advisors were supporting the Taliban with expertise and materiel and, no doubt, sending a steady stream of intelligence back to Islamabad. We also knew that thousands of Pakistanis, some from prominent families, had taken up arms to defend the Taliban.

After four days of sporadic fighting, bombing and negotiations, several thousand Taliban fighters inside Kunduz laid down their arms and were taken into custody by the Northern Alliance. Thousands of others, including foreigners like John Walker Lindh, soldiered on. Among those killed in subsequent air strikes was Juma Namangani of the Islamic Movement of Uzbekistan, who was a deputy of bin Laden's and had been sent to Konduz to lead the al-Qaeda force.

When an AC-130 Spectre gunship approached the city and General Dostum threatened to kill every last holdout, Taliban Commander Mohammed Fazal finally threw in the towel. U.S. Special Forces soldiers conducted house-to-house searches to root out foreign stragglers, while the Northern Alliance tried to process the huge influx of prisoners. Thousands were dispatched south to Sherberghan prison in everything from Russian-made military trucks, to flatbeds, to container trucks. Hundreds more were sent to Qala-i Jangi fortress ten miles west of Mazar-e Sharif.

Unlike the U.S. military, NA commanders did not follow careful protocols for searching prisoners. Nor did they have sufficient supplies of food, water and medical care. Many captured al-Qaeda and Taliban soldiers in need of medical attention died en route to prison. Hundreds of others asphyxiated in stifling, overpacked container trucks.

Unfortunately, none of our personnel in-country were present to monitor the processing of enemy combatants. The few U.S. boots we had on the ground were busy trying to keep on top of a military situation that was shifting fast.

* * *

Bilal, Amir and Hoss rocked and jostled their way north into the Panshir Valley. Their objective: an unnamed prison just twenty kilometers north of the village of Astana, near our first compound.

The ██████-born Amir had traveled the road many times. Still,

I provided him with a backup vehicle with two Afghan soldiers and warned him to expect little security from the Northern Alliance guards at the prison.

They drove all day and arrived at dusk. The prison consisted of stone buildings surrounded by a concrete wall topped with barbed wire. Typical of the lax security we had seen previously, it was situated next to an ammunition dump. As Amir, Hoss and Bilal approached the site, they saw several hundred men walking idly up from the river. Remarkably, neither Hoss, nor Bilal, nor Amir could identify a single guard.

"What the hell's this?" asked Bilal, who quickly foresaw the potential for disaster. As Amir stopped the vehicle, the several hundred prisoners continued to approach.

"Lock and load!" Bilal barked to his colleagues.

The former Navy Seal, ████████ American former Marine and Arab-American readied their weapons, hurried from the truck and quickly took up firing positions. The two Afghans in the vehicle behind them did the same. Each man held three magazines of twenty for their AK-47s and three magazines of fifteen for their Glock 9mm pistols.

In Arabic, Bilal ordered the prisoners to hit the ground and pumped his hand up and down to show them what he meant. Out of the large group of Pushtun speakers, only a few understood colloquial Arabic. For the rest, the AK-47s pointed at them had the desired effect. They fell to the ground immediately. Bilal then ordered the men to return to the prison in groups of twenty. Halfway through this procedure the chief NA guard emerged to ask what all the fuss was about.

Bilal tried speaking to him in Arabic. That didn't work. Then he tried English. The guard held up his hand, as if to say, Wait. He then ducked back into the prison and reappeared with a well-groomed young man in his late twenties. The man introduced himself in excellent English as Aziz.

███

Aziz asked if Bilal could arrange for his release to work as a transla-tor for the Americans.

"I'll put in a good word for you if you help us," the thickly built ex-Marine offered. He explained that he wanted to interview the foreign fighters among the prisoners to see if any were willing to volunteer in-formation. Aziz went to talk to the guard.

[*NOTE TO READER:* The redacted section above deals with Bilal's interviews with Arab prisoners.]

15

QALA-I JANGI FORTRESS

"The true Muslim is the one from whose hand and tongue other Muslims are safe."

—*the prophet Mohammad*

*   *   *   *   *   *

It was Sunday morning, November 25, 2001, and CIA officers Mike Spann and Dawson were up at dawn. They drove from their base in Mazar-e Sharif ten miles west to Qala-i Jangi fortress. What they found there looked like something out of the Middle Ages: a massive fortress made of mud surrounded by two sets of thick walls topped with ramparts and turrets. Up until recently, it had been used exclusively to stable General Dostum's horses, thirty of which still lived there in mud stalls.

Now it was crammed with five hundred Taliban and al-Qaeda prisoners who'd been trucked in the night before following the fall of Kunduz. They poured in fifty at a time on flatbed trucks. In a gesture of reconciliation, General Dostum's soldiers told the prisoners that Afghan members of the Taliban would soon be set free to return to their families, while foreigners would be turned over to the UN.

Very few of the prisoners had been searched prior to their arrival. Some concealed weapons and explosives under their clothes. A few managed to strap their weapons under the carriages of the trucks.

Upon entering the fortress, the tired, hungry POWs couldn't help but notice that they outnumbered their Uzbek guards five to one.

When the Northern Alliance commander of Qala-i Jangi, Nadir Ali, ordered prisoners to turn out their pockets, one of them pulled the pin on a grenade he was hiding, killing the commander and himself. Later that night another prisoner blew himself up along with Hazara commander Saeed Asad. As a result, the POWs were herded into cells in the basement accessed from south of the fortress, where—with no food and little water—they spent a cold, dark night.

Foreign al-Qaeda prisoners huddled together, separate from the rest. Only weeks ago they'd been regarded as respected guests and leaders by their Taliban hosts in a historic fight against the West. Now that the tide of war had turned against them, the Afghans viewed the foreigners from as far away as Yemen and Western Europe with suspicion and hostility.

*   *   *

After Dawson exchanged a few words in Uzbek with the Northern Alliance guards, the two Americans were let in. ██████████████████ ██ ██ ██ ███████████████████████████

[*NOTE TO READER:* This redacted section concerns Dawson's background.]

Mike Spann, who hailed from Alabama, was a thirty-two-year-old former Marine Corps officer in top physical condition. He had just completed the Agency's Career Service Training program and was serving his first assignment in the field. Both men had wives and children.

The two ████████ officers entered the northern half of the fortress and walked past the prison governor's office through a large opening in the wall and continued south. First, they were struck by the strong smell of horses coming from the stables on their immediate left. They then passed a low building on their right and another on their left, before arriving at an L-shaped building. Past it about one hundred al-Qaeda prisoners were seated in rows on the ground with their elbows tied behind their backs. They'd been brought up from the basement one-by-one by NA guards.

Behind the prisoners rose the southern walls and ramparts of the fortress. A mere thirty yards away stood the prison armory stocked with racks of weapons, ammo, rockets and mortars. A double set of metal stairs at the southern end of the fortress led to cells underground.

Mike and Dawson knew that the mission they'd been sent to undertake was dangerous, but absolutely had to be done. They were in Qala-i Jangi to identify foreign fighters with knowledge of future al-Qaeda attacks against the West. If one of the five hundred prisoners revealed a future hijacking or dirty bomb attack, hundreds, or even thousands, of innocent lives could be saved.

They couldn't wait until General Dostum's men imposed stricter order or more guards were called in. So they dove in, going from prisoner to prisoner. CNN reporter Robert Young Pelton recorded Dawson asking in Farsi: "Why are you here? Why have you joined the Taliban?"

"To kill you!" came the answer from Arabs, Chechens, Pakistanis, Uzbeks and even a few Europeans. Both Mike and Dawson were stunned by the depth of hatred directed towards the U.S.

[*NOTE TO READER:* CIA censors redacted the next two pages. The same scene was recorded by CNN reporter Robert Pelton and broadcast on TV. The source of the following description and partial transcript is his TV report.]

███

███

As they moved through the prisoners, Mike Spann noticed a pale young man with long hair who was trying to look invisible. "Hey, you, right there with your head down," Spann called. "Look at me. I know you speak English. Where'd you get that British military sweater?"

Twenty-one-year-old John Walker Lindh continued to stare at the ground. So Mike Spann had one of the guards pull Lindh to his feet and drag him over to a blanket that had been spread over the dirt. As John Walker Lindh knelt, his long hair fell over his face. "All I want to do is talk to you and find out what your story is," Mike Spann explained in English.

Lindh remained silent. Dawson walked over and said, "We can only help the guys who want to talk to us."

"Do you know that the people you're working with are terrorists and have killed other Muslims?" Mike asked. "Do you know that there were several hundred Muslims killed in the attack on New York City?

Is that what the Koran teaches? I don't think so. Are you going to talk to us?"

Lindh remained silent. Finally, Dawson said, "Fine. You got your chance," and moved on.

On a signal from Dawson, an Uzbek guard pulled Lindh to his feet and shoved him into a group of previously interrogated prisoners. All the young American had to say were three words: "I'm an American," and he would have been whisked from the fortress, cared for, questioned and fed. But he chose not to.

The frustration on Mike Spann's face was captured on videotape by reporter Robert Young Pelton, who'd been given permission to enter the fortress by General Dostum. As Dawson walked away, Pelton's camera recorded his saying, "The problem is, he needs to decide if he wants to live or die, and die here. We're just going to leave him, and he's going to fucking sit in prison the rest of his fucking short life. It's his decision, man. We can only help the guys who want to talk to us." Mike and Dawson moved on.

*　*　*

It was 0900 hours when George and I discussed intelligence we'd both received which reported the movement of bin Laden and a large group of his followers into the mountains south of George's position in Jalalabad.

██

██

████████████████████████████████

[*NOTE TO READER:* CIA censors redacted this section dealing with the distribution of resources to the newly formed Eastern Alliance headed by Babrak and Nuruddin.]

"We're repositioning ourselves south of Jalalabad at the foot of the White Mountains so we can be within striking range," George continued. "We're packing the vehicles as I speak."

"Good man," I said. "How are our Afghan allies equipped?"

"They've got weapons and ammo, but not much else."

I had a feeling that would be the case. I said, "I'll call Hank and see what I can get. Contact me again once you're set up."

It was midnight back at CTC/███, but I called anyway. A senior ops officer answered the phone and went secure.

"How are you doing out there?" he asked.

"You'll see two more intel messages tracking bin Laden. George is moving Jawbreaker Juliet down to the foot of the mountains along the Pak border. ████████████████████████████████████, but more important, I don't want to have to wait for them to purchase gear. Can you order say three hundred sets of uniforms, boots, parkas, sleeping bags etc. and get them to me ASAP?"

"No problem, Gary," he answered. "It'll probably take a few days to purchase, ship and put in your hands, but I'm on it."

*   *   *

Dawson looked down at his watch, then around the dusty courtyard of Qala-i Jangi prison. It was 11:15 A.M. It had been a frustrating morning so far. He and Mike had questioned dozens of foreign prisoners, but hadn't gotten much back except for dirty looks and curses. At least the sun had warmed up the courtyard a bit.

Dawson stood holding Mike's AK-47, when he looked over at his partner approximately five meters away, leaning over and talking to a kneeling prisoner. Without warning, an explosion rocked the courtyard sending him back on his heels. A Chechen near Mike had detonated a grenade. More grenades thudded in the southern stairway and prisoners yelling "Allah u Akbar!" started swarming up the stairs.

Before Dawson and Mike knew what was happening, rows of prisoners in the yard rose to their feet and charged. A half dozen of them wrapped their legs and half-bound arms around Mike and tried to bring him to the ground. Spann squeezed off two rounds from his Glock 9 millimeter pistol, killing two of his attackers.

Behind him, prisoners poured up from the south stairway and attacked the Uzbek guards. Amid terrified shouts in a polyglot of languages, prisoners scurried like crazed rabbits searching for weapons and untying one another. One charged straight at Dawson firing a pistol. As bullets whizzed by ███████████, Dawson raised his AK-47 and dropped the prisoner. He then turned to Mike, who was engulfed by a frenzy of men. He quickly shot three of the Arabs on top of Mike, before turning back to face the surge of prisoners coming towards him.

As chaos engulfed the dusty courtyard, John Walker Lindh sat by the southern wall looking for a way to escape. When he started to stand, a bullet hit him in the foot. He screamed out in pain, then decided to lay motionless and pretend he was dead as the riot grew more savage.

Everywhere Dawson looked the Uzbek guards were being disarmed and shot to death with their own weapons. And the torrent of angry men continued to surge up from the basement. Dawson quickly calculated that they'd already murdered the small contingent of Uzbek guards who'd been guarding them, then freed their Taliban and al-Qaeda compatriots.

As he backed up, Dawson fired nonstop into the wall of prisoners. He felt sick to his stomach because he couldn't see his partner, Mike, who'd disappeared in the melee of dust and men. Dawson kept backing towards the north side of the fortress and firing his AK-47 until it was empty. Throwing it aside, he drew his Glock and squeezed off more rounds.

Now a prisoner started coming at him with a grenade in one hand and his other arm around the neck of an Uzbek guard whom he was using as a shield. The guard's eyes bulged out in terror. Dawson backed up further as the volume of fire directed his way increased. He faced a choice: he could either die in the courtyard, or turn and run for cover in the north end of the fortress. He turned and ran.

Behind him prisoners savagely killed and stripped the guards in front of the armory. Then, smashing in the doors, they helped themselves to racks of weapons and ammunition.

The few Uzbek guards who managed to escape fell back into the remaining building in the southern half of the prison. A few scaled the wall that split the prison into southern and northern halves and laid down a deadly field of fire into the courtyard below. Thousands of rounds of gunfire ricocheted in all directions as Taliban and foreign fighters scrambled for cover. The prisoners wrested control of the armory, stables, the L-shaped building in the center and the entire southeastern end of the fortress. In less than ten minutes a full-scale battle was underway.

Dawson burst into the prison governor's office where the prison Governor was cowering with two Red Cross officials. "GET OUT!" he screamed in Uzbek at the top of his lungs. "THE PRISONERS HAVE KILLED AT LEAST TWENTY GUARDS AND ARE TAKING CONTROL OF THE FORTRESS!"

The two men immediately climbed up the fort's parapet and slid down the sixty-foot inclined wall to safety. Dawson stayed. His partner had been lost in the chaos and he was hoping somehow to call in forces to quickly retake the southern half of the prison so he could go back for Mike. Just then two camera crews who were trapped in the fortress burst into the main building where Dawson was hiding.

Fortunately, a member of one of the camera crews was carrying a satellite phone. Dawson used it to call the ██████████ in Tashkent. He spoke to the Defense Attaché who was the officer on duty, then called his wife. Trying not to frighten her, he explained that it was very important that the ████ Tashkent call him immediately. She carefully wrote down her husband's number and passed along his message. Soon help was on its way.

While Dawson waited in the main building on the northern perimeter, wounded John Walker Lindh lay in the yard along the southern wall next to another wounded prisoner and continued to play dead. The fighting continued nonstop.

Shortly after 1400 hours Dawson received an urgent call over his small handheld radio. A combined U.S.-British Special Forces team with a close air support contingent had landed outside the prison. They told him to stay put and then set about doing what they did best: responding to a highly chaotic combat situation with minimal preparation. Using a SOFLAM they lit up targets in the southern half of the fortress for incoming aircraft, which started killing the revolting prisoners in large numbers. By the time darkness fell, seven waves of air strikes had pounded the fortress. One bomb hit a building on the southern perimeter that housed a number of Uzbek guards, killing several and wounding others.

Dawson and the journalists used the cover of darkness to slip over the northern wall. Fourteen hours after the battle had begun, John Walker Lindh's comrades dragged him back into the basement where he remained throughout the remainder of the revolt.

The Special Forces team had hoped initially that they could get to Mike before the night was over and recover his body. But the fighting raged on.

*　　*　　*

Hundreds of miles to the southeast, George and Jawbreaker Juliet arrived quietly at the foot of the White Mountains as the sun started to set. Babrak had arranged for them to bivouac in a vacant brick school with no running water, no toilets and blown out windows covered with cardboard located in the sparsely populated hill town of Agam. From there they looked out on foothills to the right and snow-covered peaks due south. Babrak's men referred to the highest snow-covered peak as "the white sheik."

An imposing man with a tight, curly beard and gentle eyes, Babrak had already deployed into the remote mountain communities of

Pacheer and Agam soldiers who now returned with information. Hundreds of Arab al-Qaeda members fleeing Kabul and Jalalabad had retreated into camps nearby and more Arabs and other non-Afghans were arriving every day.

George asked Babrak if he could provide guides to lead his men forward to find a defensible observation point. Babrak said that he could because his soldiers knew the mountains well. The big Texan stroked his mustache and decided on the spot to deploy a team right into the heart of the al-Qaeda sanctuary. In addition to himself, George had three other Agency officers, three JSOC soldiers and an SF medic. Babrak, though he claimed to command hundreds, appeared to have at most forty to sixty soldiers with him at the time.

The Texan asked Babrak through Babrak's translator for the name of the area where al-Qaeda was gathering. The Pashai warlord fingered bright blue prayer beads as he answered: "Tora Bora," which translated into English means "black dust."

16

TORA BORA

*"It is a principle of human nature to hate those
whom you have injured."*

—*Tacitus*

*   *   *   *   *   *

We listened helplessly from Kabul as the fighting continued in Qala-i Jangi. When Hamid, who'd been a classmate of Mike Spann's at the Farm, volunteered to join the battle, I reminded him that the fortess was six hundred miles away.

Throughout the night U.S. air strikes pounded the south side of the fortress, which allowed the Uzbeks to regroup and establish a command post in the northeast tower. Shortly after 10 A.M. additional Special Forces soldiers and eight men from the 10th Mountain Division arrived in trucks. Two Special Forces soldiers armed with radios and an all-important SOFLAM inched their way along the northern parapet. "Be advised," said one soldier over his radio as he watched from below, "you're dangerously close. You're about a hundred yards away from the target."

"I think maybe we're a little too close," replied the spotter. "But we have to be to get the laser on line."

SF spotter: "Be advised we have new coordinates, north 3639996, east 066558866. We're about ready to pull back."

Pilot: "We're ready to release."

Spotter: "Two minutes."

With bullets and RPG rounds exploding around them, the SF spotter lit up the target and withdrew seconds before a U.S. rocket slammed into a nest of armed Taliban and al-Qaeda rebels.

The battle had turned into an inverse castle siege with the rebels holding the interior of the fortress and our Uzbek allies and Special Forces troops controlling the walls and surrounding fields. Despite the nonstop air assault, the enemy had a huge supply of ordinance, which they had grabbed from the armory.

At 1053 hours an errant Air Force missile tore into the north wall ten meters from the combined Uzbek-U.S.-British command post and exploded. An Uzbek tank positioned next to the tower flew in the air and flipped over, ripping off its gun and killing the crew. Uzbek soldiers began sliding down the side of the fort and staggering into surrounding cotton fields, blood dripping from their ears and eyes. British SAS and American SF soldiers emerged from the fort's entrance choking and spitting mud. Dozens had to be dug out of the rubble. "We have one down, semiconscious, no internal bleeding," a British soldier reported over the radio net. The casualties and wounded were quickly loaded into jeeps and minibuses and driven to a base in Mazar-e Sharif. Five Americans and another five British SAS soldiers were later medivaced to Landstuhl Regional Medical Center in Germany.

In the first twenty-four hours of the battle, thirty of our Uzbek Northern Alliance allies had died and another fifty were wounded. Below in the courtyard lay the mangled remains of two hundred Taliban and al-Qaeda fighters along with a number of Dostum's thirty horses. It was a gruesome scene.

*   *   *

George selected four men to deploy forward: Parker, the former SF officer who had entered Kabul with Bismullah Khan's men; Dusty, a former JSOC soldier who'd retired to become an Agency contractor; Reno, an Air Force combat controller assigned to JSOC who'd come to Afghanistan to support the Shelter Now International rescue effort; and Lance his JSOC Army partner. Accompanying Juliet Forward, as the team was called, were ten of Babrak's soldiers to serve both as guides and provide additional firepower should they be attacked by al-Qaeda.

They packed onto mules weapons, ammo, food, communications equipment, sleeping bags and the SOFLAM that had been lent to them by Lt. Colonel Haas and prepared to follow a primitive dirt road to a valley higher up in the mountains.

George called me to review the state of play. "I'm ready to send a team into the mountains to find al-Qaeda for the purpose of attacking them with airpower," he reported.

"Excellent," I said. "What else can I do to support you?"

"We need to be thinking ahead past the point we make contact," he responded.

"If you engage the enemy, I should be able to convince Colonel Mulholland to deploy an SF team to join you."

"My men leave within the hour," George said. "Tomorrow Babrak, Nuruddin and the others will start moving their troops to block al-Qaeda escape's to the east and west. Our aim is to pin the enemy with their backs against the mountains to the south."

"Sounds like a good plan, George. Jawbreaker out."

Colonel Alexander, who commanded the latest SF team to arrive in-country, stood at my side. "I guess we won't be training counter-terrorism pursuit teams this week," he said with a grin.

"No," I answered. "I suspect you'll be busy doing something else. Prepare your men so you're ready to deploy as soon as I get the nod from Mulholland."

*   *   *

As evening of the twenty-sixth fell over Qala-i Jangi, the nonstop shooting from Taliban and al-Qaeda rebels finally let up. At midnight an AC-130 gunship started to circle the fortress and direct awesome firepower on several southern-perimeter buildings held by the rebels. One SF soldier wearing night vision goggles shouted: "It's going to be quite a show!" Powerful 30mm guns and cannons shredded the walls of the armory setting off a massive explosion that lifted the entire fortress in air. The blast blew open doors ten miles away. Secondary explosions lit up the night sky for miles around and continued for hours. A foreign fighter who escaped was captured by local residents and hung from a tree.

Downstairs in the southern basement hundreds of foreign fighters, including John Walker Lindh, huddled against the walls with their hands over their ears as the ceiling rumbled and quaked overhead.

Tuesday morning, one hundred Uzbek Northern Alliance soldiers dispatched by General Dostum scaled a tower on the southwestern wall. Slithering into position on their stomachs, they began to lay down a wall of machine gun fire that killed anything in the courtyard that moved.

Nearby, a U.S. soldier greeted an SAS comrade who had been trapped in the errant air strike the day before. "How's your hearing today?" he asked. The British soldier pretended that he was deaf. "I said, How's your hearing?" shouted the American. The Brit pointed to his ear and shook his head.

Dawson returned to the fortress praying that through some miracle his buddy Mike Spann was still alive. In the afternoon, a force of Uzbeks soldiers burst into the southern courtyard led by a tank that blasted volley after volley into the last rebel-held building. The Uzbeks picked their way carefully through hundreds of charred bodies, mangled buildings and blast craters, stopping to strip bodies of guns, ammo, money and sneakers. Mike Spann's body was found by Special Forces soldiers with a booby-trapped Taliban body placed on top of him prepared to go off. He had been executed with two bullets to the head.

In a basement room of one of the buildings, four foreign fighters were discovered alive and dragged out. But in the southern basement armed al-Qaeda soldiers refused to be coaxed out.

*　　*　　*

That same morning, the twenty-seventh of November, thirty-two Afghan delegates representing four different political factions met in Bonn, Germany, in a conference organized by the UN. The Northern Alliance, which now controlled half of the country, sent a team of eleven delegates led by Interior Minister Younis Qanooni made up of Tajiks, Uzbeks, Hazaras and Pushtuns. The official political leader of the Northern Alliance, former President Burhanuddin Rabbani refused to attend, insisting that any talks about the future of Afghanistan should take place inside Afghanistan. Eighteen outside countries, including the U.S., sent representatives to monitor the talks.

Besides the Northern Alliance, the other Afghan political groups were the Cypress group comprised of exiles with ties to Iran, the Rome group loyal to former King Mohammad Zaher Shah and the Peshawar group made up mostly of Pushtun exiles based in Pakistan. Taliban delegates were excluded from the talks.

Hamid Karzai addressed the opening session of the conference via satellite phone from inside Afghanistan. He made an impassioned plea for the various factions to set aside their differences for the sake of the whole nation. "This meeting is the path towards salvation," he said.

U.S. Special Representative Jim Dobbins was surprised at how warmly delegates from the different factions greeted one another. "There was no animosity and some affection," he said later.

UN Ambassador Mohammad Fadhel Brahami, who presided over the conference, quickly got the delegates to agree to form an interim administration that would run the country for the next three to six months, until the traditional Afghan grand council of ethnic leaders called the *loya jirga* could be called into emergency session. It would be the responsibility of the *loya jirga* to chose a transitional government and draft a new constitution.

Ethnic rivalries and suspicions flared over three points: peacekeeping forces, the leader of the interim administration and the distribution of cabinet ministries among the different factions. The Northern Alliance felt that they should continue to provide security for Kabul. But the three other factions, fearing the type of abuses that occurred when Northern Alliance warlords controlled Kabul after the Soviet withdrawal in '89, favored a UN peacekeeping force.

Initially former King Mohammad Zaher Shah appeared to have wide support to lead the interim government. But he was strongly opposed by Rabbani and other members of the Northern Alliance. Eventually the choice came down to two candidates: Pushtun leader Hamid Karzai and an ethnic Uzbek proposed by the Rome group by the name of Abdul Sittar Sirat. Former King Zaher Shah made clear that he had no personal political ambitions, and agreed to withdraw his name and preside instead over the *loya jirga* when it convened.

After intense negotiation and threats by some Northern Alliance representatives to quit the talks, the delegates agreed to form a twenty-nine-member interim government to be headed by Hamid Karzai and a UN force to provide security for Kabul.

The last remaining and most contentious issue was the distribution of ministries. On the last night of the conference, U.S. Special Representative Dobbins and UN Ambassador Brahami called together the Russian, Iranian and Germany ambassadors to meet with the leader of the Northern Alliance delegation Younis Qanooni. They haggled until two in morning. The Northern Alliance, which had gone into the meeting demanding twenty of the twenty-nine positions in the interim government, agreed to take seventeen. The Northern Alliance delegates to the interim government would include General Fahim (Defense), Dr. Abdullah Abdullah (Foreign Affairs) and Younis Qanooni (Interior).

The UN Security Council quickly approved the deployment of 3,000 to 5,000 peacekeepers to be led by 1,500 soldiers from Great Britain's International Security Assistance Force (ISAF), which would protect Afghan dignitaries who assembled in Kabul for Karzai's inauguration on December 22.

*　　*　　*

George contacted me by radio from the schoolhouse at the foot of Tora Bora. "Gary, this is George," he said solemnly. "We have a delay in moving our team forward."

"What kind of delay?" I asked.

"It seems that a member of the Afghan security detail didn't pack the mules as well as he should have. One of them carrying an RPG-7 round detonated halfway up the mountain blowing the mule to pieces and killing two of Babrak's men."

"Holy shit! Are any of our guys injured?"

"Apparently not," he answered. "But we have to bring the bodies back down to a location where Babrak's men can get them. These Afghans are all related to each other, one way or another."

I immediately thought of the word friction. According to the great Prussian military strategist Carl von Clausewitz, friction was the enemy of every army on the march. Friction was when a wheel broke off a towed artillery piece, or when a supply cart fell into the river, or men were stricken with disease. It was a commander's responsibility to anticipate and guard against friction. In the case of our ongoing Afghan campaign, friction had manifested itself in the form of an exploding mule!

"Was the team's entry into the mountains discovered because of the explosion?" I asked.

"It doesn't appear so," George answered. "The team's preparing right now to return the bodies for a proper burial."

"Please pass on my condolences to Babrak. Jawbreaker out."

I looked at my watch, which read 2330 hours. The only other person in the Station was Billy Waugh, who was reading the incoming traffic. He must have seen the concern in my eyes.

"You want some coffee, Chief?" Billy asked.

"Thanks, Billy," I said. "I can get off my butt and pour it."

"I got it. You just take cream, don't you?"

"That's right."

Setting down the coffee, he said, "You're doing a good job. I've spent more than thirty years in the Army and finished as a Command Sergeant Major in Special Forces. I know what I'm talking about."

"Thanks."

"Sending George down into Jalalabad to lead was real smart. He's good."

"How do you know George?" I asked.

██

██

████████████████████████████████████

"George never said anything about that," I replied.

"That's the kind of guy he is. Quiet. Does his job with courage, intelligence and a minimum of bullshit," Billy said. "I can tell that you trust him, which is real important. In this business you have to trust men and then send them forward with the authority to make decisions. Success in life is the same. Nobody can do it all. Trust is what allows men and women to get the really difficult things done. "

The seventy-two-year-old former Command Sergeant Major and I sat up and talked for another ninety minutes. Billy had seven combat tours under his belt and something else that doesn't necessarily come with them: wisdom. Anytime he made a recommendation, I took it under careful consideration.

*   *   *

General Dostum was red hot. He'd hurried back to Mazar-e-Sharif and gone straight to Qala-i Jangi fortress to survey the destruction. It pissed him off to no end that the Taliban and their foreign partners had tried to break out.

Initially, he'd been led to believe that fewer than a dozen holdouts remained in the basement. He sent a team of local health workers to speak to the armed, barricaded and desperate men. When the rebels fired on the health workers, General Dostum sent in two mullahs to try to convince the holdouts to surrender. This failed as well.

That's when Dostum turned to coercion. First, he had his men drop live grenades through the vents, then they fired rockets. Several more rebels were killed, but still no surrender. Losing his patience, the barrel-chested Uzbek commander ordered his men to dump diesel fuel in the basement and set it on fire. Screams rose from below as a number of the rebels burned alive and others were overcome by fumes. But the holdouts still wouldn't surrender. Finally, General Dostum had his men pump in ice cold water with the aim of drowning some and freezing out the others in the midst of the Afghan winter.

One night of waist-high freezing water did the trick. On the morning of November 30 eighty-six Taliban and al-Qaeda fighters emerged from the basement and surrendered. They were ghastly looking, hungry and covered with shrapnel wounds and burns.

Among the foreign fighters was John Walker Lindh, who suffered from severe hypothermia, shrapnel wounds in the upper right thigh, and grenade shrapnel in the back. Also, part of the second toe on his left foot had been shot away. The prisoners were fed bananas, apples, pomegranates and bread and given clothes before being loaded onto three trucks and driven to Sheberghan prison.

Asked in the prison hospital by reporter Robert Pelton if the jihad had been a good cause for him, John Walker Lindh answered: "Definitely." He said he was from Washington state and had come to Afghanistan to help the Taliban build a perfect Islamic government, but refused to give his name.

One week later, Mike Spann was buried with full military honors at Arlington cemetery. "Not everyone is skilled or has the desire to go to faraway places to fight in wars, but all of us have the skills and should have the desire to serve our country by being good," his wife, Shannon, said in her eulogy. "Mike served his country by being good."

All of us on the Agency teams were stricken by the news of Mike Spann's death. He'd become the first U.S. casualty in Afghanistan, but wouldn't be the last.

17

THE BATTLE OF MILAWA

*"The fact that slaughter [battle] is a horrifying spectacle
must make us take war more seriously, but [it does] not
provide an excuse for gradually blunting our swords in the
name of humanity. Sooner or later someone will come
along with a sharp sword and hack off our arms."*

—*Carl von Clausewitz*, On War

*   *   *   *   *   *

The four men from Jawbreaker Juliet returned with the dead from Babrak's security detachment, then turned around and humped back into the mountains with their mules. Ahead of them lay large trails and, even, roads, which they avoided for fear of being detected by an enemy that outnumbered them by at least 100 to 1.

Babrak's guides knew exactly where to go, leading them through a primitive agricultural area towards a valley high in the mountains nestled between two sharp sets of peaks. Parker, Dusty, Lance and Reno were at over 10,000 feet and counting. With increasing frequency they stopped to examine hilltops through their binoculars and scopes.

Climbing into the thinning oxygen for two days, they stopped at a bluff overlooking a valley with small villages and primitive farms. Babrak's guides pointed to a military camp built into an embankment, where they spotted trucks, houses, command posts, checkpoints, machine gun nests, an obstacle course and hundreds of bin Laden's men.

"Bingo!" Parker exclaimed.

Carefully, they moved their mules out of sight and established a position behind rocks and some scrawny trees where they couldn't be seen. They instructed the ten Afghan guides to stay below and defend possible avenues of approach.

Parker wasted no time establishing communications with both George and me. "I'm ready to establish sat-com and start calling in JDAMs," he said excitedly.

We gave him a big thumbs-up. Meanwhile, Dusty and Lance hauled the gear they needed, including weapons and ammunition, to the observation post. There, they set the SOFLAM on its tripod, and Reno, the combat controller, dialed up his radio and established communications with an AWACS. "We'll have bombers in thirty minutes," he announced.

Parker reported to me and George: "We're set up and ready to begin."

Dusty and Lance peered through the SOFLAM's rubberized scope. The accompanying wire and trigger were tested and ready. The spindly looking contraption could fire a laser as far as ten thousand meters and mark a target for incoming smart munitions. Reno picked up a device that looked like a gigantic Palm Pilot, which he used to insert coordinates and provide additional guidance to incoming aircraft. As a combat controller his job was essentially that of an air traffic controller for combat missions.

"Thunder, Juliet," Reno said over the radio to airplanes above. "The coordinates are north 3639116, east 0666875, elevation 11,298 feet."

After receiving a report from the pilot, he turned to Dusty and Lance and said: "Three minutes."

"Two minutes."

They lit up the target.

"Thirty seconds."

A great arrow-shaped missile zoomed by, screeching like a car in high gear. A loud explosion shattered the quiet and echoed through the mountains. Shrapnel burned through the air. Before the al-Qaeda soldiers knew what hit them, smart bombs from a B-1 started thundering around them, throwing trucks in the air and ripping apart buildings and bunkers.

Dusty, Lance, Reno and Parker watched the pandemonium below as al-Qaeda soldiers tried to reorganize, seek cover and attend to their wounded all at once. This wasn't a faceless enemy as portrayed in movies or on TV, but real flesh-and-blood soldiers suffering a grizzly death.

Working nonstop, the four men directed strike after strike by B-1s, B-2s and F-14s onto the al-Qaeda encampment with incredible precision. Somehow through the massive bureaucracy, thousands of miles of distance, reams of red tape and a diffuse system of command that had been hastily assembled and never used before, the U.S. had managed to place four of the most skilled men in the world above the motherload of al-Qaeda, with a laser designator and communications system linked to the most potent air power in history. Al-Qaeda soldiers who'd once dreamed of wreaking havoc on the West were now paying with their lives.

As I listened over our encrypted radio network, one word kept pounding in my head: *revenge*. I thought, *Let's do this right and finish them off in the mountains.*

Meanwhile, pilots were flashing strike reports back to General Franks and his CENTCOM staff in Tampa, Florida. CENTCOM brass was excited to learn that we'd established an observation point smack in the middle of al-Qaeda's hideout. They reacted rapidly, shooting all available air assets to Jawbreaker Juliet.

Even though their legs were numb and their eyes bleary and red, Dusty, Lance, Reno and Parker called in air strikes throughout the night. Since their communication system ran on batteries, we could only be in contact with them at four-to-eight-hour intervals. I left someone next to our radio twenty-four hours in case they called for help.

In the morning, Parker was describing the destruction resulting from a new wave of air attacks when his voice suddenly rose in pitch.

"What's wrong, Parker?" I asked.

"An al-Qaeda tank has just moved into our field of vision from left to right," he said excitedly. "I think they might have found us!"

"Have the JSOC guys light it up," I shouted.

"They can't! They can't! It's no longer in our field of vision!"

Reno immediately radioed aircraft overhead and asked a pilot to find and destroy the tank. The pilot refused, saying that the rules of engagement only allowed him to attack targets that were either designated with SOFLAMs or had been pretargeted before the mission. Reno explained that the tank was now concealed behind a hill so the team could not light it with the laser. "I'm sorry," the pilot said. "I've got strict orders to follow the rules of engagement."

The rules had been set to reduce friendly fire incidents. But these four men were all alone in the midst of a hornet's nest of hardened al-Qaeda fighters.

I radioed Parker and told him I would try to help. Almost immediately I was on the phone with our Agency rep to the SF teams in ███████████████████████████, just across the border. I was more than a little distressed.

"Relax, Gary," the rep said. "I'll take care of it. I know you're damn busy down there. Keep hammering away."

George prepared a combined team of Americans and Afghans to conduct a rescue of his isolated four-man team. A CIA Special Activities Division contractor who'd recently arrived in Tora Bora volunteered to lead the mission. But scouting reports from the Afghan guides indicated that the team hadn't been discovered.

Within twenty-four hours the rules of engagement for Tora Bora were altered and the tank destroyed. This time, the lumbering Department of Defense bureaucracy moved quickly.

Since there were only four men and the SOFLAM and accompanying commo equipment were relatively light, the team was able to move
about the promontory to gain better views of the camp below. Dusty,
Lance, Reno and Parker had been calling in air strikes for a day and a
half when I received a phone call from CTC/███. It was about 9 P.M.
in Afghanistan.

"Hello, Gary," I heard Hank say.

"What's up?"

"Gary," he said clearing his throat. "It's apparent that you have a
team up near Tora Bora and they're calling in a lot of air strikes."

"Yeah, that's us."

"Good for you. Based on the intel and intercepts from our end it
appears that bin Laden is up there, too."

"That's correct."

I could hear Hank chuckle with approval on the other end. "Good
job. I'm proud of you. Keep it up."

I said, "I'm seeing Colonel Mulholland tomorrow morning. I want
to insert Colonel Alexander's SF team—the one you sent me to
train counterterrorism pursuit teams—into the mountains. They have
enough men for at least three observation points, so we can increase
our air attacks. We can train the Afghan pursuit teams later. I want to
kill as many al-Qaeda as I can in Tora Bora right now."

"Do it!" Hank exclaimed. "Don't wait." Then he turned somber.
███
███
████████████████████████████

"Thanks for the warning. I'll handle the prisons question here. It
won't stop us from exploiting possible leads. Don't worry."

"Okay," Hank said. "CTC/███ out."
███
███

████ The order was a knee-jerk response to Mike Spann's death.

I called everyone in for a meeting, including Bilal, Hoss and Amir, who'd returned from the Panshir where they hadn't found any information about possible future attacks against the West. More than a dozen officers packed into our workspace.

"Gentlemen," I said. "I have a cable here which prohibits our entry into prisons to speak to prisoners. ███████████████████████████ ███████████████████████████████."

A collective groan rose from the men.

"Hold on a minute," I continued. "I need to explain a few things. First, Mike Spann did nothing wrong by going into Qala-i Jangi fortress. We have two hundred and seventy million citizens counting on us to uncover the next attack and Qala-i Jangi, Sheberghan prison and the various prisons in Kabul are likely to produce a lead that could help us. Mike was a very brave man."

They all nodded.

"I don't give a rat's ass what the DCI or DDO think about us going into the prisons," I said. "███████████████████████████ ████████████████████████ We have too many missions and there are too few of us to have additional security measures layered onto us from five thousand miles away. I decide what happens here. If anyone has a problem with that speak up now and tell me."

Nobody said a word.

███
███
███
███
████████████████████

[*NOTE TO READER:* CIA censors redacted my instructions to my team regarding the care I wanted them to use in dealing with prisoners and what I thought of the order we had received from headquarters.]

The following morning Colonel Alexander and I set out to Bagram to see Colonel John Mulholland, who knew by now that our forward team was directing air strikes against al-Qaeda in the mountains near

Tora Bora. Both Alexander and Mulholland were full colonels and had been friends for years. Colonel Mulholland had turned down my request a few days ago to send an SF team into Jalalabad. Now Colonel Alexander was asking him to send his team on a close air support mission into the belly of the beast.

"How will you deploy?" Colonel Mulholland asked.

"By MH-47 helicopter," Colonel Alexander answered.

Mulholland thought out loud: "That'll be our first helicopter combat mission into Nangahar province."

Mulholland took a minute to consider. He had SF teams scattered all over the country conducting combat operations against a far more numerous enemy. The margin for error was slim. He turned to me and said: "You can have the team."

"Thanks, John," I said.

Back at the guesthouse in Kabul, Colonel Alexander's twelve-man team starting packing gear. They thought they'd come to Afghanistan to train Northern Alliance soldiers. Now they were getting a chance to go after bin Laden. They couldn't have been more pumped up.

Parker called on the radio from Tora Bora and said, "We're going to shut down now and catch some sleep."

"What?" I responded. "What the hell do you want sleep for? You're killing the enemy!"

"Chief, I'm sorry," Parker explained. "But we've been doing this for fifty-six hours straight. Before that we had to hump up here. We're wiped out."

Everyone in the office broke out laughing. They thought that I was a maniac. Colonel Alexander had to cover his face because he was laughing so hard. "Chief, you should let them sleep," he argued.

Realizing I was being unreasonable, I relented: "Okay, Parker. I'm sorry. Get some rest. Help's on the way. We'll have an SF team there in less than forty-eight hours."

"That's great news," Parker responded. "We'll be back up on the air in six hours. Juliet forward, out."

"Jawbreaker, out."

*　　*　　*

Prior to departing at dawn the next morning Colonel Alexander stopped by to express his gratitude. Over the years he had prepared many times to go after bin Laden only to have the missions scrapped at the last minute.

"Nobody's going to stop us now," I told him. Three of Majid's men were joining him for the drive to the school at the foot of the White Mountains. His SF team would follow later in the day by helicopter.

Parker, from the front, reported that the vast majority of al-Qaeda in Milawa valley had started retreating south into caves and bunkers. Others were moving farther back into the snow-covered mountains.

George, from the schoolhouse at the base of Tora Bora, assured me that his Afghan blocking force had slowly begun to move into place.

"Is there any way to light a fire under them?" I asked.

"We are in the holy month of Ramadan now, Chief," George answered in his drawl. "A large number of these guys fast during the day, then leave their positions at night to go back to their families and eat. Also, a number of our new Eastern Alliance partners are complaining ████████████████ about promised resources."

I explained that Majid had been hesitant to send ██████████ (resources) by road. That's when I remembered Colonel Alexander's team at Bagram getting ready to helicopter down to Tora Bora. "Hold on, George," I said. "I've got a plan."

I quickly called ahead to Bagram and told the helicopter to wait. Besides Major General Dell Dailey, commander of JSOC (Joint Special Operations Command), had arrived and wanted to meet me. I would kill two birds with one stone.

Davis and I arrived at dusk carrying the ████████████ in a duffel bag. Guards from the U.S. Army 10th Mountain Division waved us in. We drove directly to the tarmac where the MH-47 helicopter had already fired up its engines. The rear hatch door was down and soldiers were still loading gear.

Over the roar of engines, I said, "Let me talk to one of the officers. "

One of the soldiers answered: "One minute, sir." Then jogged to the helicopter and entered its belly.

Out came a young SF officer I recognized from the guesthouse. I said, ███

███

███

███

████████████████████████████████

[*NOTE TO READER:* This redacted section deals with a transfer of resources to the Eastern Alliance.]

They made the trip that normally took eight hours by road in less than an hour. George and his men designated a landing zone using infrared lights. ████████████ was safely handed over. After a good night's sleep in the schoolhouse, Colonel Alexander's twelve-man team was ready to deploy forward.

My meeting with Major General Dailey took place in the same building we had initially used as our staging area. Now it housed the U.S. Army's command and communications center. They had upgraded it with sofas to form a waiting area, barbed wire surrounding the building and armed guards at the door.

General Gary Harrell, CENTCOM's Director of Joint Security who'd been sent to direct the humanitarian effort, made the introductions. General Dailey, who had spent most of his career as a helicopter pilot, was interested in the Afghan response to the British arrival and wanted to know if I thought we should include the British in U.S. combat operations.

"Not until the Afghans accept the fact that the British are here to help and are operating under our umbrella," I answered. I told him that I thought the Afghan reaction to the British had been petty, but it was their country.

Major General Dailey had been thoroughly briefed by Colonel Mulholland about Jawbreaker Juliet's ongoing activities and expressed his approval.

*   *   *

Following the U.S. air bombardment, bin Laden and his men abandoned their Milawa camp and retreated farther into the White Mountains. George ordered Dusty, Parker, Lance and Reno down from their observation post, while Babrak sent small scouting teams forward to search for al-Qaeda's new location. It wasn't long before they discovered new encampments in an area surrounded by caves.

George, Colonel Alexander and Babrak drank green tea and pored over maps. Colonel Alexander had initially planned to establish three new observation points, but decided that two were better suited to the difficult terrain and new sets of targets. The idea was to trap bin Laden and his fighters in a kill box between three promontories manned by SF teams. Two new teams would be positioned on peaks south and west—one on Tonga Mountain, another closer to Slinga farther south—while the original post near Milawa would be reestablished to the east.

With Babrak's men serving as guides Colonel Alexander's team split into two groups, and, avoiding the hordes of journalists who had pitched tents around the schoolhouse, drove the dirt road to Milawa. There, in the deserted valley, they saw the devastation of the U.S. air strikes—trees shredded to knee-high stumps, smalls caves and tunnels destroyed, huge craters bored into the rocky ground and mud buildings blown to bits. Bundling themselves against the bitter cold, they climbed into the mountains.

Within a day the teams—code named Black, Silver and Red—established posts on ridges and began calling in air strikes. CENTCOM responded with a full compliment of B-52 and B-1 bombers from bases in the U.S. and fighters stationed on aircraft carriers in the Persian

Gulf. AC-130 Spectre gunships lumbered in at night to lay down a lethal blanket of machine gun and cannon fire.

This time, al-Qaeda fighters sought temporary refuge in caves before retreating farther into the mountains under the cover of darkness.

George positioned Nuruddin forces in the west—to his right looking south—Babrak to his center and Haji Qadir's son, Haji Mohammed Zahir, to the east. Haji Qadir was the older brother of Abdul Haq, the Pushtun tribal leader who had been hanged by the Taliban ███████████. The idea was to pin bin Laden's force against the mountains.

From the start it was clear that the men leading this new Afghan force did not have the same desire we did to pursue and destroy al-Qaeda. And many of their foot soldiers were followers of local religious leader Maulawi Mohammad Younus Khalis, who had instructed them to allow al-Qaeda to escape.

"My father told me, 'Just go,'" Haji Zahir later explained to Susan B. Glaser of the *Washington Post*. "So I left for Tora Bora with seven hundred soldiers. We got there, but I don't know what for. We had no food or anything. We just got there with nothing but these seven hundred soldiers."

It wasn't a perfect arrangement to say the least. No sooner did Eastern Alliance soldiers advance into the mountains than they started to receive fire from al-Qaeda. Bin Laden had ordered elements of his forces to slow the Eastern Alliance advance.

*   *   *

George and I spoke frequently over our encrypted radio net. He told me that soon after Colonel Alexander's arrival, the ██████████ drafted a five-paragraph "operations order" delineating the tactics and goals of the military operation. I received the document the morning of December 3 and quickly reviewed it with J.P., ████████████ in CIA Special Activities Division, who had arrived in Kabul. Special Activities had jurisdiction over ███████████ which had provided the paramilitary officers on my team. It only took ten minutes of discussion for us to establish that we were of the same mind regarding the conduct of the campaign and Jawbreaker's pursuit of al-Qaeda into Tora Bora.

J.P. noted that this was the first time in at least a century and a half that a civilian, George, was in charge of a battlefield. When I showed the document to Lt. Colonel Mark Sutter of JSOC, he suggested we change the language to read that George would remain in command until he could be relieved by an appropriate military officer.

Thirty minutes later Major General Dailey arrived to discuss the issue of including the British in his operations. I told him that if he wanted to use the British, he should, but it was more important that he read the operational order drafted by Colonel Alexander and ████████ . He refused.

I tried to hand him the order and said, "General, we're involved in a very important combat operation down in Tora Bora and I would like you to read this document."

"No, thank you," he responded.

J.P. looked at me as if to say, *I can't believe this.*

I was ready to raise my voice, when Lt. Colonel Sutter stepped in covering for his boss, "I've seen it, sir. It's fine."

After General Dailey departed, I turned to J.P. and said, "I don't get it! Why wouldn't he read the order?"

J.P. who knew Defense Department politics better than I did, answered, "If things go badly in Tora Bora, he won't have his fingerprints on it. If they go well, they'll have a party for him at the Pentagon."

I went down to the office with J.P. to greet Parker and Dusty, who had just returned from Juliet Forward in the mountains of Tora Bora. We assembled the men and opened a case of beer that J.P. had brought with him from Dushanbe.

"I would like to make two toasts," I called out.

"First, a toast to our Commander-in-Chief. God bless him for being a man who is not afraid to fight."

"To the President!" several men yelled out.

"Next, I would like to toast Cofer and Hank for their intelligence and courage."

"To Cofer and Hank!" they all responded.

We spent the next thirty minutes drinking beer and relaxing before everyone returned to their posts. Then, I turned to Parker and Dusty and said, "I need your assessment now. What do we have down there? How can we kill more of al-Qaeda and faster? How do we make sure that bin Laden and his men won't escape?"

In his thick southern accent, Dusty described the terrain and the large number of possible escape routes. Then, he gave his assessment of our allies, which was not encouraging. He said that a battalion of U.S. Army Rangers would be an immeasurable help. He recommended that Rangers be dropped behind al-Qaeda positions to block their escape to Pakistan. It would be a difficult and daring mission, Dusty explained, but the kind that the Rangers were trained to do. And Dusty knew what he was talking about. He'd spent his entire career in the Army and served as a Delta Force officer.

Billy Waugh standing next to me agreed. "The trick," he noted, "will be to get the Army to agree. There will be resistance."

I instructed Parker and Dusty to .

[*NOTE TO READER:* CIA censors redacted a critical request for help on the battlefield that was made by me and distributed to CIA headquarters.]

18

ADAM KHAN

"Hero-worship is the strongest where there is the least regard for human freedom."
—*Herbert Spencer,* Social Statistics, IV

*   *   *   *   *   *

There was no immediate reply to my appeal for U.S. Rangers, but CTC/███ did respond ███████████████████████
███████████████████████████████████████
███████████████████████████████████████
████████████████████

[*NOTE TO READER:* This redacted section deals with supplies for the Eastern Alliance.]

The five men from Team Delta were waiting to see me. So I wished Bilal and Hoss good luck and sent them on their way. "We're all set," Special Activities officer Klesko said. ████████████████████
████████████████████ The walled city of Ghazni, one hundred and thirty miles south of Kabul, had been the site of the SNI hostage rescue.

"Great."

"If ██████ is willing to help us capture bin Laden, we'll do business with him and let him go," Klesko continued excitedly. "If he jerks us around, we'll take him prisoner."

"Sounds fine by me." I knew that neither headquarters nor CENT-COM would approve such an off-the-cuff operation. The guys on Team Delta wouldn't be able to assess the value of the mission until ███ showed up.

I said: "Use your best judgment. Remember, ███████ and his senior guys will most likely lead the insurgency against the new government when this war is over. If you can't negotiate bin Laden's capture or if he refuses to meet with you and you can get a fix on his position, ████████████████████████████████████ I don't want to give him an opportunity to lead an insurgency against us later. Am I clear?"

The entire team nodded. Some said: "Yes."

"Stop at Bagram before you leave. Hank's deputy, John, just arrived to help the military set up an intel cell. Tell him what you're doing. He's smart and aggressive. I'd trust him with my life."

"We will."

The guys on Team Delta were about to go into the Taliban stronghold of Ghazni where we had no support. The mission was fraught with risks. But Ghazni was probably one of the only places that ███████ would show his face.

I decided not to draft an operational message describing Team Delta's mission. Hank wouldn't have a problem with it, but others might read the document and find reasons to pull back. I was on the ground to be aggressive, take reasonable risks and seize opportunities that people sitting at headquarters weren't in a position to evaluate as fully. Just as I had sent men into Jalalabad and Tora Bora, I would send Team Delta into Ghazni to take a shot at ███████████.

On the afternoon of the fourth, a second Agency flight arrived at Bagram bringing my old friend Adam Khan. Since our meeting in the hall at Langley over a month ago, this rare, talented and very valuable ██████ Pushtun speaker had been stuck in CTC's language unit translating documents. Enraged at the way he was being misused, Adam Khan marched into CTC's front office and said, "Send me to Kabul, or I'm gone."

He was dispatched to Kabul immediately. "Finally!" I shouted as he strode into the guesthouse.

"What an idiotic waste of my time the last four weeks have been," he exclaimed taking my hand.

"You just missed Bilal, who's on his way to Tora Bora. I'll send you tomorrow."

Adam Khan laughed. "I knew I could count on you to send me forward. Thanks."

"Get some rest, you're going to need it. George has his hands full with a bunch of tricky Pushtuns."

"I'll handle them," Adam said. "Don't worry."

"I'll feel a lot better with you, George and Bilal down there. All former Marines."

"*Semper fideles*, baby," he answered with a grin.

*   *   *

George was having a hell of a time dealing with our new Pushtun allies. Most of Nuruddin's men were from the local Khungani tribe and many of them had been on bin Laden's payroll in recent months, hired to dig caves. One of them, Haji Nazir, later claimed to reporters that he was sent by Nuruddin into the mountains to warn al-Qaeda forces about what was coming and "give them some options." After making radio contact with al-Qaeda, Nazir and the men accompanying him were given safe passage forward. "We saw a man," Nazir explained to Anthony Loyd of the London *Sunday Times*. "He was an Arab. We told him that he had three days to either leave with his men, surrender or get ready to fight." The Arab told Nazir that they would fight and Nazir returned to Nuruddin who reportedly said, "The warning was my Pushtun responsibility. Now it is fulfilled and we shall fight."

The most reliable of the three warlords seemed to be Babrak, but his translator spoke very limited English. So communicating the complexities of an ever-evolving battlefield was very challenging. Also,

George received two reports that Nuruddin's men had fired on Babrak's forces in an effort to slow down their advance. When confronted, Nuruddin professed his innocence. Complicating an already difficult situation was the fact that the two warlords saw themselves as rivals for military control of a post-Taliban southeast.

When George expressed his frustration over our radio net, I told him that Adam Khan, a ██████ Pushtun-speaking former United States Marine, was on his way to help him.

"Where in the world did you find someone like that?" he asked.

"It's a long story, but don't worry. He'll be of enormous help."

That afternoon I drove to Bagram to meet John (Hank's CTC/██ deputy) who arrived for a one-week visit. I thanked him for his support, then listened with great interest as he filled me in on the mood and concerns back at Langley.

Prior to heading back to Kabul with John, General Dailey stopped me and told me that he planned to dispatch a six-man JSOC advance team to Tora Bora.

"We can use all the help we can get," I answered.

On our way back into the city, John and I were forced to stop at gunpoint at a Northern Alliance checkpoint. After confirming our identities, the soldiers explained that Taliban stay-behinds were planning to launch attacks in the city.

Back at the guesthouse, John addressed the men. At midnight, several new U.S.-made pickups arrived with the six-man JSOC advance team that was on its way to Tora Bora. I asked the team leader to wait, then hurried inside to wake Adam Khan. "You're leaving a couple hours earlier than I expected," I told him.

Ten minutes later he was ready to go. I assigned two of my Afghan drivers who knew the roads well. The thirteen-hour trip to Jalalabad was ███████████████████████████████████████. First, their convoy was almost ambushed by troops loyal to Pushtun warlord Gulbuddin Hekmatyar, who'd once been an ally of Abdul Rashid Dostum, but now professed loyalty to Osama bin Laden. After talking his way past Heymatyar's men, Adam Khan's truck broke down. He radioed back to Kabul and asked me for permission to commandeer another.

I said: "Do whatever you have to do."

*   *   *

Bilal and Hoss had started down to Tora Bora with four Afghan guards on the morning of the third in two trucks packed with hundreds of uniforms, blankets, boots and MREs. It took them ten hours to negotiate the potholed road to Jalalabad, where just days before foreign journalists had been killed in an ambush. At sundown their Afghan guards stopped by the side of the road to break their fast.

After a few hours sleep at Babrak's safehouse in Jalalabad, they drove another two hours east to the L-shaped schoolhouse at the foot of Tora Bora. There they met Babrak and two dozen of his men wrapped in scarves and blankets.

On the morning of the fifth, Hoss and the four Afghans started back to Kabul, while Bilal climbed into a pickup with a group of Babrak's men for the drive into the mountains. Their biggest problem initially was evading dozens of journalists who had camped near the schoolhouse and desperately wanted to know what was going on. Bilal covered himself with a tarp to evade their cameras.

Babrak's men drove as far as the Milawa camp, which lay in ruins, then continued climbing on foot. Ahead of them B-52s from Berkstram Airbase in Missouri and F-14s from aircraft carriers stationed in the Gulf of Oman were pounding al-Qaeda positions. During a break in the air assault, Bilal radioed Colonel Alexander's SF team up on a promontory ahead, to tell them that he was deploying forward.

A tough, aggressive former Marine, Bilal climbed the rolling hills, while two of Babrak's soldiers followed a dozen feet behind him. The first thing he encountered was scores of Afghan scavengers who ran towards him trying to hawk notebooks, videotapes and scraps of clothing that they had recovered from al-Qaeda caves. Some even offered to sell bodies for three hundred dollars apiece. Another thing Bilal noticed were foreign journalists being driven around in Toyota trucks rented from Nuruddin's men.

Clutching his AK-47, Bilal picked his way over the rolling, dusty hills and ravines until he came to the first set of al-Qaeda caves cut into the limestone. Some had been formed naturally by rainwater; others were man-made. Some had steep sloped entrances to guard against missile attacks. Some were connected to other caves to provide a means of escape in case of attack. But these were nothing like the elaborate facilities with elevators, sleeping quarters and cargo bays for receiving trucks that Bilal had read about in *Time* magazine. Instead they were barely big enough to accommodate half a dozen men. Outside each group of four or five caves, Bilal saw a common kitchen with a campfire and crude implements. Lying around, he found al-Qaeda bodies that had been stripped of their boots and uniforms, sleeping mats and cases of Russian-made ammunition.

Bilal, who was in constant communication with the SF teams, waited for the next wave of B-52 strikes to pass. Winding his way forward through a valley, he arrived at a recently bombed al-Qaeda encampment that had been abandoned in haste. One mangled body clutched a Japanese-made hand-held Yazoo radio—the kind sold in electronic stores in the States. Listening, Bilal realized that it was tuned to the al-Qaeda frequency. He heard men talking excitedly in Arabic: "Bring the food!" "We need water." "Kill the Americans!"

It became clear immediately from their communications that the al-Qaeda fighters were in desperate need of food and water, which was only available in the valley. They also expressed surprise that the Americans had found them so fast.

As a slow-moving Spectre AC-130 gunship circled overheard firing its 30mm canons at a target over the next ridge, Bilal listened to Arabs on the radio refer to it as "the water buffalo." After the Spectre cleared the area, Bilal heard a voice he recognized from dozens of tape recordings. It was Osama bin Laden telling his troops to keep fighting. Someone asked bin Laden in Arabic: "Are you okay?"

Another fighter asked, "Zamat, how is the sheik?"

Someone answered, "The sheik is fine."

* * *

As Adam and the six-man JSOC contingent started the final thirty-mile drive from Jalalabad to Tora Bora on a road built by Osama bin Laden, they were stopped by armed soldiers loyal to Nuruddin, who demanded the equipment and uniforms they had in the truck. Once again guns were drawn and Adam Khan had to talk his way past hostile, armed men. Only this time they were supposedly on our side.

Early in the morning, Adam Khan and the six men from JSOC arrived at the schoolhouse, where George waited with Colonel Al and Babrak. The JSOC team leader immediately huddled with George and Colonel Alexander to review the disposition of the battlefield. Adam Khan, meanwhile, introduced himself to Babrak, who greeted him in his native Pashai. Adam experienced a moment of shock, because the words from Ali's mouth were unintelligible to him. *Have I been away so long that I've forgotten how to speak the language?* Adam asked himself.

Babrak repeated the words again. "I don't understand," answered Adam Khan in Pushtun.

Babrak shook his head. "I speak Pushtun as well," said the commander shifting to Pushtun from his native Pashai. A greatly relieved Adam Khan handled all communications between the Americans and the Afghans at Tora Bora from then on.

* * *

I'd just sat down to breakfast after a few hours sleep when I noticed one of Bismullah Khan's Northern Alliance subcommanders, General Sharifi, milling about the lobby. Outside the window, I saw soldiers

from Chief Warrant Officer David Diaz's Triple Nickel SF team loading equipment into a truck. So I got up to see what was going on.

"We're going out with General Sharifi to do some airstrikes," one
of the guys from Triple Nickel said.

I found this extremely interesting, because up until then, General
Fahim's Northern Alliance had wanted nothing to do with attacking
the Taliban in the South. "Who're you fellows planning to hit?" I
asked.

"Some warlord named Razzak, who's important down in Ghazni.
He has some forces just southwest of here."

"Interesting," I said. "Very interesting." Razzak was the ████████
warlord who'd been working with Team Delta. "Promise me you won't
go anywhere for the next five minutes."

"Yes, sir."

I went inside and found Lt. Colonel Haas eating breakfast in the
dining room. "I need to talk to you privately," I told him.

With the door to my room closed, I said, "Chris, I have a little problem. I have a team down in Ghazni with a warlord named Razzak, who
is supposed to introduce them to ███████████, the chief of Taliban
████████. My team is either going to convince him to help us capture
bin Laden or snatch him."

"Sounds like a winner to me," Lt. Colonel Haas answered.

"The problem is that I just found out that Triple Nickel is loading
up outside to go with General Sharifi and call in airstrikes against
Razzak when my men are with him."

Chris Haas stood and said, "I'll take care of it immediately." At the
door he stopped and turned back. "One other thing," he added.
"Please let me know when you have something like this going on and
I'll make sure my teams don't kill any of your friends."

"You've got a deal."

In the volatile political landscape with warlords vying for power,
desperate bands of Taliban and al-Qaeda still roaming the country

and more U.S. combat teams arriving every day, I couldn't take my eye off the ball for a second.

That night around 2300 hours, I'd just laid down to sleep when I heard a knock on my door. It was one of my officers telling me that CTC/▓▓ was on the phone with something important. I hurried to the office where Todd stood with a STU-111 satellite phone.

"Is this the leader of Jawbreaker?" a young woman on the other end asked.

"Yes, this is Gary. How can I help you?"

"You have a team stuck down near Ghazni and the military won't pick them up."

"What?" I asked, still a little groggy.

"Your team's stuck near Ghazni and CENTCOM refuses to send a helicopter."

"Thanks for the call," I said. "I'll get back to you." I hung up and hurried to the radio net.

Team Delta hadn't wasted any time. "This is Jawbreaker," I said into the radio. "Do you read me?"

"This is Team Delta," Klesko replied. "We read you."

"What's your status?" I asked.

"The principal target didn't arrive. Instead, he sent his number two and number three men. We have them both in custody and need a lift out." Klesko then relayed their coordinates, which Todd wrote down.

"We're having a little problem getting a bird," Klesko added.

"Hang on," I said. "I'll get back to you. Jawbreaker out."

I called CTC/▓▓ and asked for Hank. He was out, so I explained to his executive officer that Team Delta had Qari Amadullah's number-two and number-three in custody down in Ghazni and needed a lift.

"That's great," he replied. "I'll call CENTCOM right now to make sure this is taken care of."

"Thanks." I got back on the radio and informed Team Delta that a helicopter would be coming. "Sit tight."

[██]

[█████████████████████████████████]

[*NOTE TO READER:* CIA censors redacted the details of Team Delta's mission.]

When word reached CENTCOM that an Agency operation was underway in Ghazni, senior staff expressed anger that they hadn't been informed and refused to send a rescue team. From their narrow bureaucratic perspective, if the Agency wanted to conduct operations without them, then the Agency could organize their own transportation. What CENTCOM didn't realize was that three of the five men on Team Delta were active duty military officers—one Navy Seal, one Marine and one Army. I would have gladly sent my own helicopter to pick them up, but it had a bum tail rotor that needed to be replaced.

After making Team Delta wait several hours in very dangerous territory, CENTCOM changed its mind and sent a helicopter. Team Delta threw the keys to their vehicles to their Hazara allies and loaded their prisoners on the bird for the trip to Bagram.

A few hours later, I spoke to Hank, who said that CENTCOM was still pissed, but would get over it. "Congratulate Team Delta for me," he said. "Capturing the number two and three in Taliban intel was a good day's work."

[██]

[██]

[██]

[██]

[█████████████████████]

[*NOTE TO READER:* This redacted section deals with handing the prisoners over to proper authorities.]

After crawling out of the basement of the Qala-i Jangi fortress, John Walker Lindh had been transported to Sheberghan prison where he received medical treatment, was identified, taken into U.S. custody and moved to Kandahar. Neither I, nor any of the men under my command, had ever set eyes on him.

* * *

The following day, December 5, as I was following events in Tora Bora, Craig, our team leader with Hamid Karzai and ODA 574 twenty-five miles northwest of Kandahar, spoke over the Agency radio net. In a very strained voice he reported that they had just been struck by a large explosive device, which he thought was a thousand-pound car bomb. Survivors of the blast were administering first aid to the critically injured and a number of men from the Special Forces Team ODA 574 were dead.

We later learned that the two-thousand-pound bomb was delivered by one of our B-52s, which had been given the wrong grid coordinates by men on the ground. Craig was meeting with Hamid Karzai and several tribal leaders to plan an assault on Kandahar when it struck. He instinctively threw his body on Karzai and tried to shield him. The Pushtun leader escaped with slight shrapnel wounds to his face. Master Sergeant Jefferson Donald Davis, Staff Sergeant Brian Cody Prosser and Sergeant First Class Daniel H. Petithory, who had all fought valiantly in the defense of Tarin Kowt, died along with three of Karzai's mujahideen fighters. Five minutes after the blast, a shaken Karzai received a satellite phone call informing him that he'd been selected to lead Afghanistan's new interim government.

* * *

[*NOTE TO READER:* CIA censors redacted this section dealing with a bureaucratic tie-up at headquarters that had put our whole operation at risk.]

19

HAMID KARZAI

*"There is a tide in the affairs of men,
Which, taken at the flood, leads on to fortune."*
—*William Shakespeare,* Julius Caesar

*   *   *   *   *   *

On the afternoon of December 7, George called me over the radio net from Tora Bora. "There's been a cessation in the fighting," he announced in his Texan drawl.

"What the hell are you talking about?" I asked.

"Al-Qaeda has sent someone out to say they want to negotiate."

"Screw that," I responded. "We came here to kill them."

George said, "I told the Afghans to keep fighting, but al-Qaeda sent someone who is talking to Nuruddin. I told them: 'No negotiations!' But Nuruddin and commanders affiliated with him demanded that I send the al-Qaeda offer up my chain of command."

"Fine," I said. "You've done that. My response to al-Qaeda is, 'Screw you! We're going to kill all of you.' And that's our final position. Make sure Adam Khan translates that one clearly."

"Will do."

"And one more thing. Tell them your commander is from New York. I want them all dead!"

"I got the message," George said. "Juliet out."

I quickly called CENTCOM and spoke to our Agency rep.

"I have al-Qaeda trying to draw our Afghan allies into negotiations. I have refused. You need to talk to CENTCOM and throw as much air power at them as quickly as possible. Guys who fly airliners into skyscrapers don't negotiate. They're trying to reduce the intensity of our attacks so they can slip out. "

"I'll go see General Kimmons, the J-2, right now."

"Thanks. Jawbreaker out."

I'd learned that Afghans love to negotiate. I also knew that as far as our Eastern Alliance allies were concerned, they would be happy to take our money and let al-Qaeda slip away.

The next eight hours were extremely dangerous for Team Juliet and the handful of U.S. soldiers in Tora Bora, since they weren't sure if our Eastern Alliance allies had sided with the enemy.

Day and night, I kept thinking, *We needed U.S. soldiers on the ground! We need them to do the fighting! We need them to block a possible al-Qaeda escape into Pakistan!* I'd sent my request for 800 U.S. Army Rangers and was still waiting for a response. I repeated to anyone at headquarters who would listen: "We need Rangers now! The opportunity to get bin Laden and his men is slipping away!!"

Apparently, the U.S. Rangers weren't coming. CENTCOM commander General Tommy Franks later explained to *Frontline:* "The Afghans themselves wanted to get into Tora Bora. They wanted to do it very quickly. At that time, our Special Forces troopers were not yet in large numbers, even with those forces that we were providing support to. So rather than taking a decision that said: Let's take a break for some prolonged period of time and try to introduce large numbers of non-Afghan coalition forces, the determination was made. I made it, and I think it was a pretty good determination, to provide support to that operation, and to work with the Pakistanis along the Pakistani border to bring it to conclusion."

He was either badly misinformed by his own people or blinded by the fog of war. I'd made it clear in my reports that our Afghan allies were hardly anxious to get at al-Qaeda in Tora Bora. So why was the U.S. military looking for excuses not to act decisively? Why would they want to leave something that was so important to an unreliable Afghan army that'd been cobbled together at the last minute? This was the opportunity we'd hoped for when we launched this mission. Our advantage was quickly slipping away.

* * *

Several hours later George called again to report that the fighting had resumed. "Gary," he continued. "Babrak allowed a source from Jalal-abad to go into Tora Bora and deliver water and food to bin Laden's men. He gave us an excellent description of three prominent Arabs, one was extremely tall, definitely bin Laden, another older man probably Ayman al-Zawahiri (bin Laden's deputy). The third man slightly resembled the tall one and was approximately 20 years old. I suspect he's bin Laden's son Saad."

"Did Babrak's source give us a position?" I asked.

"We have coordinates near some large caves where they met," George answered. "I want to use a BLU-82."

"Great idea." I thought quickly and remembered that there was still one in theater that wasn't dropped on the Shomali Plains. "Give me the exact geo-cords," I said, "and I'll work with the military and CTC/█."

"Thanks. Juliet out."

A BLU-82 would make things interesting. I quickly sent the proposal to CTC/█, which promised to work with CENTCOM. Almost immediately, the word came back: the BLU-82 will be ready to be dropped the morning of December 9. I couldn't wait.

* * *

The few brave members of Babrak's troop who went forward with Bilal on most days stayed ten or more yards behind him. And each night they returned with the rest of Babrak's men to eat and sleep with their families. It was still the holy month of Ramadan. In dark rooms lit by kerosene lanterns, Afghan fighters loyal to Babrak, Haji Zahir, and Nuruddin would lean their rifles against mud walls, place their prayer mats in the direction of Mecca, bow and pray:

> *In the Name of Allah, the Beneficent, the Merciful*
> *Praise be to Allah, Lord of the Worlds,*
> *The Beneficent, the Merciful,*
> *Owner of the Day of Judgment*
> *Thee alone we worship; Thee alone we ask for help.*
> *Show us the straight path,*
> *The path of those who Thou hast favored;*
> *Not the path of those who earn Thine anger nor of*
>   *those who go astray.*

Then they'd sit, drink tea and eat pomegranates. After a night's sleep with their families, they'd bundle up against the bitter cold and return to the front in the mountains where they met with their commanders. This meant territory that was seized from al-Qaeda one day had to be taken again.

It was hardly an ideal way to fight a war, thought Bilal, the former Marine, who couldn't help but imagine how quickly a battalion of Marines could finish off what was left of the enemy. Still, the air strikes continued to be devastating. The terraced slopes he stood on proved that. A recent al-Qaeda camp was now pockmarked with bomb craters fifty feet wide and twenty feet deep. Strewn across the rubble were shattered trees, torn strips of Arabic training manuals, shreds of clothing, white boxes filled with dates, metal boxes of Russian ammunition, a set of parallel exercise bars and fragments of U.S. bombs. Of approximately one thousand al-Qaeda fighters that Bilal estimated were present with bin Laden in the mountains, approximately five hundred had been killed since the bombing began on November 30.

Continuing to listen to al-Qaeda communications over the seized Yazoo radio, Bilal heard bin Laden's men discuss the need for water and food. He also learned that bin Laden no longer trusted the Taliban or other non-Arabs and had surrounded himself exclusively with Saudis and Yemenis. Increasingly fearful of being betrayed by his own men, the al-Qaeda leader had split his al-Qaeda force in two. The Pakistanis, Algerians, Chechens, Egyptians and other al-Qaeda soldiers were fighting on their own.

Meanwhile, farther down the mountains, the gray-bearded Nuruddin was holding his daily press briefing with reporters. He said, "I'm an optimist. We need to do two things. We need to bomb them again and again. And we need to encircle them." But he wasn't doing either. At the same time, the Iran Press Service reported that al-Qaeda fighters were "insisting on surrendering to United Nations officials with the presence of foreign observers."

Hours later, when a tank creaked up a steep road to Nuruddin's position, he ordered it to open fire on al-Qaeda snipers higher up in the mountains. But, according to reporter Susan B. Glaser of the *Washington Post*, the tank driver balked because he reported to Babrak and wouldn't fire until he got the order from him.

As Adam Khan, Babrak and several JSOC officers bounced up the Agamtangai River valley their four four-wheel drive vehicle came under constant shelling from al-Qaeda soldiers in the hills above. At one point the fire was so heavy that they sought refuge in a large ditch until U.S. airpower destroyed the al-Qaeda artillery.

On the way back that night Adam Khan, Babrak and the two JSOC officers found themselves abandoned behind enemy lines. Babrak's fighters had left the battlefield to break their fast. U.S. airplanes could not provide cover since clouds had moved in preventing pilots from flying lower than thirty thousand feet. With less than an hour's worth of ammunition among them, the plight of Adam Khan, Babrak and the two JSOC officers looked bad. The JSOC commander at the schoolhouse assembled a team of JSOC soldiers to attempt a rescue. Meanwhile, Adam Khan, Babrak and the two JSOC officers very quietly picked their way out of the mountains.

Khan had stopped earlier in the day to buy recovered al-Qaeda material from local villagers. Among them was a notebook with cell and fax numbers for Mullah Omar, Osama bin Laden and top al-Qaeda commanders. He had them in his possession now. After a tense two hours, the JSOC rescue team reached Adam Khan, Babrak and the two U.S. officers and led them to safety. Later a grateful Adam Khan wrote up the JSOC soldiers for Silver Stars for bravery under fire.*

* * *

During the afternoon of the eighth we learned that a Pakistani prisoner with a Singaporean passport named Muhammad Aslan Yar Ali Khan confessed to ███████████ that he was part of a major al-Qaeda plot to attack United States, British, Australian and Israeli interests in Singapore. I felt something ease in my chest. This was the break I'd been hoping for. ██ ██

The next day Singaporean authorities arrested thirteen al-Qaeda and allied Jemaah Islamiyah Islamic terrorists who were in the process of procuring twenty tons of explosives to bomb the embassies of the U.S., Australia, Great Britain and Israel and the USS *Carl Vinson*, which was scheduled to dock in late December.

On October 7, 2001, a thirty-year-old Indonesian traveling on a false Filipino passport (known as Mike) and a Kumati traveling on a fake Canadian passport (Sammy) had entered Singapore for the purpose of activating an al-Qaeda sleeper cell and planning the bombings. A backup unit was later arrested in Malaysia. Another terrorist was seized in Manila with a ton of Anzomex explosive, three hundred detonators and six 400m rolls of detonating cord.

*Based on interviews conducted by Ralph Pezzullo.

In all, thirty-three men were arrested as part of this plot, which was scheduled to be al-Qaeda's follow-up to 9/11. ██████████ ████████████████████████████ *

*   *   *

Without news of incoming U.S. Rangers, all I could do was wait with hope and anticipation for the morning of December 9. George had positioned himself on a promontory with Babrak where they watched the C-130 approach.

Through binoculars they saw a 15,000-pound BLU-82 the size of a car fall out of the back of the plane. They heard an explosion rumble through the mountain, followed by a huge sucking, whooshing sound. But the mushroom cloud they expected to see rise over the mountains didn't appear.

George called me on the radio and said, "I don't know if it went off. I think we dropped a dud."

All of us in the guesthouse standing around the communications gear looked at one another in consternation. "Is that possible?" I asked out loud.

"I suppose, anything's possible," one of my men answered.

I called CENTCOM and spoke to our Agency rep.

"I know this might sound strange but that BLU-82 that was just dropped either didn't explode or just partially exploded. Can CENTCOM send some additional big-ass bombs to that same location A-S-A-P?"

"I'll have to see what we have in the air," he answered. "Don't hang up." Ten minutes later he was back on the line. "Gary, there are three B-52s on their way to Afghanistan which CENTCOM will vector into Tora Bora in one hour. Each B-52 has forty-five hundred pounders, which is a lot of steel. Will that do?"

"Wonderfully! Have a nice day."

*Based on Associated Press and CNN news reports.

I got back on the horn to George, who was pleased. I also told him that forty U.S. Army JSOC soldiers would arrive at Bagram in a day or so. I'd make quick arrangements for trucks and escorts to send them his way.

*   *   *

It had taken weeks for Davis and Storm from SAD to hammer out arrangements with the Hazara ████████ to escort a team into Lowgar province directly south. This new team, called Jawbreaker Romeo, would include Davis, Storm, Marlowe, Hamid, Billy Waugh and sixty armed Hazaras to provide security. Their first mission was to set up a base south of Gardez.

As the men loaded a truck with equipment, several of our Northern Alliance intel counterparts came to me and said, "Mr. Gary, you cannot go south without Engineer Aref's approval and the establishment of a formal agreement with someone affiliated with us in that sector."

██

████████████ I said, "The hell I can't. My men are going."

A half hour before Jawbreaker Romeo was to launch, I received a STU-111 call from Hank.

"Hello, Gary," he said. "I want to chat with you about a few things."

"What's up?"

"First, CENTCOM reviewed the satellite photos and the BLU-82 did go off."

"I'll tell George."

"I completely agree with your decision to ask for more firepower," Hank continued. "The B-52s were a nice add-on."

"Thanks."

Journalists who later visited the al-Qaeda camp hit by the BLU-82 described a path of devastation in a daisy pattern five football fields wide. NBC reporter Kevin Sites found "nothing but scorched earth. Trees burned down to their roots, trucks, tanks, weapons—incinerated."

I heard Hank clear his throat. ████████████████████████

████████████ "We've selected a permanent chief, which will allow you to return to your post in South America."

I took a deep breath. It felt as though someone had just thrown a bucket of cold water in my face. I couldn't believe they were doing this in the middle of the most important battle of the war. "Who's the new chief?" I asked, trying to keep my composure.

The room turned silent as everyone stopped what they were doing to listen to Hank's answer. "It's Rich, the chief of the ████████████," Hank answered.

Men around me slapped their hands over their heads and groaned.

"When will he arrive?" I asked.

"He should get to you by the fourteen of December." That was five days away.

"I'll meet him at Bagram on arrival," I said. "What about George?"

"Rich is bringing his own deputy who will arrive soon. I want you to know we all think you've done a remarkable job," Hank continued. "You've seized control of almost the entire country and have al-Qaeda by the throat down in Tora Bora. . . ." I didn't hear the rest.

As I put down the phone, still stunned, several of the men approached me and asked, "Are you done?"

I was struggling with the same question.

"No disrespect to Rich," said some of the men, "but when you leave, we leave. We came together; we leave together. We're pulling out! "

Watching Jawbreaker Romeo depart with their Hazara escorts, I wished I'd been given another month to get the job done. Clearly, headquarters thought the war in Afghanistan was winding down. They were wrong.

As I tossed and turned that night, I remembered that Rich had served on the staffs of both DCI Tenet and DDO Pavitt. I suspected they felt more comfortable with him in charge.

Still, it didn't seem right. My men and I had risked our lives to do something that few people in Washington had thought possible and succeeded in record time. Now that we finally had bin Laden and his al-Qaeda cadres trapped in the White Mountains why was headquarters pulling us out? And why was Washington hesitant about committing troops to get bin Laden? These were the questions that kept me up at night.

*   *   *

Early in the morning of December 10, the forty-man JSOC unit arrived at the base of the White Mountains. The JSOC commander who'd been working alongside George since his arrival with the six-man advance team asked George to turn over the command of the battlefield to him. George forwarded his request to me.

I said, "We welcome his command," still stewing from the news of the day before.

George and the remainder of Jawbreaker Juliet would stay on to support the campaign with intel and to coordinate with our partners in the Eastern Alliance.

Without delay, the JSOC commander deployed his men forward in teams attached to elements of Babrak, Nuruddin and Haji Zahir's troops. As I listened on the military radio net, one vehicle of four JSOC soldiers was stopped at an Eastern Alliance checkpoint where our allies asked for a toll of fifty U.S. dollars per person before they were let through. I heard JSOC soldiers asking each other for tens and twenties as they tried to make change.

Lt. Colonel Mark Sutter from JSOC, who was standing beside me listening, looked at me with disgust.

"Welcome to Afghanistan," I said.

An hour later, Lt. Colonel Sutter and I drove out to Bagram to see how John (the deputy from CTC/█) was progressing with the intel cell he was setting up for General Gary Harrell. Thirty minutes later I walked to an adjacent building to drop in on General Dailey. He apologized for the military's delay in picking up Team Delta and the two Taliban prisoners outside of Ghazni. I told him it was imperative that the Agency and military cooperate and share across the board.

Entering General Dailey's JSOC headquarters, I was greeted by an impressive array of computers, communications systems and satellite coverage of Tora Bora. A Lt. Colonel proudly showed me leaflets that they were planning to drop on the battlefield urging al-Qaeda fighters to surrender.

"What the hell do you want to do that for?" I asked him.

The Lt. Colonel didn't expect that response.

"The bastards will surrender," I shouted, "and if they do, they'll get a goddamn army of lawyers to defend them and in five years we'll be the ones who are considered guilty. Don't drop the leaflets or invite them to negotiate! They came to fight, didn't they? So let's oblige them. No damn leaflets! Let's fight the war!"

Several soldiers standing nearby expressed their agreement with my position. Later, I reiterated to General Dailey that I thought that the leaflets were a stupid idea. I also informed him that I'd sent a message to Langley requesting the introduction of ground forces into Tora Bora. He said, "Gary, you've done great down there. Now we'll finish it off."

"With what?" I asked, venting my frustration. "Forty JSOC soldiers and a dozen SF troops? You think that somehow they're going to block escape routes across hundreds of miles of caves and mountain passes? It's not enough."

It didn't take a great military strategist to figure out that bin Laden was looking for a way out and would ultimately succeed in escaping. It was a twenty-four-hour climb through the White Mountains from Tora Bora to Pakistan. Yet, General Dailey and CENTCOM continued to ignore my request for eight hundred U.S. ground troops.

Meanwhile, in the White Mountains, Colonel Alexander's Special Forces Team called in as many as one hundred air strikes a day against al-Qaeda soldiers, as they retreated higher and higher into the snow-covered peaks.

"We'd soften them up," one Special Forces Sergeant told *Frontline*, "then General Babrak's troops pushed forward. It was kind of a leapfrog type of thing. We'd spot al-Qaeda's troops and target them with SOFLAMs, and after the air strikes, Babrak's troops would advance again."

George described "a wolfpack style of fighting." A bold subcommander from either Babrak's, Nuruddin's or Haji Zahir's forces would lead the charge against al-Qaeda positions and a group of his men would follow. But absent an aggressive leader, the Afghans would hang back and wait.

One such aggressive subcommander went by the name of Crazy and was attached to Babrak. He boasted that he'd recovered bin Laden's camouflage jacket from a recently bombed camp. Later, he led an attack on the village of Alif Khil, high up in the mountains, capturing twenty-two al-Qaeda prisoners, including Libyans, Yemenis and Kuwaitis. Before the prisoners were turned over to us, some of them spoke to Haji Zahir, who told *Sunday Times* reporter Anthony Loyd: "They told us that Osama had drunk tea with them and told them: 'Fight against the Americans. Fight on.' Then he left and headed up Tora Bora with a party of fighters and mules."

Still, Afghan warlords Haji Zahir and Babrak fought over who would control the prisoners. A similar scene played out a few days later between Haji Zahir and Nuruddin. When Nuruddin caught someone trying to reinforce al-Qaeda positions, he was stopped by Haji Zahir and a group of his men who wanted the prisoner. Wrapped in a brown blanket, Nuruddin refused to turn him over. Guns were drawn on both sides and fighters for the two warlords took cover behind rocks.

"Hold your fire," Zahir said, according to Phillip Smucker of the *Christian Science Monitor.*

"The Taliban gave that man five hundred weapons, and we stopped him from trying to supply al-Qaeda," the elderly Nuruddin explained. "I told my people to catch him. Zahir said that he was their man. That is a lot of crap. I don't care who is supplying al-Qaeda. We must stop them."

"It was a very hit-and-miss operation," Bilal said later. ███████

███

███████████████████████████████

"Babrak's lines were real thin," reported a second SF team member. "Al-Qaeda started retreating backwards and Babrak's troops would push forward for about a three-day period."

"They fought very hard with us," said one of Babrak's commanders. "When we captured them, they committed suicide with grenades. I saw three of them do that myself. The very hardest fighters were the Chechens."

*　　*　　*

On the evening of December 12, 2001, Lt. Colonel Mark Sutter and I drove to Bagram to receive the incoming chairman of the Afghan Interim Government, Hamid Karzai. Arriving at 2100 hours we found two hundred Northern Alliance Afghan soldiers lined up on the tarmac in their best dress uniforms. Large spotlights, powered by generators, lit up the scene. I spotted Bismullah Khan and his senior staff and went over to shake hands. Farther down the tarmac stood General Fahim and other NA leaders in civilian clothes.

We stood no more than five minutes when a USAF C-130 touched down and taxied to a stop 150 yards away. General Fahim strode towards it and the hundred Afghan soldiers armed with AK-47s broke from their positions and started running towards the plane. Luckily the propellers stopped spinning before the C-130 was engulfed.

Turning to me, Lt. Colonel Sutter remarked, "Complete and utter chaos. This doesn't look good."

"No kidding."

In the distance, we saw the mob force its way into the side door of the aircraft.

"I'm sure the aircrew is loving this," Lt. Colonel Sutter said.

"I bet."

After a few moments, the swarm of uniformed men armed with

AK-47s spread chaotically and started to move towards us. At its center stood a slight man in a long Uzbek coat—Hamid Karzai. Just ahead of him stood my ███████ American friend Bassam.

"What the hell are you doing here?" I asked Bassam, a former Farsi language instructor and case officer, who had been deployed down south.

"Gary, you want to meet Hamid?" he yelled from ten yards away.

"Not now," I shouted back. "Too many people running around here with guns. Let's get him in a car first."

It was clear that the man who embodied the future of Afghanistan had no security detail. I didn't want him shot or trampled before he reached Kabul. As the mob of soldiers ran alongside the interim prime minister, jostling one another to get a look at him, I spotted a line of SUVs parked to the side of the tarmac and yelled at Bassam: "Right there!"

Bassam opened the door of one of the SUVs and helped Karzai in.

General Fahim and other VIPs loaded into other vehicles and together they sped off in a long line, while Bassam and I exchanged hugs.

It was midnight when we arrived at the gates of the presidential palace, where two guards with rifles provided the only external security. Inside the palace stood another Afghan soldier with a revolver.

I introduced myself to Hamid Karzai as Gary the leader of the Agency's largest team that handled all of eastern Afghanistan. "Ambassador James Dobbins has primary responsibility for policy discussions between the United States and the interim government," I explained. "I'm available as a conduit for secure communications with Ambassador Dobbins until the arrival of officers from the Department of State and reestablishment of the United States Embassy."

Hamid Karzai said, "Gary, please pass on my best to Ambassador Dobbins and to President Bush. Please tell them that the Afghan people and I are grateful for the sacrifices your men have made in blood to free the Afghan people from the tyrannical rule of the Taliban. Tell Ambassador Dobbins and President Bush that I'll never forget the bravery of the Agency teams and the Special Forces soldiers that fought alongside my men and me."

He then sat down and wrote a note to Craig—the Agency team leader in Kandahar and the man who had shielded him from the B-52 bomb—inviting him to his inauguration.

Hamid Karzai stood out from every other Afghan leader I'd met so far. He was humble, well educated, intelligent, brave and sophisticated and also seemed to radiate a quality that I'd rarely seen in Afghanistan: hope.

I realized that since the tragedy of 9/11 and my entry into Afghanistan, I'd done everything I could to harden myself. Sitting across from me was a man who was doing the exact opposite: trying to embrace all those who opposed him in order to unite his country. He'd proven that he could be tough on the battlefield. Now he spoke about the need for healing and compassion.

I was deeply impressed, but took the opportunity to point out the need to develop a strong personal security detail for himself and his family. Karzai agreed that despite the warm welcome he'd received at Bagram, he had plenty of enemies and said he would promptly take steps to defend himself and his new government.

"Please do."

*   *   *

The following morning I received another urgent call from headquarters. *The Wall Street Journal* had contacted CENTCOM to tell them that one of their reporters in Kabul, Alan Cullison, had come into the possession of a computer that'd been used by senior members of al-Qaeda. [*NOTE TO READER:* This section has been redacted by CIA censors.]

Alan Cullison in an article entitled "Inside Al-Qaeda's Hard Drive" published in the September 2004 issue of *Atlantic Monthly* magazine reported how three CIA officers appeared at his hotel in Kabul. In the article he explained how his laptop had been destroyed a couple of weeks earlier when the truck he was riding in slammed head-on into

into a Northern Alliance fuel truck in the Panshir Valley. After arriving in Kabul, he purchased an IBM desktop and Compaq laptop computer from a computer dealer, who had an office overlooking Kabul's central park. The dealer told Cullison that he regularly serviced computers for the Taliban and al-Qaeda.

Cullison wrote that the computer dealer claimed he stole the forty-gigbyte IBM desktop and Compaq laptop from al-Qaeda's central headquarters on the night of November 12. He wanted money so he could travel to the U.S. and meet girls. *The Wall Street Journal* reporter asked the CIA officers to copy the hard drives before he handed them over.

He thought the computers might hold information about plans for a future al-Qaeda attack against the United States. He quickly copied the hard drive of the IBM desktop for his own records and surrendered both computers to the CIA.

Months later he learned that the computers had in fact been used by the number-two and number-three men in Osama bin Laden's organization—Ayman al-Zawahiri and Mohammad Atef.

Among the items found on the hard drives was a memo from Mohammad Atef to Ayman al-Zawahiri dated April 15, 1999 that, according to the article in *Atlantic Monthly*, read: "A germ attack is often detected days after it occurs, which raises the number of victims. . . . Defense against such weapons is very difficult. . . . I would like to emphasize what we previously discussed: that looking for a specialist is the fastest, safest and cheapest way. . . ."

Subsequent correspondence on the computers revealed that al-Qaeda did hire an expert named Midhat Mursi (a.k.a. Abu Khabab), built a rudimentary laboratory and created a charitable foundation to serve as a front for their program to develop chemical weapons. According to Cullison, a videotape later recovered from al-Qaeda's Darunta training camp outside Jalalabad showed Mursi and several students performing chemical experiments on dogs.

Thank you, Alan, for being a dedicated reporter and a great American.

20

ESCAPE

*"A sadder and wiser man,
He rose the morrow morn."*
—*S.T. Coleridge,* The Rime of the Ancient Mariner

*   *   *   *   *   *

Even though the JSOC commander was directing the battlefield in Tora Bora, George and I were still very much involved. I spoke again with Hank at CTC/■■ and asked one more time for the U.S. military to deploy ground troops to trap bin Laden and the remnants of his force in the White Mountains. Hank assured me that my request had been forwarded to CENTCOM and the seventh floor. He explained: "Unfortunately, it's not my call."

"What about placing forces to block the mountain passes into Pakistan?" I asked him.

He said that the government of Pakistan had already deployed four thousand soldiers from their Frontier Force to do the job. They weren't the U.S. troops I had requested, but they were better than nothing.

Meanwhile, in Tora Bora, a Russian-made tank commandeered by Eastern Alliance fighters blasted valleys between snow-capped ridges high up in the mountains as B-52s rained bombs from above. According to reports in the *Christian Science Monitor* and *Washington Post,*

Babrak paid a lieutenant named Ellias Khan 300,000 Pakistani rupees ($5,000) to block the main escape routes into Pakistan. But Ellias Khan, who had earlier fought for Taliban commander Awol Gul took the money and satellite phone he was given and disappeared.

"Our problem was that the Arabs paid him more," explained Babrak deputy Mohammed Musa.

A month earlier, another Nuruddin subcommander, Spin Gul had been fighting in a Taliban trench outside of Mazar-e Sharif that had been hit by an American airstrike. "Twenty-five out of thirty in my bunker were killed by the Americans," Gul told *Christian Science Monitor* reporter Phillip Smucker. "I'll never forgive them." Yet now he was being paid to fight for our side.

*   *   *

Midday on the fourteenth, I was at Bagram to meet Rich, who was arriving on a commercial turboprop to establish the CIA ▮▮▮▮▮ in Kabul. Rich thanked me for the work I'd done and asked me to serve as his deputy.

I said, "Hank told me that you're bringing in your own deputy."

"That's right."

"Then how is this going to work?"

Rich didn't have an answer. I explained that being the kind of officer I was, I'd be pushing him 24/7. "We can only have one leader, and I can't let up."

"I've heard."

"I don't think it will work. You pushed for the job," I told him, "now it's yours. I'll stick around a few days until you get up to speed."

Rick said he understood, but didn't look happy.

"It's time for me to leave."

The next day both Major General Dell Dailey and Brigadier General Gary Harrell traveled to the guesthouse in Kabul to welcome Rich. During the meeting I insisted strongly that CENTCOM insert U.S. troops on the ground in Tora Bora immediately.

General Dailey and General Harrell both assured me that things had gone extremely well in Tora Bora and I'd done an excellent job.

"Gentlemen, we need to do more than an excellent job," I responded. "Don't you get it? We need to make sure that not one single member of al-Qaeda gets out of there alive!"

General Dailey said that he was against introducing U.S. troops for fear of alienating our Afghan allies.

"I don't give a damn about offending our allies!" I shouted. "I only care about eliminating al-Qaeda and delivering bin Laden's head in a box!"

General Dailey made it clear that CENTCOM's position regarding the introduction of ground troops was unchangeable.

"Screw that!"

*   *   *

Later the afternoon of the fifteenth Bilal and Adam Khan in Tora Bora were listening to the Yazoo radio Bilal had picked up from a dead al-Qaeda soldier when they heard Osama bin Laden speak. Bilal immediately recognized the al-Qaeda leader's voice because he'd heard it more than fifty times before in taped interviews and intercepts.

As Bilal and Adam Khan listened, bin Laden addressed his men in Arabic. "Forgive me," he said. He went on to apologize for getting them trapped in the White Mountains and pounded by American airstrikes. Then, he gathered them together in prayer. Next, Bilal and Adam Khan heard the sound of mules and a large ground of people moving about. Then the radio went dead.

Bin Laden split his force in two. One group, numbering 135 men, headed east into Pakistan where they ███████████████████████ ███ ███ ███████████████ . A number of al-Qaeda detainees later confirmed that bin Laden escaped with another group of two hundred Saudia and Yemenis by a more difficult eastern route over difficult snow-covered passes into the Pushtun tribal area of Parachinar, Pakistan. He was guided by members of the Pushtun Ghilzai tribe, who were paid handsomely in money and rifles.

*   *   *

After breakfast on the morning of the sixteenth, I packed my things, then drove to the market, where I purchased several prayer rugs made in Herat. After lunch, I stopped at the U.S. Embassy to meet with Ambassador Jim Dobbins, who'd arrived to open the Embassy.

As the stars and stripes was raised into the brilliant blue sky, the men on my team and a group of Special Forces soldiers stood in a large circle around a group of seated VIPs. One of Dobbins's assistants came over to ask me to sit with the dignitaries. I told him I'd rather stand with my men.

I was still pissed off. After all we had gone through to get a shot at bin Laden, we were letting a golden opportunity slip away.

SF Colonel John Mulholland delivered a short, moving speech under a cloudless sky that finished with:

> "I ask you to share a moment of silence with me in memory of the countless innocent Afghanis who have suffered so long and for the fallen in New York and in Washington and for the fallen of the 5th Special Forces Group who gave their lives so that this day could become a reality."

Then Colonel Mulholland and I shook hands. "Your men really distinguished themselves here, Colonel," I said.

He answered: "Yours did, too."

The shotgun marriage between the SF and Agency teams had worked. According to Bob Woodward in his book *Bush at War*, in less than two months, approximately 110 Agency officers and 350 SF soldiers on the ground with seventy million dollars and the support of

U.S. airpower and the help of our Afghan allies had wrested control of the country from the Taliban and destroyed a good part of al-Qaeda.

Bob Woodward quotes President Bush, calling it one of the biggest "bargains" in history.

He was right.

Back at the guesthouse, I joined Davis, Hamid, Amir, and Marlowe and A.C. from Science and Technology, who were also leaving, for the trip to Bagram airport. We traveled silently, lost in our separate thoughts.

As Amir looked out the window, he saw children flying kites and playing soccer—two activities that had been prohibited under the Taliban. It brought a smile to his face. The first day he arrived in Kabul he hadn't seen a single civilian on the street. Now he saw families, friends and lovers walking, shopping, eating, talking and laughing as they enjoyed the afternoon sun. We passed a throng outside a movie theater showing a Bollywood movie. Amir felt tremendous satisfaction. He had fought his "good fight" and won.

My thoughts were more shaded with gray. Mostly, I felt frustration. *If only headquarters had given me and my team another month. If only CENTCOM had sent the Rangers I asked for to block and hunt bin Laden.*

"If onlys" had haunted me throughout my career. They were hounding me again.

When will we learn? When will the bureaucrats back in Washington face the real challenges and respond appropriately?

Waiting at Bagram stood Lt. Colonel Chris Haas. I shook his hand then took a last look around at the dusty Shomali Plains and the rugged Hindu Kush mountains. Climbing the steps to the civilian turboprop aircraft, I bid a silent "Good luck" to the tough, resilient Afghan people.

Once in the air, I reflected on the past six weeks. Many better men than I had come to Afghanistan to wage war and remained buried under its unforgiving rocky landscape. But maybe none had come with a stronger sense of purpose.

To the credit of our President, our government and the citizens it serves, we'd responded to an attack on our shores with intelligence, drive and strength. But we'd failed to finish the job. I understood that this was just the end of the first chapter in a long, difficult struggle against al-Qaeda and other terrorist organizations that we would have to wage diplomatically, culturally and militarily throughout the world. As we passed over the peaks of the Hindu Kush mountains, I prayed we'd never lose our will.

It was a bittersweet moment, to say the least. I'd begun my career with the Agency almost twenty years earlier with the expectation that I would serve, struggle and somehow make the world a better place. Part of that dream had been realized, but other important pieces of it had slipped away.

21

CONCLUSIONS

"Ignorance is an evil weed, which dictators may cultivate among their dupes, but which no democracy can afford among its citizens."
—*Lord William Beveridge*

       ✱   ✱   ✱   ✱   ✱   ✱

The bombings of the American Embassies in Nairobi and Dar es Salaam in August 1998 were a wake-up call that went unheeded. The attack on the USS *Cole* in the port of Yemen two years later was wake-up call number two. Rarely in history has a great power like ours received two such warnings and failed to act to defend itself. The price our country paid was huge.

Many CTC unit leaders and Chiefs of Stations in the field begged for an opportunity to respond. But CIA leadership was unwilling to fight the bureaucratic battles necessary to win Clinton administration approval to defend the United States. The *9/11 Commission Report* and Richard Clarke's *Against All Enemies* show that DCI Tenet and DDO Pavitt constantly downplayed the Agency's ability to launch a successful attack against al-Qaeda.

As a twenty-year veteran of the clandestine service, I can tell you unequivocally that the Directorate of Operations had (and still has) the skill sets needed to undertake almost any type of operation in any part of the world. But intelligence officers like myself can only engage an enemy when we're given the go-ahead by leadership on the seventh floor. The seventh floor, in turn, depends on approval from the President. It's CIA leadership's job to honestly report the capabilities of its own Agency, which it failed to do before the World Trade Center attacks.

Let's hope that the World Trade Center tragedy has taught us once and for all that we must be aware of threats against us, heed those threats and act against them without delay. The world's too small and interconnected, societies too fragile and technology too lethal to do otherwise. If we want the values we believe in to prevail and our country to survive, we simply have to do a better job of defending ourselves.

The challenge we face involves not only thwarting potential attacks against us with more intelligence and vigor, but also engaging the world in a more skillful and comprehensive way. How can we know what's going on in countries that mean to do us harm if we're not there? Closing Embassies and pulling CIA Stations out of hostile countries should only be an option after we've declared war. We must have people in every corner of the globe listening, observing, making friends and educating other people about our society, warts and all. We need trained experts who speak the languages and show sensitivity to native cultures. And we should promote student, cultural and scientific exchanges and cooperation between ourselves and other societies on every level possible.

The speedy success of the war in Afghanistan took most people by surprise, including many of our leaders in Washington. According to Bob Woodward in his book *Bush at War*, it took a little more than two months, for 110 CIA officers and 350 Special Forces soldiers allied with roughly 15,000 Northern and Eastern Alliance Afghans and supported by as many as 100 combat sorties per day, to defeat a Taliban army estimated at 50,000 to 60,000 plus several thousand al-Qaeda fighters.

New York Times correspondent Nicholas Kristof reported that as many as 8,000 to 12,000 Taliban soldiers were killed and another 7,000 or more taken prisoner. In addition, a majority of the 4,000 to 5,000 al-Qaeda fighters either perished or were taken prisoner.

Michael O'Hanlan of the Brookings Institution in his *Foreign Affairs* article "A Flawed Masterpiece" concluded that: "It [the Afghan war] may wind up being more notable in the annals of American military history than anything since Douglas MacArthur's invasion at Inchon in Korea half a century ago." What he fails to mention and what makes the Afghan war even more remarkable is the fact that a large number of the decisions on the ground were made by civilians in the CIA.

Several important factors contributed to its success:

a. INTELLIGENCE-DRIVEN WARFARE. Each CIA team in the field (including Jawbreaker) was equipped with highly trained officers who knew the language, history and culture and could communicate effectively with our Northern Alliance counterparts. They also guided and assisted the Special Forces teams assigned to them with high-value targets and resources, focusing the SF teams where they were most effective.

b. PARTNERSHIP WITH THE NORTHERN ALLIANCE. This political decision, made at the White House, provided us a native army to work with and an extremely valuable intelligence network to link into. The very effective NA intelligence network helped us support the rescue of the SNI hostages, capture top Taliban intel officials and track bin Laden and his al-Qaeda fighters into Tora Bora.

c. TECHNOLOGY. The advantage provided by SOFLAMs, smart bombs, laser-guided munitions, Spectre A-130 gunships, Predator drones, sophisticated communications equipment, etc. tipped the balance militarily, enabling the outnumbered Northern Alliance to defeat the Taliban army. Superior technology also gave us the ability to kill hundreds of al-Qaeda fighters in Tora Bora with as few as four Americans on the battlefield.

d. ABILITY OF TEAM LEADERS TO MAKE QUICK DECISIONS ON THE
GROUND. Team leaders like myself were given the resources and
authority to take advantage of the quickly evolving situation on the
ground. Hank and CTC/■ instructed me to be aggressive and
backed me up. As a result, I was able to react immediately to incoming intelligence, which allowed us to inflict considerable damage on our enemies.
e. THE MUSLIM AMERICANS ON OUR TEAM. Hamid, Amir, Bilal, Adam
Khan and others contributed enormously to our success in Afghanistan because of their language skills and familiarity with the native
culture.
f. LEADERSHIP. General Tommy Franks, Vice Admiral Bert Calland,
Chief CTC Cofer Black, Chief CTC/■ Hank and DC/CTC/■
John devised an effective strategy, deployed teams with the requisite skills in the field, supported those teams with the right resources and, for the most part, worked together seamlessly.

The biggest and most important failure of CENTCOM leadership
came at Tora Bora when they turned down my request for a battalion
of U.S. Rangers to block bin Laden's escape.

Before the U.S. Senate Armed Services Committee on July 31, 2002,
General Tommy Franks explained: "On Tora Bora, early December
2001, the United States at that time had about 1,300 Americans in-
country in seventeen different locations. Kandahar was, as of that time,
still not fully under control. We had our Marine forces acting out of
Camp Rhino, which was our initial point of entry into Afghanistan. We
were very mindful—and I guess I'll take credit or blame for this—I was
very mindful of the Soviet experience of more than ten years, having
introduced 620,000 troops into Afghanistan, more than 15,000 of
them being killed, more than 55,000 of them being wounded.

"It was the Afghans who wanted to attack in the Tora Bora area. We
had Special Forces troopers with those Afghans, to be sure. We had
linkage with the Pakistanis, who some would say, although not much

reported at the time, had in the vicinity of 100,000 troops on the western Pakistani border along a great many points of exfiltration."

Franks went on to say: "I am satisfied with the decision process that permitted the Afghans to go to work in the Tora Bora area."

Not me.

Three months after Tora Bora, General Franks and CENTCOM did step up, sending combined light infantry from the 10th Mountain and 101st Airborn Divisions after al-Qaeda and Taliban forces south of Tora Bora in Shah-i-Kot Valley. Together with British, Australian, German, Danish, Canadian, French and Afghan troops, Operation Anaconda succeeded in killing hundreds of Taliban and al-Qaeda fighters and destroying bin Laden's last major sanctuary in Afghanistan.

In comparing the conflicts in Afghanistan and Iraq, I need to point out an important difference: in Iraq we didn't have an indigenous army like the Northern Alliance to work with, which forced us to adopt a different strategy. Whether or not you agree with the decision to invade Iraq, the absence of an indigenous force that could feed us intelligence, provide security once Saddam Hussein's army was defeated, and form the backbone of a new government, helps explain the complicated and dangerous situation we now face on the ground.

Where is bin Laden? He's hiding among the millions of Pushtuns who live along the mountainous Afghan-Pakistan border and believe it's their tribal duty to protect him from outsiders. Will we ever catch him? If we're creative, aggressive and not afraid to take risks, yes!

I suggest each and every American read the *9/11 Commission Report*. In clear language it explains the challenges faced by an open society as it tries to defend itself against a lethal enemy and the need for leaders who are willing to take risks.

Terrorism won't be stopped by intelligence collection and military force alone. Compassion in trying to feed the world's hungry, heal its sick and support peoples' search for freedom and dignity must remain at the core of our international goals. The challenges we face as we enter the 21st century are daunting. We have a lot of work to do.

INDEX

Abdullah, Abdullah, 203, 204, 208–13, 217–20, 222, 224–25, 230–31, 235, 260

A.C. (Jawbreaker team member), 84, 161, 162, 167, 173, 184, 207, 215, 309

Afghan war: Berntsen's request for ground troops in, 277, 278, 290, 295, 305, 306–7, 309, 314; British forces in, 202–3, 209–10, 219, 253, 256, 258, 273, 276, 315; Iraq war compared with, 315; logistical problems in, 83; opening days of, 77–79, 82–83; spies in, 111, 239; U.S. casualties in, 64, 82, 256, 264, 288, 313; U.S. strategy for, 74–75, 82–83, 84, 89–93, 105, 111, 141, 149, 314; as U.S. success, 312–14; winding down of, 297–98. *See also specific person, city, or topic*

Afghan warlords, 48–49, 75, 76, 99, 147, 154–57, 240, 285–86. *See also specific person*

Afghanistan: Berntsen's journey to, 88–101; Berntsen's return from, 308–10; as bin Laden/al-Qaeda base, 67; British occupation of, 72, 99, 180; civil war in, 125; Dobbins as special representative to, 203–4; geographic location of, 83; interim governing authority for, 203–4, 208–11, 217–20, 222, 223, 224, 230, 231, 235, 259–61, 288, 301–3; maps of, 110, 177, 193, 195, 239, 240; overview of, 72; politics in, 91, 94, 125–26, 155, 208–11, 216, 219, 230, 231, 235, 259–61; Soviet invasion of, 49, 58, 66–67, 72, 99, 126, 155, 194, 240, 260, 314; Sunni Jihadists in, 18; 2000 CIA team in, 43–64; U.S. embassy in, 194–95, 302, 308. *See also specific person, city, or topic*

Afghans: bartering of hostages by, 180; Berntsen's views about, 48, 58, 157; Fraser's comment about, 154; as negotiators, 92–93, 290; response to British forces by, 203, 219, 273; views about U.S. of, 42, 62, 94, 125–26, 142, 147. *See also* Afghan warlords; *specific tribe*

al-Qaeda: and Afghan allies of U.S., 292, 300; and Afghan war as U.S. success, 312; Afghanistan as base for, 67; Amir's views about, 155; in Balkans, 43; Berntsen's assessment of, 307, 310; Berntsen's strategy for locating, 125; casualties among, 160, 173, 283, 292, 313, 315; caves of, 283; cell and fax numbers of, 294; chemical weapons program of, 304; Clinton administration response to, 31–33, 311; computers used by, 303–4; and defection of Taliban commander, 159, 160; and disputes among Afghan warlords, 300; and East Africa bombings, 31; and Eastern Alliance, 290, 305; escape into Pakistan of, 277, 290, 299–300, 305–6, 307–8; founding of, 67;

and Franks' Tajikistan meeting, 90, 91; future plans to attack West by, 229–30, 247, 304; hostages of, 142–43; inspection of sites used by, 196; intelligence reports about, 110, 126, 213; Jalalabad as stronghold for, 186, 225; and Kabul offensive, 173; and Kabul security, 219; leaflets urging surrender of, 299; Massoud's assassination by, 69–70; materials seized from, 225, 228, 294, 303–4; in Milawa valley, 272, 282; military camps of, 183–84, 283, 292, 296; mission of, 67; negotiation attempt by, 289–90; and NGOs, 26–27; and planning and organization for Jawbreaker, 73; as prisoners, 74, 196, 204–5, 229, 242, 245–53, 256, 257–58, 263, 294–95, 300, 301, 313; Pushtuns as supporters of, 280; radio interception of communications from, 283, 284, 293, 307; reluctance of Afghan allies to search for, 290–91; retreat of, 142, 192, 194, 202, 206, 254, 274, 275, 299, 301; rewards for capture of, 115; rumors of surrender of, 293; safehouses of, 179, 184, 189, 192, 206–7; search for, 192, 208, 212–14, 256–57, 265–72, 274–75, 282–84, 293–300, 305–6, 313, 314–15; and September 11, 2001 bombings, 71; on Shomali Plains, 128; Singapore plot of, 294–95; sleeper cells of, 294; and SNI hostages, 118, 121; sources of information about, 155, 156; splitting of, 293, 307; spread of, 67, 69; suicide among members of, 301; supplies and equipment for, 283, 291, 300; Taliban's relationship with, 62, 90, 101; Tenet declares war on, 28, 33, 36; Tenet's downplaying of CIA ability to attack, 311; training facilities of, 32, 48, 67, 155, 192, 196, 206–7, 240, 241, 304; and 2000 Jawbreaker team, 48, 54, 60, 62; U.S. air strikes against, 32, 77, 140, 180, 206, 266–71, 274–75, 282, 283, 290, 292, 293, 299, 300, 305, 307; and U.S. strategy, 90, 91; and USS *Cole* attack, 66. *See also specific person*
Alexander, Colonel, 192, 228, 276; Berntsen's first meeting with, 211–13; and Eastern Alliance, 272, 273; and search for al-Qaeda/bin Laden, 211–13, 269, 270–71, 272, 274, 275, 282, 284, 299; and terrorist pursuit teams, 191, 212, 257; Uzbekistan trip of, 217, 218, 223–24
Amadullah, Qari, 114, 178, 179, 208, 286
Amir (Jawbreaker team member), 78, 95, 97, 98, 115, 225, 228, 309, 314; Afghan warlord meeting with, 155–57; background of, 39,

155; and future al-Qaeda/bin Laden, 230, 269–70; and Jawbreaker headquarters at Bagram, 169, 170; and Kabul offensive, 160–61, 162, 176–77; motivation for joining Jawbreaker of, 155; and prisoners, 204–5, 207–8, 211, 228–29, 238, 242–44, 269–70; recruitment and training of, 38–39, 68, 84
Andy (SF Sergeant), 175–76, 177, 185–86, 187–89
Arab Americans: and Afghan war as U.S. success, 314; harassment of, 226; recruitment of, 68–69
Aref, Engineer: and Babrak, 197; Berntsen's assessment of, 219; and bin Laden search, 197; and British in Afghanistan, 203; and defection of Taliban commander, 158; and Franks' Tajikistan meeting, 89, 91, 92, 93; friends of, 151; and interim governing authority, 208–11; Kabul headquarters of, 163, 165, 179–81, 182, 199; and Kunduz, 149, 210; and Mazar–e offensive, 143, 144; and NDS, 122, 153, 163, 182, 208; and Northern Alliance–CTC team relations, 107; and operations in southern/eastern Afghanistan, 296; Schroen's comments about, 122, 153, 163, 182, 201; and Shomali Plains offensive, 143, 144, 149; and SNI hostages, 117–18, 120–21, 145–46, 159, 180; and 2000 Jawbreaker team, 48, 49, 54, 55, 56, 57, 60; and U.S. financial commitment to Northern Alliance, 112–13; and U.S. strategy, 89, 91, 92
Atef, Mohammad, 67, 114, 206, 304
Atta, Mohammad, 136, 138, 237

Babajan, General, 111–12, 165, 171, 174, 184
Babrak (Pashai warlord): Aref's tracking down of, 197, 199; Diane's briefing about, 197; disputes with other warlords of, 300; and Eastern Alliance, 240, 249–50; explosion kills troops of, 261; Jalalabad safehouse of, 282, 293; and Team Juliet and search for al-Qaeda/bin Laden, 197, 213–15, 225, 238, 253–54, 257, 265–66, 274, 275, 280–81, 282, 284, 291–95, 298–301, 305–6
Badr al–Din, Mustapha, 6, 9–10
Bagram Airbase: Alexander at, 211–13; Babajan as commander of, 111–12, 171, 174; British forces at, 202–3, 209–10, 219; conditions at, 184, 187, 218–19, 273; Dailey–Berntsen meeting at, 272, 273–74; Dobbins–Abdullah press conference at,

Bagram Airbase (*cont.*)
222, 224–25; Dobbins' considers talks at, 218–19; Franks at, 231; and Franks' Tajikistan meeting, 91, 93; importance of securing, 116; as Jawbreaker headquarters, 169–76, 183; journalists at, 172; and Kabul offensive, 164; and Karzai return to Afghanistan, 301; Marlowe's assessment of, 152; Northern Alliance retaking of, 58; Rich arrives at, 306; and search for al-Qaeda/bin Laden, 270–71; Sutter meeting at, 233–34; Waugh and Hoss at, 190
Bamian province, 56, 80, 147, 193–94, 199, 200, 226, 237
Beirut, Lebanon, 6, 7, 9, 33
Berntsen, Alexis (daughter), 3, 4, 45, 69, 87, 98, 163, 221
Berntsen, Barbara (sister), 85
Berntsen, Gary: early CIA career of, 5–6, 30–31; education of, 29, 30, 223; ideals/expectations of, 310; leadership style of, 31, 35–36, 124–25, 214, 271, 279; military career of, 29–30, 70, 97; personal background of, 28–29, 52; praise for, 149, 307; rank of, 123
Berntsen, Rebecca (wife): courtship and marriage of, 30; and Gary's 2000 Afghanistan assignment, 43, 44, 45; and Gary's East Africa assignment, 1, 2–3, 4, 10; and Gary's second Jawbreaker assignment, 72, 85, 86, 87, 163; and Gary's thoughts about al-Qaeda, 98; Gary's Uzbekistan call to, 220–21; in Latin America, 69, 71, 85, 86, 87; sees Gary on CNN, 220; and September 11, 2001, bombings, 71
Berntsen, Susan (sister), 85
Berntsen, Thomas (son): and Gary as CIA agent, 3; and Gary's 2000 Afghanistan assignment, 43, 44, 45; and Gary's car, 4; Gary's climbing in Nepal with, 162; Gary's exchange of books with, 52; and Gary's second Jawbreaker assignment, 72, 85, 86, 87, 162, 163; and Gary's thoughts about al-Qaeda, 98; in Latin America, 69, 71, 85, 86, 87; and September 11, 2001, bombings, 71
Bilal (Jawbreaker team member), 39, 228, 314; background of, 34–35; and Balkan al-Qaeda operation, 43; and Eastern Alliance, 278; and future bin Laden/al-Qaeda plans, 230, 269–70; joins second Jawbreaker team, 225–26, 227–28; and prisoners, 228–29, 238, 242–44, 269–70; radio interception of al-Qaeda by, 307; and search for al-Qaeda/bin Laden, 280, 282–84, 291–92, 293, 301; and 2000 Jawbreaker team, 34–35

bin Laden Group (CIA), 32, 59–60
bin Laden, Osama: Afghanistan as base for, 67; Afghanistan sponsor of, 115; in Alif Khil village, 300; Berntsen's assessment of location of, 315; Berntsen's strategy concerning, 108, 211, 307; birth of, 66; cell and fax numbers of, 294; CIA intelligence expert on, 10, 18; comments about U.S. of, 65; criticisms of Saudi Arabia by, 67; destruction of last Afghanistan sanctuary of, 315; early career of, 66; and East Africa bombings, 7, 25; escape of, 299–300, 305–8, 314; family background of, 66; intelligence reports about, 108, 126, 154–55, 156, 213, 238; and Jawbreaker mission and organization, 73, 86, 100; and Northern Alliance, 90; orders to slow Eastern Alliance by, 275; Pakistani support for, 240; Pushtuns as supporters of, 280, 281–82, 308, 315; radio interceptions of, 284, 307; retreat of, 239–40; search for, 114, 189, 196–98, 200, 208, 211, 213–14, 225, 233, 235, 239–40, 249–54, 265–72, 278–79, 285, 290, 295–300, 305–6, 309, 313, 314–15; and September 11, 2001, bombings, 71; and SNI hostages, 114; and Soviet invasion of Afghanistan, 66–67, 240; splitting of al-Qaeda forces by, 293, 307; in Sudan, 67; and Taliban, 90, 108, 293; turning point for, 66–67; and 2000 Jawbreaker team, 43, 48, 59, 60, 62; U.S. bounty on, 48. *See also* al-Qaeda; Team Juliet
Black, Cofer, 170, 277, 314; background of, 36; and Berntsen's assignments, 37, 41, 63, 86; and Berntsen's frustrations with CIA, 36–37; calls for Lawrence's dismissal, 63; and Jawbreaker's mission and organization, 73, 77, 78, 86–87; praise for Berntsen's team from, 149; and recruitment of language officers, 37, 40–41, 68; and 2000 Jawbreaker team, 41, 43, 44, 59, 60, 63
Black Team (Jawbreaker), 274
BLU–82 bomb, 137–38, 144, 168, 291, 295–96
Bonn, Germany, conference in, 230, 231, 235, 259–61
Breen (Special Activities officer), 104, 108, 112, 141–42
British forces: in Afghan war, 202–3, 209–10, 219, 253, 256, 258, 273, 276, 315; Afghans response to, 203, 219, 273; and operations memo for Jawbreaker, 276; at Qala-i Jangi fortress, 253, 256, 258
Brock (2000 Jawbreaker team member), 43–46, 48–50, 53–55, 57–60, 62, 63, 64
Buckley, William F., 5, 6, 9, 33

Bunch, Peter, 181–82. *See also* Shelter Now International
Bush, George H.W., 3, 194
Bush, George W., 73, 103, 164, 209, 211, 226, 276–77, 302–3, 309

Calland, Albert, 93, 95, 98, 103, 108, 111, 112–13, 314
CENTCOM (U.S. Armed Forces Central Command): and al-Qaeda's attempt to negotiate, 290; Berntsen's frustrations with, 307, 309; and Berntsen's request for ground troops, 299, 305, 306–7, 315; and BLU–82 bomb incident, 295–96; CIA relations with, 105, 287; and Cullison's computer finds, 303–4; failure of, 314–15; forwarding of intelligence to, 143; intelligence reports from, 123; and Jawbreaker planning and organization, 75; and JSOC–Jawbreaker relations, 233; and Kabul offensive, 141, 165, 166, 168; and Khan–Berntsen meeting, 150; and Mazar-e Sharif offensive, 136, 138; and opening of Friendship Bridge, 141; and search for al-Qaeda/bin Laden, 279, 295–96; and Shomali Plains offensive, 131, 141; and Taliban retreat, 148; and Taloqan air strikes, 141; and Team Delta rescue at Ghazni, 286–87; and U.S. air strikes against Taliban and al-Qaeda, 128, 141, 150, 153, 157, 165, 166, 168, 180, 206, 237, 267, 274–75, 290; and U.S. strategy, 105. *See also specific person*
chemical weapons, 304
children: tank shells exploded by, 232
CIA (Central Intelligence Agency): and Afghan war as U.S. success, 312, 313; and al-Qaeda–Taliban relationship, 101; Berntsen considers leaving, 36; Berntsen recruited by, 30; Berntsen's early career with, 30–31; Berntsen's frustrations with, 32–33, 36–37, 68–69, 72, 80; Berntsen's views about leadership at, 60, 311, 312; bin Laden bounty on officers of, 48; and Clinton administration, 311; and Cullison's computer finds, 303, 304; cutbacks at, 32, 33, 35, 37; FBI relations with, 3, 10, 31; Karzai's praise for, 303; media portrayals of, 5; military/CENTCOM relations with, 75, 86–87, 120, 287, 298; and NDS, 122, 153, 163, 182; Northern Alliance relations with, 45, 46, 81, 102–3, 104, 105, 107, 113–14, 127–29, 130, 131, 313; organization of, 4; and politics, 36, 37; public trust in, 124; recruitment of Arabs by, 37–40, 68; Special

Forces' relationship with, 308–9, 313. *See also specific person or division*
Clinton administration, 4, 9, 25, 31–33, 63, 67–68, 85, 311
CNN: and BLU–82 bomb incident, 295; East Africa bombings reports on, 4, 5, 7, 16; and fall of Kabul, 172; and interim government in Afghanistan, 223; and interviews of prisoners, 247, 249; Rebecca's viewing of Gary on, 220; Taliban regrouping report on, 223; and USS *Cole* attack, 66; and World Trade Center bombings, 70
Coleman (Tanzania embassy employee), 11, 12, 14–15
Counter–terrorism Center, CIA. *See* CTC
Craig (CIA Team Leader), 288, 303
Crumpton, Henry A., 75, 85
CTC (Counter–terrorism Center, CIA), 1, 4, 9, 31, 33, 36, 71–72, 77. *See also* Jawbreaker; *specific person*
Cullison, Alan, 303–4
Curry, Dayna, 119, 181–82, 187, 192, 198. *See also* Shelter Now International

Dailey, Dell, 272, 273–74, 276, 281, 298–99, 306–7
Davis (Jawbreaker team member): and Abdullah–Berntsen meeting, 230–31; Afghan warlord meeting with, 154, 155–57; and al-Qaeda/bin Laden search, 196, 197, 200; and Atef's death, 206; background of, 84; and Berntsen in Panshir Valley, 102–3, 106; and Berntsen's strategy, 143; and Eastern Alliance resources, 272–73; and intelligence reports, 149; and Jawbreaker Romeo, 296; and Jawbreaker's move to Bagram Airbase, 169, 170, 173; and Jawbreaker's move to Kabul, 190; joins Jawbreaker team, 84; Kabul activities of, 191–92, 194; and Kabul offensive, 169; and Khan–Berntsen meeting, 149; and Lowgar province, 296; and Majid's friends, 151; and Northern Alliance–CTC team relations, 107; and Pushtun warlord killing, 147; and Rahman's son, 228–29; and relationships among Jawbreaker team members, 129, 141, 146–47; responsibilities of, 107, 114, 115; return from Afghanistan of, 309; and stolen gun incident, 188; and supplies and equipment, 116, 117; in Uzbekistan, 217
Davis, Jefferson Donald, 288
Dawson (Jawbreaker team member), 245–49, 250–53, 258
Defense Department, U.S., 101, 268, 276

Delta Force, U.S., 82, 213, 233, 277

Deutsch, John, 9, 32

Diane (Afghanistan expert), 76, 197

Diaz, David, 109, 111–12, 131–32, 165, 172, 285

Directorate of Intelligence (DI), CIA, 78–79, 175, 270

Directorate of Operations (DO), CIA, 4, 30, 37, 68, 78, 124, 175, 270, 311–12

Division Chief, Latin America, 69, 71, 86

Division Chiefs, CIA, 32–33, 78

Dobbins, James, 203–4, 208–13, 217–20, 222, 224–25, 230, 231, 235, 259, 260, 302–3, 308

Donna (intelligence analyst), 10, 18, 22

Donovan (CIA support officer), 218, 220, 226

Dorothy (CTC employee), 1, 2

Dostum, Abdul Rashid: allies of, 136, 256, 258, 262–63, 281; assaults against Taliban in southern Afghanistan by troops of, 94; background of, 74; and Franks' Tajikistan meeting, 91; and Hekmatyar, 256, 258, 262–63, 281; and Jawbreaker planning and organization, 74, 78, 80; and Kabul battle in 1990s, 177; and Kunduz offensive, 141, 142, 149, 210, 240–41, 242; and Mazar-e Sharif offensive, 133–34, 135, 137, 138, 139–40; and Qala-i Jangi fortress, 245, 247, 249; and R.J., 74, 78, 80, 94, 133, 135–36, 137, 138, 139, 141, 149; size and spirit of army of, 135; supplies and equipment for, 135, 136; and 2000 Jawbreaker team, 55; U.S. air support for, 138, 139; and U.S. attacks on Taliban, 135; and U.S. strategy, 91; and Uzbeks as part of Northern Alliance, 125

Duerrkopf, Silke, 181–82. See also Shelter Now International

Dusty (Jawbreaker team member), 256–57, 265, 266, 267–69, 274, 276, 277

East Africa, U.S. embassy bombings in: al-Qaeda as responsible for, 31; arrests and convictions in, 24–26, 27; casualties in, 2, 7, 11, 12, 19, 27; CIA briefings and instructions concerning, 5, 7–8; EDTs for, 7, 9, 11–22; and FBI–CIA relations, 31; historical background about, 10–11; journalists in, 12–13; sale of information about, 23–24

Eastern Alliance, 240, 249–50, 272–73, 275, 278, 290, 298, 305, 312

embassies, U.S., 6, 7, 33, 40, 194–95, 223–24, 294–95, 302, 308, 312. See also East Africa, U.S. embassy bombings in

Fahim, Mohammed Qasim: Berntsen's assessment of, 219, 235–36; and British forces in Afghan war, 203, 219; CIA relations with, 147; and Dobbins meeting, 208–11; and Franks at Bagram, 234–35, 236–37; and Franks–Berntsen meeting, 235–36; and Franks' Tajikistan meeting, 89, 90, 91–94, 105, 237; and interim governing authority, 204, 220, 260; and Jawbreaker planning and organization, 73; Karzai interrogation by, 81; and Karzai's return to Afghanistan, 301, 302; and Kunduz offensive, 210; negotiation attempts by, 92–93; and Northern Alliance–CTC team relations, 107; as Northern Alliance leader, 70, 125; and politics, 94, 125, 235; and supplies and equipment for Northern Alliance, 124; and Taliban in southern Afghanistan, 285; and Team Juliet, 236; and U.S. air strikes on Shomali Plains, 149; and U.S. strategy, 89, 90, 91–93, 105, 234

FBI (Federal Bureau of Investigation), 4–5, 37; CIA relations with, 3, 10, 31; and defection of Taliban commander, 157–58; and East Africa bombings, 7, 8, 15, 18, 20–21, 25, 26, 31. See also specific person

5th Special Forces Group, U.S., 93, 308

Fischer, Ursula, 181–82. See also Shelter Now International

Franks, Tommy: and Afghan war as U.S. success, 314; in Afghanistan, 231, 233–37; Berntsen's meeting with, 234–36; Berntsen's views about assessment by, 290–91; and CIA–military relations, 120; and ground troops for Tora Bora mountains, 290–91, 314–15; and Kabul offensive, 168; and planning and organization Jawbreaker, 75; and search for al-Qaeda/bin Laden, 290; Tajikistan meeting of, 88–93, 111, 141, 237; and Taliban in southern Afghanistan, 149; and U.S. air strikes against Taliban and al-Qaeda, 153, 180, 267; and U.S. financial commitment to Northern Alliance, 112; and U.S. strategy, 89–93, 105, 111, 141, 149

Friendship Bridge: opening of, 141

Frontline, 216, 290, 299

Gardez (city), 199, 204, 206, 214, 296

George (Jawbreaker team member): and al-Qaeda's attempt to negotiate, 289; background of, 84; and Bagram base of Jawbreaker, 184; Berntsen's briefing by, 104–6; and Berntsen's early days in Panshir Valley, 104–6, 108–10; and Berntsen's replacement, 297, 298; and Berntsen's strategy, 113, 124, 144; and Berntsen's trip to front lines, 131; Berntsen's views about, 185; and BLU–82 bomb incident, 296; and CIA–military relations, 120; and Eastern Alliance, 240, 272, 273, 298; and Haas–Berntsen meeting, 108–10; Jawbreaker training of, 84; and JSOC, 298; Kabul activities of, 192; and Kabul as Jawbreaker base, 184–85; and Kabul offensive, 160, 164, 165, 167, 169, 172, 173, 174; and Khan–Berntsen meeting, 149, 150; and Nuruddin, 238; and Pushtuns, 280–81; and relationships among CTC team members, 129; responsibilities of, 105, 107, 114–15; and search for al-Qaeda/bin Laden, 196–97, 249–50, 268, 272, 274, 275, 284, 291, 295–96, 298, 300; and Stan–Northern Alliance relations, 128; and Team Juliet, 212, 215, 217, 225, 238, 240, 249–50, 253–54, 256–57, 261–62, 266, 268, 272–76, 280, 284, 289, 291, 295–96, 298, 300

Ghazni (city), 186–87, 192, 198, 278, 279, 285, 286–87, 298

Glaser, Susan B., 275, 293

Gold Falcon (code name), 118, 120–21, 124, 145–46, 153, 159, 167–68, 170, 180

"government managers" incident, 189–90

Great Britain: International Security Assistance Force (ISAF), 261; occupation of Afghanistan by, 72, 99, 180; Singapore embassy of, 294–95. *See also* British forces

Haas, Chris: Berntsen first meets, 108–9; Berntsen's coordination with, 192, 194–95; and Berntsen's early days in Panshir Valley, 108–10; and Berntsen's return from Afghanistan, 309; and Berntsen's trip to front lines, 131; and Berntsen's trips to Shomali Plains, 150; and CIA–military relations, 120; and Gardez trip, 204; and Ghazni–Razzak situation, 285; and Jawbreaker move to Bagram Airbase, 169; and Kabul offensive, 164, 165, 175–76; language abilities of, 105; loans Team Juliet supplies and equipment, 257; and SNI hostages, 168; as Special Forces commander, 104; and stolen gun incident, 185, 188; supplies and equipment for, 117

Hafiz (Northern Alliance officer), 160–62, 189–90

Halsey (2000 Jawbreaker team member), 45–46, 50, 51, 53, 54–55, 60, 62, 63

Hamid (Jawbreaker team member), 73, 95, 97, 98, 105, 110, 114–15, 131, 184, 314;

and battles of Dostum's forces, 95; and Berntsen's strategy, 113; and CIA–military relations, 120; and Franks' Tajikistan meeting, 88, 89, 91, 92, 93; and "government managers" incident, 189; and Jawbreaker Romeo, 296; Jawbreaker training of, 84; Kabul activities of, 191–92; and Kabul offensive, 164, 165; and Khan–Berntsen meeting, 149, 150; and Khan–CIA relations, 147; and killing of Pushtun warlord, 147; and Northern Alliance–CIA relations, 128; and relationships among Jawbreaker team members, 129, 146–47; return from Afghanistan of, 309; and search for bin Laden, 197, 225; and Shomali Plains offensive, 147; Spann as friend of, 95, 255; and stolen gun incident, 185–86, 187, 188–89

Hank (CIA officer): and Afghan war as U.S. success, 314; and Bagram Airbase as Jawbreaker headquarters, 170; and battles of Dostum's forces, 94–95; and Berntsen's Latin America assignment, 86; Berntsen's relationship with, 124–25, 191; and Berntsen's request for ground troops, 305; and Berntsen's Jawbreaker replacement, 296–97; and BLU–82 bomb incident, 296; calls for Lawrence's dismissal, 63; and CIA–military relations, 120; and defection of Taliban commander, 159, 160; and Franks' Tajikistan meeting, 88, 89, 91, 92, 93; and Jawbreaker move to Kabul, 189, 190; Jawbreaker responsibilities of, 85; journey to Afghanistan of, 94, 95, 98–112; and Kabul as Jawbreaker base, 184; and Kabul offensive, 175; and Khan, 68; and Kunduz battle, 149; and Mazar-e Sharif offensive, 138; and money for Jawbreaker activities, 106; and money for return of SNI hostages, 145; in Panshir Valley, 103–4, 108, 111; and planning and organization for Jawbreaker, 73–75, 76–77, 78, 79, 80, 82, 83–84, 85, 87; and search for al-Qaeda/bin Laden, 269, 305; and September 11, 2001, bombings, 72; and strategy and tactics in Afghan war, 77, 84, 85, 91, 92; and supplies and equipment for Jawbreaker, 250; and supplies and equipment for Northern Alliance, 124; and Taliban collapse, 167, 170; and Taliban retreat, 148–49; and Team Delta, 279, 286, 287; and terrorist pursuit teams, 191, 212; toasts to, 277; and 2000 Jawbreaker team, 43, 44, 59, 60, 63; and U.S. air strikes against Taliban, 153; and U.S. financial commitments to Northern Alliance,

Hank (CIA officer) (*cont.*)
112–13; and U.S. strategy, 141; and USS
Cole attack, 67
Harold (Berntsen's CTC deputy), 9, 34–35
Harrell, Gary, 189, 203, 213, 273, 298, 306–7
Hazara tribe: Aref's briefing about, 55–56;
Berntsen's assessment of, 219; and interim
governing authority, 259; and Jawbreaker
Romeo, 296, 297; Khalili as commander of,
55; Massoud's followers' killing of, 63; as
members of Northern Alliance, 55, 125; as
part of Afghanistan population, 72, 224;
and Tajiks, 179, 199; and Taliban collapse,
167; Taliban killing of, 49, 55, 57; and
Team Delta, 80, 193, 287
Hekmatyar, Gulbuddin, 125, 126, 281–82
Hezbollah, 1, 6, 7, 9, 15, 18, 25, 31, 35, 36.
See also Islamic Jihad Organization (IJO);
specific person
Hoss, Lt. Commander, 190, 238, 242–44,
269–70, 278, 282
hostages: of al-Qaeda, 142–43; bartering of,
180; SNI, 112, 113, 117–22, 124, 145–46,
152–53, 159, 167–68, 170, 180, 181–82,
186–87, 192, 198–99, 201, 233, 278, 313
humanitarian relief effort, 189, 203, 213, 237,
273

International Security Assistance Force
(ISAF), British, 261
Iran, 6, 49, 66, 83, 152, 259, 293
Iraq, 9–10, 315
Islamic Jihad Organization (IJO), 1, 6

Jalalabad: al-Qaeda in/near, 186, 206, 213,
225, 304; al-Qaeda retreat from, 254;
Babrak's safehouse in, 282; and Nuruddin,
238; and search for al-Qaeda/bin Laden,
196, 197, 239; Special Forces in, 270–71;
Taliban in, 225; and Team Juliet, 212,
213–14, 215, 220, 225, 233, 236, 237, 240,
262; U.S. air strikes against, 239
Jawbreaker: and Afghan war as U.S. success,
313; Bagram Airbase as headquarters for,
169–76; Berntsen as leader of team for, 73;
Berntsen leaves, 308–10; Berntsen's biggest
mistake concerning, 238; and Berntsen's
leadership style, 124–25; Berntsen's responsibilities with, 73–74, 76, 85, 108, 123–24,
302; Berntsen's speech to teams of, 84–85;
Berntsen's strategy for, 113–16, 124–25,
143–44; and CIA–military coordination, 75;
expansion of activities of, 191; explosion at
Kabul headquarters of, 231–32; functions

of teams for, 75; Kabul as base for, 171, 183,
184, 189–201; mission of, 86–87, 100, 103,
114, 115–16, 191; operations memo for,
275–76; planning and organization for,
72–87; Rich as replacement for Berntsen at,
296–97, 306–7; selection and assembling of
teams for, 73–80; Special Forces coordination with, 192; supplies and equipment for,
95, 96, 97, 100, 106–7, 116, 167, 193–94,
217, 228, 250; training of teams for, 84;
2000 team for, 43–64, 127; and U.S. strategy
for Afghan war, 74–75
Jawbreaker Romeo, 296, 297
Jelinek, Kati, 181–82. *See also* Shelter Now
International
Jemaah Islamiyah Islamic terrorists, 294–95
John (Hank's CIA deputy), 73, 77, 80, 81,
83–84, 124, 167, 174–75, 279, 281, 298, 314
Joint Forces Air Component Command
(JFACC), 157, 165, 216
Joint Special Operations Forces (JSOC):
Dailey as commander of, 272; and Jawbreaker move to Bagram Airbase, 170, 173;
and leaflets urging surrender of al-Qaeda,
299; Silver Stars for, 294; and SNI hostages,
119, 120, 121, 152–53, 168; and Team Juliet
and search for al-Qaeda/bin Laden, 215,
236, 254, 268, 281, 284, 293–94, 296, 298,
305. *See also specific person*
journalists: al-Qaeda terrorists pose as, 69; at
Bagram, 172, 184; and BLU–82 bomb incident, 296; and East African bombings,
12–13; Iranian, 142; killing of, 215, 282;
and Massoud's death, 155; and Nuruddin,
283, 293; and Pushtuns as bin Laden supporters, 280; at Qala-i Jangi fortress, 252,
253; and Rahman's son, 229; and search for
al-Qaeda/bin Laden, 239, 274, 282, 296;
terrorists posing as, 115; vehicles for, 106
Juliet Forward. *See* Team Juliet

Kabul: al-Qaeda safehouses in, 179, 184, 189,
192; as allied victory, 237; Aref's occupation
of, 153; Berntsen's leaves, 308; Berntsen's
trips into, 175; and Franks' Tajikistan meeting, 91; and Hank in Panshir Valley, 104;
importance of, 91; intelligence reports
about, 141; as Jawbreaker base, 171, 183,
184, 189–201, 202, 231–32; and Jawbreaker
mission, 115–16; maps of, 79, 144, 145, 161,
177, 184; nine1990s battle for, 177; Northern Alliance takeover and control of, 150,
153, 163, 173, 177–81, 199–200, 235; Northern Alliance–U.S. offensive against, 164–81;

prisoners in, 229, 270; Rich as leader of CIA operations in, 306–7; security for, 219, 260–61; and Shomal Plains offensive, 144–45; SNI hostages in, 112, 117–18, 119–22; and Soviet invasion of Afghanistan, 260; Special Forces in, 228; spies in, 111; Taliban/al-Qaeda evacuation and withdrawal from, 168–70, 173, 174, 235, 254; Taliban attacks on, 281; Taliban meetings in, 160–62; Taliban takeover and control of, 98, 131, 141, 155, 177, 178; and 2000 Jawbreaker team, 59; and UN, 116, 150, 166; U.S. air strikes against, 119, 141, 144–45, 161–62, 165–67, 168, 173; U.S. embassy in, 194–95, 302, 308; and U.S. strategy, 91, 105

Kandahar, 79, 80, 82, 165, 186, 202, 287, 288, 303, 314

Karzai, Hamid, 81–82, 125, 202, 215–17, 224, 259, 260, 261, 288, 301–3

Khalili, Karim, 55, 80, 167, 193, 200, 237

Khan, Adam, 225, 284, 314; and al-Qaeda's attempt to negotiate, 289; background of, 40; joins Jawbreaker, 279–80; and Pushtun paper, 79–80; and radio interception of al-Qaeda, 307; recruitment and training of, 40, 68; and Team Juliet and search for al-Qaeda/bin Laden, 281–82, 284, 293–94

Khan, Berryelah, 91–92, 141–42, 241

Khan, Bismullah: Berntsen's meetings with, 130–31, 149, 150–51; and defection of Taliban commander, 160; on foreign troops in Afghanistan, 183; and Kabul offensive, 150–51, 160, 164, 165, 166, 169, 172, 173, 174–75, 177; and Kabul takeover by Northern Alliance, 180–81; and Karzai's return to Afghanistan, 301; and Mazar-e Sharif offensive, 141, 143, 144; Shomali Plains as base for, 111, 130, 131, 143, 144, 147, 149, 150–51; and Shomali Plains offensive, 131, 141, 150–51; subcommanders of, 284–85; U.S. air support for, 151, 173

Khan, Ismael, 125, 167, 237

Kharruti warlord, 154–57

Khobar Towers (Dhahran, Saudi Arabia): bombing of (1996), 7, 33, 68

Kimmons, General, 93, 168, 290

Klesko (SAD paramilitary officer), 193–94, 200, 278, 286

Kristof, Nicholas, 313

Kunduz: battle for, 141–43, 148, 149, 240–42, 245; and Kabul offensive, 165; Northern Alliance concern about, 210; Taliban/al-Qaeda in, 140, 141, 142, 210, 240–42

Kuwait, 6, 9–10

Lance (Jawbreaker team member), 257, 265, 266, 267–69, 274

language officers. See translators

Latin America: Berntsen as Chief of Station in, 63, 69–72, 73, 86; Berntsen's return to, 297; Division Chief for, 69, 71, 86

Lawrence (CIA officer), 45, 46, 59, 62, 63

leaflet incident, 299

Lindh, John Walker, 241, 242, 248–49, 251, 252–53, 258, 263, 287

Lowgar province, 196, 197, 206, 212, 214, 296

Loyd, Anthony, 239, 280, 300

Majid (Northern Alliance officer): and Berntsen's arrival in Panshir Valley, 100–101, 103, 106–7; and Berntsen's meeting with allied intelligence officials, 118; and British in Afghanistan, 203; and defection of Taliban commander, 158, 160; and Eastern Alliance, 272; friends of, 151; and Hazara incident, 199; and interim governing authority, 204, 208–9, 230; and Kabul as Jawbreaker base, 183, 184, 190; and Kabul offensive, 168–69, 170, 175–77, 178–79, 181; and Khan–Berntsen meeting, 149; and Kunduz offensive, 149; and Northern Alliance–CIA relations, 130; in Panshir Valley, 110; and prisoners of war, 196, 229; reports from, 112; and search for al-Qaeda/bin Laden, 196, 239, 272; and Shomali Plains offensive, 144; and SNI hostages, 117, 120, 159, 170; and stolen gun incident, 186, 187–88; and supplies and equipment for Northern Alliance, 125; and Taliban hostages, 142–43; and Taliban retreat, 148; and Team Juliet, 215; and 2000 Jawbreaker team, 48, 49, 50, 51, 52, 54, 55, 57, 61, 62; views about U.S. of, 125

Marlowe (Jawbreaker team member), 63, 152, 184, 309; background of, 45, 84; and findings from al-Qaeda safehouses, 207; and Jawbreaker Romeo, 296; and Kabul offensive, 167, 173; and 2000 Jawbreaker team, 45, 46, 53, 54, 57, 59, 60, 61

Mary (Chief of Career Service Trainee program), 37–38, 68–69, 157–58, 160

Massoud, Ahmad Shah, 88, 118, 177; death of, 69–70, 73, 101, 115, 155, 209; and Iran, 49; as member of Rabbani government, 155; as Northern Alliance leader, 62–63, 69–70; and Soviets, 58, 126; and Taliban capture of Taloqan, 98; and 2000 Jawbreaker team, 48, 49, 53, 62–63; views about U.S. of, 42

Mazar-e Sharif: as allied base, 256; allied offensive against, 133–40; Berntsen's assessment of operations in, 237; and Franks'
Tajikistan meeting, 90, 91; maps of, 79;
Northern Alliance capture of, 139–40, 143,
237; and supplies and equipment for
Northern Alliance, 124; and Taliban collapse, 167; Taliban retreat from, 139–40,
150–51, 157, 210, 240; Taliban seizes, 49;
U.S. air strikes against, 137–38, 139, 144,
149, 306; and U.S. strategy, 90, 91, 105, 111,
131, 136–37, 141, 143, 149, 234
McQueen (CIA employee), 10, 16, 17,
18, 22
medics, 116, 170, 173, 207–8, 211, 215, 229,
236, 254
Mercer, Heather, 119–20, 121, 181–82, 198.
See also Shelter Now International
Mercer, John, 121
Milawa Valley, 272, 274, 282
military, U.S.: CIA relations with, 75, 86–87,
120, 298. See also CENTCOM
Mohammad (Taliban commander): defection
of, 157–59
money: for Afghan warlords, 157; and attempt to block passes to Pakistan, 306; and
Berntsen's arrival in Panshir Valley, 106;
and bin Laden's escape into Pakistan, 308;
and buying of prisoners, 229; and Cullison's computer finds, 304; and defection
of Taliban commander, 158, 159; as reward
for capture of al-Qaeda members, 115;
and rewards for help to Americans, 149;
and SNI hostages, 118, 120–21, 124,
145–46, 159, 167–68; for Special Forces,
109, 117, 192; and stolen gun incident, 186,
187; Storm as responsible for, 107; and
supplies and equipment for Jawbreaker,
117; and supplies and equipment for
Northern Alliance, 124; for tolls, 298; and
U.S. financial commitment to Northern
Alliance, 112–13; and U.S. strategy for
Afghan war, 75
mujahideen, 67, 155, 238, 288
Mulholland, John, 109, 167, 308; Berntsen's
meetings with, 213–14, 237; and Franks'
meetings, 93, 234; and Mazar-e Sharif
offensive, 136; and security for teams in
southern Afghanistan, 204; as senior Special Forces officer in Afghanistan, 93, 204;
and stolen gun incident, 185, 187; and
Team Juliet and search for al-Qaeda/bin
Laden, 213–14, 236, 257, 269, 270–71, 274
Mustapha (Egyptian), 22–24

Nairobi, Kenya: bombing of U.S. embassy in,
2–4, 7, 8, 9, 16, 18–20, 25, 26, 206, 311
Nangahar province, 186, 196, 213, 235, 236,
238, 240, 270–71. See also Jalalabad
narco–trafficking, 47, 50, 56, 63, 95
National Directorate of Security (NDS), 122,
153, 163, 182, 208
Nelson (Jawbreaker team member), 16–17,
206–7
9/11 Commission Report, 311, 315
non–governmental organizations (NGOs),
18, 22, 26–27, 83
Northern Alliance: and Afghan war as success, 312, 313; and Atef's death, 206;
Berntsen's assessment of, 218, 220; bin
Laden's relations with, 90; CIA relations
with, 45, 46, 81, 102–3, 104, 105, 107,
113–14, 127–29, 130, 131, 313; and comparison of Afghan and Iraqi war, 315;
Fahim as leader of, 70; and Franks' Tajikistan meeting, 89–93; and Hank in Panshir
Valley, 103–4; and humanitarian relief effort, 203; intelligence reports from, 110,
113–14; and interim governing authority,
235, 259, 260; and Jawbreaker planning
and organization, 73, 80; and Jawbreaker's
mission, 115–16; Kabul takeover and control of Kabul by, 177–81, 199–200, 235; and
Karzai's return to Afghanistan, 301; Khan
as leader of, 88; and Massoud's death, 69–70;
and MOIS, 49; and opening of Afghan war,
78; in Panshir Valley, 100, 103–4; and politics, 91, 125, 224, 235; prisoners of, 196,
204–5, 207–8, 229, 238, 242–44; Rabbani as
political head of, 224; reluctance to go into
southern/eastern Afghanistan of, 197, 199,
220, 285, 296; and security for Kabul, 219,
260–61; and SNI hostages, 114, 313; Special
Forces' relations with, 105; spies for, 239;
strength of, 76, 111; supplies and equipment for, 55, 57, 60–62, 64, 77, 84, 90, 92,
112, 118, 125, 127, 129, 144, 219, 313; Taliban interactions with, 110–11, 173; and
Taliban retreat, 153; Taloqan as capital for,
55, 97–98; tribes comprising, 55–56, 125;
and 2000 Jawbreaker team, 44, 45, 48, 49,
50, 54–55, 56, 57–64; U.S. air support for,
105, 111, 131, 150, 151, 165–67, 172, 216,
237; U.S. relations with, 125–26; and U.S.
strategy, 89–93, 111, 131, 141. See also
specific person or offensive
Nuruddin (Pushtun warlord), 238, 249–50,
275, 280, 281, 283, 284, 289, 292, 293, 298,
300

O'Connell, Jeff, 2, 5, 7–8, 10, 21, 33, 36, 37
Omar, Mullah Mohammed, 81, 82, 202, 294
101st Airborn Division, U.S., 315
Operation Anaconda, 315

Pakistan: and Afghan civil war, 125, 126; al-
    Qaeda/bin Laden escape into, 277, 290,
    299–300, 305–8; attempts to block passes
    into, 305–6; CIA in, 24; and deployment of
    ground troops for Tora Bora mountains,
    314–15; intelligence from, 224; Inter Ser-
    vice Intelligence Directorate (ISID) of, 241;
    Odeh's arrest in, 24; Parachinir region of,
    240, 308; Pushtun exiles in, 259; and rescue
    of Pakistani advisors to Taliban, 241; secu-
    rity agents in, 24; as source of Taliban re-
    cruits, 128; Sunni Jihadists in, 18; support
    for bin Laden in, 240, 241; support for Tali-
    ban from, 56, 128, 241; Team Juliet near
    border with, 250; U.S. relations with, 290
Pakistanis: as prisoners, 207–8, 230, 294; as
    Taliban soldiers, 128, 241
Panshir Valley: Berntsen's arrival in, 96, 100,
    102–3; as Berntsen's base, 94, 108–22,
    123–24, 141, 167; Northern Alliance in,
    49, 55–64, 100, 103–4; and planning and
    organization for Jawbreaker, 76, 80, 85;
    prison/prisoners in, 229, 242–44; survey of,
    57–58; 2000 Jawbreaker team in, 43–44, 48,
    52–64, 76
Parker (Jawbreaker team member), 84, 104,
    113, 183; and Kabul offensive, 173, 174–75,
    181; and Team Juliet, 215, 256, 265, 266,
    267–69, 271, 272, 274, 276, 277
Patricia (Tanzania embassy employee), 12,
    13–14, 15
Pavitt, James, 59–60, 62, 71, 124, 297, 311
Pelton, Robert Young, 247, 249, 263
Pezzullo, Ralph, 205, 211, 294
Phillip (Dobbins' aide), 203–4, 218, 220, 222,
    230
Phillip (East Africa contact), 17, 18, 22
Piernik, Ken, 20–21, 22, 26
prisoners: al-Qaeda as, 74, 196, 204–5, 229,
    242, 245–49, 250–53, 256, 257–58, 263, 300,
    301, 313; Americans as, 85; foreigners as,
    246, 247, 250–53, 258–59, 300; interviews
    of, 204–5, 207–8, 238, 242–44; Jawbreaker
    teams prohibited from speaking with, 269;
    in Kabul, 229; language officers needed
    for interrogation of, 74; medical care for,
    207–8, 211, 229, 242; of Northern Alliance,
    58, 196, 204–5, 207–8, 229, 238, 242–44;
    Pakistanis as, 207–8, 230, 294; in Panshir

Valley, 229, 242–44; at Qala-i Jangi fortress,
    245–49, 250–53; and Rahman's son as pris-
    oner, 229; of Taliban, 199; Taliban as, 58,
    196, 229, 242, 245–49, 250–53, 256, 257–58,
    263, 286–87, 298, 313; of Team Delta,
    286–87, 298. See also hostages
Pushtuns (Pathans): Berntsen's paper about,
    78–79; as bin Laden supporters, 280,
    281–82, 308, 315; control of southern
    Afghanistan by, 81; as exiles, 259; and in-
    terim governing authority, 224, 259; Kabul
    occupied by, 98; Karzai as leader of, 202;
    and killing of Pushtun warlord, 147; leader-
    ship of, 115; overview about, 79; as part
    of Afghanistan population, 72; as part
    of Northern Alliance, 125; reluctance of
    Northern Alliance to engage, 199; and
    search for al-Qaeda/bin Laden, 197; Tali-
    ban's hanging of, 275; and Team Juliet,
    220, 225, 280–81. See also specific person

Qala-i Jangi fortress, 242, 245–49, 250–53,
    255–56, 257–59, 262–64, 270, 287
Qanooni, Younis, 235, 259, 260

Rabbani, Burhanuddin, 155, 224, 235, 259,
    260
Rahman, Sheik Abdel, 228–29
Rangers, U.S.: Berntsen's request for, 277,
    278, 290, 295, 305, 306–7, 309, 314. See also
    specific regiment
Razzak (Afghan warlord), 285
Red Team (Jawbreaker), 274
Reno (Jawbreaker team member), 161–62,
    257, 265, 266, 267–69, 274
Rich (CIA officer), 59–60, 297, 306–7
R.J. (Team Alpha Leader), 78, 80; back-
    ground of, 74, 135–36; and Dostum, 74, 78,
    80, 94, 133, 135–36, 137, 138, 139, 141, 149;
    and Kunduz offensive, 141, 149; and
    Mazar-e Sharif offensive, 133, 134, 135–36,
    137, 138, 139, 140–41
Russia: invasion of Afghanistan by, 49, 58,
    66–67, 72, 99, 155, 194, 240, 260, 314
Russian Motorized Infantry, 96
Russians: and Massoud, 126; as Taliban pilots,
    50–51; and 2000 Jawbreaker team, 49

Saudi Arabia, 49, 67, 116, 239
Sayyaf, Abdul Rasul, 124, 177
Scheuer, Mike, 32, 43, 59
Schroen, Gary: in Afghanistan, 73, 76, 80; as
    author of First In, 115, 122, 153, 163, 182,
    201; Berntsen as replacement for, 100, 101,

Schroen, Gary (*cont.*)
104; frustrations with Washington of, 105;
and Haas, 109; and mission of Jawbreaker,
86; rank of, 123; retirement of, 100; and
U.S. financial commitment to Northern
Alliance, 112
Sean (Jawbreaker team member), 113, 170,
173
Senate Select Committee on Intelligence
(SSCI), 36
September 11, 2001, 70–72, 194, 200, 225–26,
229, 295, 303
75th Ranger Regiment, U.S. Army, 82
Sharifi, General, 105, 127, 165, 173, 284–85
Sheberghan prison, 240–42, 263, 270, 287
Shelter Now International (SNI): hostages
from, 112, 113, 117–22, 124, 145–46,
152–53, 159, 167–68, 170, 180, 181–82,
186–87, 192, 198–99, 201, 233, 278, 313
Shomali Plains: battle for, 144–45, 147; and
Berntsen's responsibilities in Afghanistan,
85; and Berntsen's strategy, 143; Berntsen's
trips to, 129–32, 149–51; and CIA–military
relations, 120; and defection of Taliban
commander, 158; exchange of SNI hostages
on, 168; and Franks' Tajikistan meeting, 90,
91; and Hank in Panshir Valley, 104, 111;
Jawbreaker activities on, 123–32; and Jawbreaker mission, 115–16; and Jawbreaker
move to Bagram Airbase, 171; and Jawbreaker planning and organization, 80;
Jawbreaker team on, 112, 114–15; and
Kabul offensive, 164, 165, 169, 172, 173,
177, 179; maps of, 79, 144, 145; and Northern Alliance–CIA relations, 127–29, 130,
149; reports from, 143; Special Forces teams
on, 78, 143; and supplies and equipment
for Northern Alliance, 124; Taliban on,
130, 131–32, 150–51, 169, 179; and 2000
Jawbreaker team, 61, 63–64; U.S. air strikes
on, 144, 149, 150, 151, 168; and U.S. strategy, 90, 91, 111, 141, 149, 234
Silver Team (Jawbreaker), 274
Singapore: al-Qaeda plot to attack targets in,
294–95
Smucker, Phillip, 300, 306
southern/eastern Afghanistan: Berntsen's assessment of, 220; creation of allied forces
in, 238; expansion of operations in, 237;
Hazaras in, 296; Northern Alliance reluctance to go into, 197, 199, 220, 285, 296;
Pushtuns in, 81; Taliban defeat in, 216;
Taliban in, 81, 94, 149, 285; U.S. air strikes
in, 94, 149. *See also specific city/town*

Spann, Mike, 95, 245–49, 250–53, 255, 258,
263–64, 269, 270
Spann, Shannon, 264
Special Activities Division, CIA, 82–83, 191,
211, 236, 268, 275–76
Special Forces, British, 253
Special Forces Team 53, 136, 137
Special Forces Team 534, 136, 138, 139, 140,
141
Special Forces Team 553, 200
Special Forces Team 555 (Triple Nickel), 78,
104, 109, 111, 131, 165, 167, 170, 173, 181,
192, 285
Special Forces Team 574, 202, 215–17, 288
Special Forces Team 585, 109, 142
Special Forces Team 595 (Tiger 2), 78, 104,
108, 133, 134, 136, 139, 140, 141
Special Forces, U.S.: Afghan relations with,
105; and Afghan war as U.S. success, 312,
313; air support for, 83, 134–35; and
Berntsen's strategy, 143; and Berntsen's trip
to front lines, 131–32; casualties among,
288, 308; CIA relationship with, 308–9, 313;
and deployment of ground troops for Tora
Bora mountains, 314; and Eastern Alliance,
272–73; and Franks at Bagram, 236; fund-
ing for, 109, 192; in Jalalabad, 270–71;
Jawbreaker coordination with, 192; and
Jawbreaker mission, 86; in Kabul, 192, 228;
and Kabul offensive, 165, 172; Karzai's
praise for, 303; and Kunduz offensive, 242;
leadership of teams in, 109; and leaflets
urging surrender of al-Qaeda, 299; and
Mazar-e Sharif offensive, 138, 139; members of teams of, 134; and membership of
Jawbreaker teams, 74, 75; meningitis case
of soldier in, 94; Mulholland's comments
about casualties of, 308; need for language
officers to work with, 109; and opening of
Afghan war, 77, 78; at Qala–i Jangi fortress,
255–56, 258; and search for al-Qaeda/bin
Laden, 213, 268–72, 274, 282, 283, 290,
299, 301; on Shomali Plains, 143; SNI
hostage rescue by, 198–99, 201; supplies
and equipment for, 109, 117; and Taliban
collapse, 167; and Taliban retreat, 148; at
Tarin Kowt, 216; and Team Juliet, 268;
and terrorist pursuit teams, 212; at U.S.
embassy in Kabul, 308; in Uzbekistan,
223–24. *See also specific person or team*
Stan (Jawbreaker team member), 104, 113,
183, 192; and Kabul offensive, 173, 174–75,
181; and Northern Alliance–CIA relations,
127–29, 130; and search of al-Qaeda safe-

houses, 206; and Special Forces team, 105, 112

State Department, U.S., 15, 19, 62, 101, 218, 231, 302

stolen gun incident, 185–86, 187–89

Storm (Jawbreaker team member), 63, 73, 107, 114; background of, 45, 84; and Berntsen's strategy, 143, 144; and explosion at Jawbreaker's Kabul headquarters, 231–32; and Jawbreaker move to Bagram Airbase, 169, 170, 173; and Jawbreaker Romeo, 296; and Kabul offensive, 176; and Lowgar province, 296; and money for Jawbreaker activities, 106, 107; prisoner interviews by, 196, 204–5, 207–8, 211, 228–29; and search for bin Laden, 196, 197–98; and Shomal Plains offensive, 144–45; and SNI hostages, 117, 118, 120, 121, 145, 152, 153, 159, 167–68, 170, 180; and 2000 Jawbreaker team, 45, 46–47, 53, 57–58, 59, 61

Sudan, 32, 37, 67

Sutter, Mark, 233–34, 237, 276, 298, 301

Tajikistan, 37, 47–49, 55; Franks' meeting in, 88–93, 111, 234; and 2000 Jawbreaker team, 44, 47–49, 62; as U.S. ally, 223

Tajiks: in Afghanistan, 55, 57, 72, 125, 147, 179, 199, 219, 224, 259. See also specific person

Taliban: and Afghan war as U.S. success, 312; al-Qaeda/bin Laden relations with, 62, 90, 101, 108, 293; Amir's views about, 155; and Berntsen's journey to Afghanistan, 97–98; Berntsen's strategy concerning, 108, 124–25, 143; Berntsen's views about, 56–57, 84–85, 98, 99–100; and Bonn conference, 259; casualties among, 172–73, 313, 315; collapse of, 167, 168–70, 237; computers used by, 304; defection of commanders in, 81, 169; Diane's briefing about, 76; early U.S. battles with, 82; and Franks' Tajikistan meeting, 90, 91, 92; Hazara's fight against, 56; intelligence headquarters of, 178–79; intelligence reports about, 110, 112, 126–27, 141, 155; and Iran, 49; and Jawbreaker mission, 103, 115–16; journalists executed by, 215; Karzai's relationship with, 81; and Massoud's death, 69–70; military camps of, 183–84; Northern Alliance beats back, 63–64; Northern Alliance soldiers' interactions with, 110–11, 173; Pakistan's relations with, 56, 241; as prisoners, 58, 140, 196, 229, 242, 245–49, 252, 256, 257–58, 263, 286–87, 298, 313; prisoners of, 199;

Pushtuns hanged by, 275; recruitment by, 83–84, 111, 128; regrouping of, 223, 237; reprisals on, 179; retreat by, 148, 150–51, 153, 157, 169, 173, 174, 194, 200, 202, 210, 235, 240; rise to power of, 48–49; Russian mercenaries as pilots for, 50–51; Saudi backing for, 49, 116; spring offensive of, 60; strength of, 76, 90, 111; supplies and equipment for, 84, 116–17, 135, 300; surrender of, 79, 83, 139; and 2000 Jawbreaker team, 48, 50, 52, 53, 54, 55, 60, 61, 62; UN sanctions on, 56; U.S. air strikes against, 77, 94–95, 112, 127, 131–32, 135, 137–44, 148, 153, 157, 161–62, 169, 170, 172, 180, 184, 200, 216; U.S. relations with, 194; and U.S. strategy, 91, 92. See also Shelter Now International: hostages from; specific person, city, or offensive

Taloqan: as allied victory, 237; attack and fall of, 141–42, 143, 149; and Berntsen's responsibilities in Afghanistan, 85; and Berntsen's strategy, 143; and Franks' Tajikistan meeting, 90, 91; intelligence reports about, 108, 143; and Jawbreaker planning and organization, 80; Jawbreaker team in, 112; as Northern Alliance capital, 55, 97–98; Special Forces in, 104, 109; and supplies and equipment for Northern Alliance, 124; Taliban assault and capture of, 55, 97–98; Taliban retreat from, 210, 240; and 2000 Jawbreaker team, 55; and U.S. strategy, 90, 91, 105, 111, 131, 141, 149, 234

Tanzania: Berntsen as head of EDT for, 7, 9, 11–18, 20–22, 27; Berntsen's return from, 31; bombing of U.S. embassy in, 2–4, 7, 10–18, 20–22, 26, 31, 191, 206, 311; historical background about, 10–11; U.S. relations with, 66

Tarin Kowt (town), 82, 202, 215–17, 288

Taubman, Georg, 181–82, 192, 198. See also Shelter Now International

Team Alpha (Jawbreaker), 80, 94, 133, 134, 136, 138, 139, 140–41

Team Delta (Jawbreaker), 80, 193–94, 199, 200, 226, 227, 278, 279, 285, 286–87, 298

Team Echo (Jawbreaker), 80, 82, 202, 215–17

Team Juliet: and al-Qaeda's attempt to negotiate, 289, 290; and Dailey, 274; and Eastern Alliance, 298; formation of, 212; and Jalalabad, 212, 213–14, 215, 220, 225, 233, 236, 237, 240, 262; and JSOC, 298; members of, 215, 236; and Nangahar, 236; near Pakistan border, 250; and Nuruddin, 238; operations for, 213–14, 275–76; and

Team Juliet (*cont.*)
Pushtuns, 220, 225, 280–81; and search for al-Qaeda/bin Laden, 225, 249–50, 253–54, 256–57, 261–62, 265–72, 291, 295–96, 298, 300; and Special forces, 233; supplies and equipment for, 249–50, 257, 281

Ted (FBI agent), 3, 5, 7–8, 9, 18–20, 31, 33

Tenet, George: and Berntsen's frustrations with CIA, 9; and Berntsen's replacement in Jawbreaker, 297; as CIA director, 32, 36; Clinton appoints, 32; and cutbacks at CIA, 33; declares war on al-Qaeda, 28, 33, 36; downplaying of CIA ability to attack al-Qaeda by, 311; and supplies and equipment for Northern Alliance, 124; and 2000 Jawbreaker team, 59, 62, 63

10th Mountain Division, U.S., 255, 272, 315

terrorist pursuit teams, 191, 212, 257, 269

terrorists: Berntsen's views about, 315; CIA's ability to attack, 311–12; U.S. infiltration of sanctuaries for, 41. *See also specific person or organization*

Thomas, Diana, 181–82. *See also* Shelter Now International

Todd (Jawbreaker team member), 95, 97, 129, 148, 170, 173, 174, 187, 190; background of, 45, 84; and intelligence reports, 149; Jawbreaker training of, 84; and Kabul offensive, 161; and Northern–Alliance CIA relations, 127; in Panshir Valley, 108; and Team Delta at Ghazni, 286; and 2000 Jawbreaker team, 45, 46, 53, 54

Tora Bora mountains: al-Qaeda/bin Laden in, 240, 254, 261–62, 265–76, 280–84, 289–92, 299–300, 305–7, 313–15; and operations memo for Jawbreaker, 276

translators: and Afghan war as U.S. success, 314; importance of, 312; and membership of Jawbreaker teams, 74; need for, 33, 37–40, 105, 109, 312; and opening of Afghan war, 78; and prisoner interviews, 244; recruitment of, 37–40, 68–69, 74, 76

Triple Nickel. *See* Special Forces Team 555

2000 Jawbreaker team: Berntsen's feelings about aborted mission of, 63–64; briefings for, 55; complaints and criticisms concerning, 59–60; end of mission of, 60–63; formation of, 43–45; journey to Afghanistan of, 45–52; members of, 45–46; mission of, 48, 54–55, 127; in Panshir Valley, 53–64

Ufundi building (Nairobi), 16, 19, 20

United Nations, 56, 116, 150, 166, 178, 245, 260–61, 293

United States: Afghans' views about, 42, 62, 94, 125–26, 142, 147; bin Laden's comments about, 65; challenges facing, 315; hatred of, 247; Northern Alliance relations with, 125–26; Pakistani relations with, 290; Taliban relations with, 194

USS *Cole*: attack on, 65–66, 67–68, 311

Ustad (Northern Alliance officer), 127, 128, 130–31

Uzbekistan: Alexander team in, 212–13; Berntsen in, 217–21, 222–23; Bilal in, 225–26; Dobbins' meeting in, 203, 204, 209, 217–20, 222, 235; Friendship Bridge between Afghanistan and, 141; history of, 47; Karamanov government in, 223; R.J. in, 74; as stop on way to Afghanistan, 44; 2000 Jawbreaker team in, 46–47; as U.S. ally, 223; U.S. embassy in, 223–24

Uzbeks: Berntsen's assessment of, 219; and interim governing authority, 259; and Mazar-e Sharif offensive, 138; as members of Northern Alliance, 55, 125; population of Afghanistani, 72, 224; at Qala–i Jangi fortress, 246, 251–52, 253, 255, 256, 258, 263; and Taliban, 57. *See also specific person*

Washington Post, 275, 293, 305–6

Washsak, John, 66

Waugh, Billy, 190–91, 238, 239, 240, 262, 277, 296

White Mountains, 253–54, 272, 274, 298, 299–300, 305, 307

Woodward, Bob, 308–9, 312

World Trade Center: bombings of, 70–72, 98, 110, 211, 225–26, 229, 312

Yale (Jawbreaker team member), 84, 168–69, 170, 173, 176, 215

Yemen, 65–67, 311

Zaher Shah, Mohammad, 230, 231, 259, 260

Zahir, Haji Mohammed, 275, 292, 298, 300

Zawahiri, Ayman al–, 67, 114, 147, 206, 291, 304